D.H. Lawrence's
Philosophy of Nature

D.H.Lawrence's Philosophy of Nature

An Eastern View

Dr. Tianying Zang

Order this book online at www.trafford.com
or email orders@trafford.com

Most Trafford titles are also available at major online book retailers.

© Copyright 2011 Dr. Tianying Zang.
All rights reserved. No part of this publication may be reproduced, stored in a retrieval
system, or transmitted, in any form or by any means, electronic, mechanical, photocopying,
recording, or otherwise, without the written prior permission of the author.

Printed in the United States of America.

ISBN: 978-1-4269-7672-8 (sc)
ISBN: 978-1-4269-7673-5 (e)

Trafford rev. 12/12/2011

 www.trafford.com

North America & international
toll-free: 1 888 232 4444 (USA & Canada)
phone: 250 383 6864 ♦ fax: 812 355 4082

Contents

Acknowledgements		vii
Foreword		ix
Introduction		xiii
Chapter I	Lawrence's Sensitivity to Nature	1
Chapter II	Man and Nature	32
Chapter III	Enigma of Nature	60
Chapter IV	Interrelationship and Individuality	88
Chapter V	Duality and the Yin-Yang Principle	109
Chapter VI	Life and Death	131
Chapter VII	Mind and Body	155
Chapter VIII	Primitivism and Theosophy	198
Conclusion		226
Bibliography		233

Acknowledgements

I would like to express my heartfelt gratitude to Professor Allan Ingram, my supervisor, for his illuminating instructions and valuable suggestions during my doctoral studies in UK. I am also grateful of the help from my dear friend Katie Knapton, an expert in English Language and Linguistics, who devoted considerable time in proofreading most of the chapters during the preparation of this book. I owe a special debt of gratitude to Mr. Keith Crombie for his substantial help, whose consistent support and kindness contributed a great deal to the completion of this book. Meanwhile, many sincere thanks also go to my Australian teacher and friend Mr. Keville Bott who shared with me his professional and philosophical insights. In addition, I want to thank my dear friends Emerald Dunn-Bahurlet and Rea Cris for their help with my English.

This book is sponsored by Jiangsu Education Institute, Nanjing, China.

Foreword

By Allan Ingram

Professor of English
University of Northumbria, UK

Man's relationship to his environment has always been crucial, not only to his survival but to the very quality of his survival. Whether he worships the sun, or an unseen deity, or the manmade products of the earth, be they goods, gold or the green world itself, environment and its well-being, its balance, inevitably impinge to a major extent on the circumstances and nature of that worship. Nowadays in particular this is not only a matter of belief or of well-intentioned assertion but of scientific fact. As climate change scientist Dave Reay in his book *Climate Change Begins at Home: Life on the two-way street of global warming* summarises, the 'the bare facts' are:

> Green house gases warm the planet.
> Global temperatures have risen 0.6°C in the last 100 years.
> Concentrations of greenhouse gas in our atmosphere are now higher than at any time in the last 420,000 years.
> Since the Industrial Revolution greenhouse gas concentrations have risen by around 50%.

And he adds:

> To recap: thousands of top-notch scientists from all over the world are warning that if we don't reduce greenhouse

gas emissions, we, our children, and our children's children, will almost certainly suffer dire consequences. Getting a wide array of science's big guns to agree on anything is like herding cats, yet on climate change they have reached this sobering consensus: most of the warming observed over the last 150 years is likely to be attributable to human activities.[1]

D.H. Lawrence above most writers was aware of the interdependence of man and nature. Like William Wordsworth, John Clare and Thomas Hardy he both experienced the natural world at close quarters, knew its rhythms and requirements, what it could give and what it demanded, while also transforming that knowledge in his thought and writing into something more: as Tianying Zang's book puts it, it became a philosophy of nature.

Our reading of Lawrence has passed through several phases since his own time. Once banned, deplored and viewed with suspicion, or with scorn, and then taken as an apostle of freedom in sexual behaviour and as an icon of a new spirit of the age, he is perhaps an ideal figure for reassessment through the recent mode of eco-criticism. A development of the last ten years or so, though traceable back to significant critics of earlier periods, not least to Raymond Williams in the 1970s, the eco-critical movement deals with the implications of a reading that relates writing to ecology and the concerns of man in relation to nature and the natural environment. Eco-criticism is not solely about climate change, and Dr Zang's book is neither exclusively eco-criticism nor a plea to save the planet, but the current background is a powerful factor in reading both this compelling account and also the work of D.H. Lawrence himself. Lawrence, after all, was more alert to the resonance of nature, both within nature and between man and his natural surroundings, than most of his contemporaries and the evidence for this is everywhere on his pages and impacts strongly on the texture and rhythms of his language, both poetry and prose. Few writers were more instinctively in tune with nature, a matter partly of Lawrence's upbringing, and partly of a temperament that took joy in seeing small, apparently inconsequential processes as having significance both within themselves and for themselves and at the same time within a much greater and, ultimately, an unfathomable wider system.

Perhaps the most distinctive feature of this book is the way it deals with such systems. I mean the extraordinary and striking parallels displayed between the core beliefs and principles of Lawrence's ideas and those Eastern philosophies and systems of thought that Dr Zang subjects to such lucid and sympathetic scrutiny. Balance is a key word here, not just between man and nature but within all aspects of man's and the universe's being. Lawrence, without precisely reading many of these eastern sources himself, was clearly working and thinking at the same fundamental level that gave rise to those religions and systems of the East. Deeply attracted, indeed, to the fundamental wherever he found it, and especially so if it involved beliefs long held by peoples he saw as still retaining a real and meaningful contact with the earth and all that it held, Lawrence would have been instinctively engaged by the thought of the East and have known immediately the depth of agreement and of consonance between it and what he regarded as knowledge.

Dr Zang has performed a considerable service to Lawrence studies in this lucid and refreshing book. No one who reads it will ever see Lawrence's work in quite the same way again, an achievement, I am sure, that Lawrence himself would have applauded. That would be the greatest accolade of all.

---

[1] Dave Reay, *Climate Change Begins at Home: Life on the two-way street of global warming*, London: Macmillan, 2005, pp. 21, 20.

Introduction

Lawrence is considered to be one of the greatest novelists, as well as perhaps the most controversial writer of the twentieth century. His works, in almost every literary form of the English language, have been most widely read, criticized and quoted since his death in 1930. In a literary career spanning only twenty years his achievement was enormous. It includes ten full-length novels, seven novellas, and some fifty short stories, which only account for little more than half of his work. His poems fill three thick volumes and his literary criticism a large book. He wrote four travel books, several plays and many miscellaneous essays and studies. Besides, his letters later collected and edited amount to seven huge volumes (Cambridge edition). Not only for the remarkable volume of his writing, but also for his technical achievement as a novelist, poet and critic, he was recognized by many prestigious critics and writers, such as Henry James, F. R. Leavis, E. M. Forster, Aldus Huxley and Richard Aldington. "Only a man of genius could equal his positive achievements", said Richard Aldington.[1] Forster wrote in a letter to the *Nation and Athenaeum* soon after his death in 1930, "All that we can do . . . is to say straight out that he was the greatest imaginative novelist of our generation".[2]

The years of Lawrence's life, from 1885 to 1930, saw a radical change from a world of apparent order and contentment to a world of chaos and spiritual disaster. Lawrence's personal troubles were the troubles of that time, and his work not only expresses his individual questions and tensions but also the problems of that age. However, in spite of his achievements, Lawrence met with strong hostility and prejudice from the literary world. The reason he was not popular seems to be that he was misread and misunderstood. Negatively Lawrence was known to the wider public only as the author of "indecent" books that were from time to time suppressed; positively he was regarded from the 1920s as a liberator and an apostle of sexual emancipation. Sexuality, however, is just one aspect of his main concern, which, as he consistently stresses, is the need for a balance between intellect and instinct, mind and body. F. R. Leavis points out in *D. H. Lawrence: Novelist* (1955) that "the questions and stresses that preoccupied him have still the most urgent relevance for us today".[3] Among those questions and stresses, man's ecological awareness in relation to the natural world, as constantly stressed in Lawrence's work, is perhaps even more urgent today, in the twenty-first century.

It is a truism to point out that no writer's work can exist or be created in a cultural vacuum. The development of Lawrence's ideas and conceptions is undoubtedly influenced by the prevailing cultural movements of his time, and is closely connected with various important cultural groups[4] of the then British literary world. Lawrence's early years were imbued with transcendental influences, and it is long since acknowledged that his conception of nature has its roots in the Romantic movement and the transcendentalists. In Lawrence's works, we have detected many preoccupations, attitudes and assumptions concerning nature in common with the Romantic writers. As Jessie Chambers records, the young Lawrence was deeply impressed by Darwin's *The Origin of Species*, Huxley's *Man's Place in Nature*, and Haeckel's *The Riddle of the Universe*. Roger Ebbatson in his *Lawrence and the Nature Tradition* expounds how Lawrence's nature philosophy is vitally shaped by the transcendental-vitalist readings of the Romantics, particularly the influences of the works of Meredith, Hardy, Hale White and Richard Jefferies. He also stresses the philosophical influence of such sages as Carlyle, Ruskin, Schopenhauer, Nietzsche and Edward Carpenter.[5] With regard to Lawrence's transcendental understanding of the organic relationship between man and nature, Ebbatson says, "he is the great inheritor of the English Nature-tradition".[6]

There are other Lawrence scholars who have explored his conception of nature. For example, Dolores Lachapelle in *Future Primitive* displays an alertness to the interplay of human and nonhuman elements in nature as written in Lawrence's essays and novels. She translates Lawrence's imaginative concepts of nature from her own ecological perspectives. *D. H. Lawrence & Susan His Cow* by William York Tindall discusses Lawrence's theory of relationship, mindlessness, blood consciousness, primitivism, animism, and his understanding of theosophy and yoga. Besides, F. R. Leavis' *D. H. Lawrence, Novelist*, and *Thought, Words and Creativity*; Graham Hough's *The Dark Sun*; R. E. Pritchard's *D. H. Lawrence: Body of Darkness*, and Daniel J. Schneider's *The Consciousness of D. H. Lawrence, An Intellectual Biography* have all made perceptive surveys of Lawrence's intuitive response to nature, his naturalistic philosophy and psychological development including his ideas about sex, education, consciousness, and man's organic relationship with nature.

In spite of the fact that Lawrence has been widely studied by critics and academics of the English-speaking world, compared with the other issues discussed, Lawrence's views about nature and its relation to human life have not received an equally adequate attention from critics. Moreover, while some books have been devoted exclusively to the discussion of this issue, on the whole it has been studied in an overall context of Western perceptions.

Although Lawrence is a product of the Christian tradition and should be seen as belonging to the heritage of his own civilization, in his long fight with Christianity he has put forward views that are radically opposed to Christian traditional thought. Many of his non-Christian perspectives concerning the universe and man's relationship with nature bear strong affinities with Eastern thought systems. There is a certain truth in Sri Aurobindo's playful remark that "Lawrence was a Yogi who had missed his way and come into a European body to work out his difficulties".[7] Lawrence's understanding of such fundamental concerns as the enigma of nature, nature's duality and oneness, mutual identity between man and nature, the issues of god and evolution, mind and body, life and death, sexuality, intuition, spontaneity and primitivism are the most representative of his romantic view of nature (I call them, for convenience, Lawrence's philosophy of nature). These concerns will be examined and discussed separately in the eight chapters of this book.

His friend Aldous Huxley said of Lawrence that "the core of his whole genius" was his "immediate sensitivity to the world at large". His "capacity to be aware of the universe in all its levels . . . was essentially the basis of his life and was his greatest gift", [8] which has its manifestation in his writings as a persistent theme. My first chapter "Lawrence's Sensitivity to Nature" will be devoted to this topic, exploring how his metaphysical awareness of the natural world is reflected in his life and works. Lawrence believes there is an organic relationship between man's life and nature in nature's unity and sacredness. "Our life *consists* in this achieving of a pure relationship between ourselves and the living universe about us", he says time and again.[9] To him, man truly alive is "living through all his senses and ideals and aspirations, living with a vital connection with . . . the whole natural world".[10] His understanding of the universal modes of interrelatedness of everything on earth and his theory of mutual identity between organic nature and the spontaneous characteristics of man including the issues of sexuality correspond to the principal doctrines of naturalism, oneness and spontaneity in Taoism. These issues will be dealt with in the second and fourth chapters of "Man and Nature" and "Interrelationship and Individuality".

Whatever his evolving opinions about society, race, education or sex, he always returns to the primal awareness of the transcendental power of the universe, an unknown power forever enveloping humanity. His metaphysical perception of the enigma of nature, including the perceptions of evolution, god, life force and creativity, finds deep affinities in Taoism, which will be discussed in the third chapter "Enigma of Nature". Nearly all aspects of Lawrence's religious vision were anticipated in Eastern literature. His almighty Holy Ghost, for example, who is responsible for the sacred underlying unity, is named Tao by Taoists, Brahman by Hindus and Dharmakaya by Buddhists. His duality, with its stress on the dynamic balance between complementary life-principles, is fully worked out in the Yin-Yang philosophy of Taoism. He believes this kind of balance existing in the whole universe should also be present in love and marriage. Lawrence's dialectical view of duality and polarity will be examined in Chapter Five entitled "Duality and the Yin-Yang Principle". Chapter Six "Life and Death" is about Lawrence's metaphorical perception of life and death, which reflects his romantic view of their mutual identity and mutual transformation in sustaining the continuum of the whole universe. His life-death insight, though in a way against Christian doctrines, perfectly matches the traditional thoughts of Buddhism. Chapter Seven "Mind and Body" is the discussion of his perspectives of the functions of mind and body which also parallel the Eastern view. Lawrence regards mental constructions as veils that must be swept away in order to allow for man's mystic communion with nature. Hence we have Lawrence's notion of believing in one's blood and flesh, instead of one's intellectual mind. His distrust of mind and mental consciousness for their limitations and falsities, his belief in intuition, instinct, impulse and unconsciousness not only have their legacy in some scientific researches, but also have long been acknowledged in Taoism and Buddhism. The mind-body argument leads to Lawrence's interpretation of the connection between the solar plexus and the whole universe. Finally, in Chapter Eight "Primitivism and Theosophy", his admiration of primitive culture is discussed. Unwilling to adjust his emotions to the industrialized civilization of the age, Lawrence takes refuge in all that seems opposite, in strange cults and mysteries, in primitivism and theosophy. For him, primitive peoples in many aspects have set examples to the modern world in their spontaneous life style and their inherent connection with nature, particularly their instinctive way of living and their cosmic consciousness. Primitivism and theosophy become his private religion. Through the revival of local cults and divinities, Lawrence hopes the decadent modern civilizations can be finally rescued.

The message Lawrence is trying to convey through his work has been received by both his Western and Eastern readers, but perhaps with different interpretations owing to their different cultural and social backgrounds. Is Lawrence an "indecent" writer for his propositions regarding sexuality? Is he talking nonsense for some of his seemingly absurd arguments concerning blood consciousness, mindlessness, primitivism and so on? Should he be sometimes regarded as a neurotic person for his "absurd" or "weird" obsession with nature as well as his unorthodox interpretations of life and death? Many of his concepts or theories are at once original and spontaneous; yet, his suspicion of reason, mind and even language itself troubled many readers of his time and later. It is true that some of his writing is inconsistent, such as his argument about the relationships between man and woman, which might account for T. S. Eliot's complaint that Lawrence had "an incapacity for what we ordinarily call thinking".[11] However Lawrence most of the time insists on trying to get his "abnormal" message across, which "is as insistent as it is inconsistent".[12] With regard to Lawrence's new and advanced world outlook, Earl Brewster, his Buddhist friend, comments that Lawrence is basically a prophet for many other writers. He recalls that Lawrence once said to him, "It would be three hundred years before his writings would be understood".[13] Though Lawrence's theories and life experience may seem abnormal to many men of letters and the public, they are illuminating to the future of mankind and thus have great value for us. John Middleton Murray acknowledges that:

> It is the abnormal men from whom we have to learn. They, and they alone, have something of import to teach us. Every man from whom humanity has learned how to make a real step forward into the future has been an abnormal man. He has been abnormal because he belongs to the future, because he was himself the soul of the future. Lawrence was the future; as much of it as we are likely to get in our time.[14]

Lawrence was attracted to India all his life, particularly by Hindu philosophy. However, we know that Lawrence's enthusiasm towards Hinduism is inconsistent: sometimes he rejects it, sometimes admires it. He admits, in January 1922, that "the fact that I have felt so spiteful against Buddha makes me feel I was unsure all the time, and kicking against the pricks". In the same letter he says, "I only know it seems so much easier, more peaceful to come east. But then peace, peace! I am so mistrustful of it: so much afraid that it means a sort of weakness and giving in."[15] In

the autumn of 1929, one year before his death, he wrote to Earl
Brewster from Germany:

> I agree with you entirely about India—but I feel I don't
> belong to the actual India of to-day. I love the Indian art,
> especially Brahmin, more every time I see it—and I feel
> Hindu philosophy is big enough for everything. Yet we
> have to bring forth some different thing, in harmony with
> the great Hindu conceptions. Which need carrying out.
> You couldn't hate the "west" machine world more than I
> do. Only it's no good running back into the past.[16]

Lawrence admired the mysterious and essential wisdom of
Hinduism. When he returned Brewster's copy of Coomaraswamy's
The Dance of Shiva, he said, "I enjoyed all the quotations from
ancient scriptures. They always seem true to me." Of J. C.
Chatterji's *Kashmir Shaivism*, he remarked: "That seems to me
the true psychology, how shallow and groping it makes Western
psychology seem."[17] I do not suggest that Lawrence was influenced
by Hinduism or some Oriental philosophies to any considerable
extent, though he was fascinated by their mysteries, and was
interested in the old Hindu hymns and familiar with Indian sage
aphorisms as Brewster suggests. While discussing Hinduism with
Brewster, Lawrence said that he did not "want to be tied to it by
the leg". He wanted to go "somewhere between east and west, in
that prophetically never-to-exist meeting point of the two". He
never found that meeting point, and was never really ready to
accept any Oriental religion or philosophy. The reason is that, as
he told Brewster, he found it difficult "entering into the thoughts
and feelings of another race".[18] Hinduism and Buddhism were no
more attractive to him than American Indian primitive culture.
He admired the Indians for their intuitive way of living, which
he believed was a necessary precondition to secure a "living
relationship" with the material cosmos. Besides, he felt far more
comfortable with pagan Greeks and Romans than the Oriental
religious world which he thought too logical and rational. From
Lawrence's upbringing and the books he read of both Romantic
and scientific writings, and of the volumes on Hinduism as
recorded, we should consider his philosophical positions to be the
outcome of the mixed influences of these literary contributions.

I would like to make a very brief introduction to the historical background and cultural context of certain Eastern religions or philosophies to which this book makes reference, such as Taoism, Buddhism and Hinduism.

In ancient Chinese society, more than two thousand years ago, there were two "philosophical" traditions playing complementary parts—Confucianism and Taoism. Confucianism is an ethical and philosophical system based upon the teachings of the Chinese sage Confucius. His philosophy emphasizes personal and governmental morality, correctness of social relationships, and justice and sincerity. Confucius' thoughts are regarded as imperial orthodoxy, which concerns itself with the linguistic, ethical, legal, and ritual conventions. These conventional restrictions force "the original spontaneity of life into the rigid rules of convention", in Alan Watts' words. Confucius' teaching greatly damaged man's "naturalness and un-self- consciousness" and caused much "conflict and pain" in human beings' everyday relationships. Whereas, "The function of Taoism is to undo the inevitable damage of this discipline, and not only to restore but also to develop the original spontaneity."[19]

Taoism is, strictly speaking, not a religion, nor a philosophy. It encompasses, however, both a Taoist philosophical tradition (called "Tao Jia", meaning "The School of Tao") associated with Laozi's *Dao De Jing*, *Zhuangzi*, and other texts, and a Taoist religious tradition (called "Tao Jiao", meaning "The Religion of Tao") with organized doctrine, formalized cultic activity, and institutional leadership. These two forms are clearly related, though at many points in tension. Traditionally, Taoism has been attributed to three sources, the oldest being the legendary "Yellow Emperor", but the most famous is Laozi's *Dao De Jing*. Laozi (the Old Master, died in 479 B.C.) is an older contemporary of Confucius.[20] The third source is Zhuangzi's untitled work. Laozi and Zhuangzi (360 B.C.), living at a time of social disorder and great religious scepticism, developed the notion of the Tao (way or path), which is a reinterpretation and development of an ancient nameless tradition of nature worship and divination. The Taoist heritage, with its emphasis on individual freedom and spontaneity, the embrace of social primitivism, mystical experience and techniques of self-transformation, represents in many ways the antithesis to Confucian concern with individual moral duties, community standards and government responsibilities.

Tao is the origin of all creation and the force that lies behind all the functioning and changes of the natural world. The main characteristic of Tao is its pervasiveness, which is manifested in two aspects. One aspect is its invisible, insensible, ineffable nature, the essence of Tao. The other aspect is the Tao as we see it in its activity in the world. Even though the Tao in itself is not sensible or describable, we can confirm its action in examples of harmony, flexibility and naturalness displayed in the world. The Yin-Yang philosophy represents the balance of opposites in the universe. In the balance and harmony of nature, Laozi saw the basis of a stable, unified, and enduring social order. The Tao of nature provides people with a spiritual approach to living: each person focuses on the immediate external world in order to understand the inner harmonies of the universe. The way to achieve one's harmonious relationship with nature is through meditation and contemplation. Taoism is a way of life. Much of the essence of Tao is in the art of Wu Wei (literally 'no-action') which actually means a practice of minimal action, or action modelled on nature. It is the art of living and surviving by conforming with the natural way of things. Spontaneity, intuition and submitting to nature are other characteristic practices of Taoism.

"De" in *Dao De Jing* means literally virtue, the power of which is the manifestation of the "Tao" (or Dao in Chinese Pinyin) within all things. Thus, to possess the fullness of De means to be in perfect harmony with one's original nature. According to Zhuangzi, an individual in harmony with the Tao comprehends the course of nature's constant change and fears not the rhythm of life and death. The individual with De must get rid of ideals and ideology, learn to embrace the primitive, reduce selfishness and have fewer desires. This free-and-easy approach to life enables one to return to the original purity and simplicity of the Tao.

The exposure of Taoists and Confucians to the main principles of Indian Mahayana Buddhism makes possible the creation of Zen Buddhism. So Japanese Buddhism, having been introduced into and remaining rooted in the culture of Japan since the twelfth century, originated from Indian Mahayana Buddhism. Zen is regarded as the fulfilment of long traditions of Indian and Chinese culture, though it is actually much more Chinese than Indian. The origins of Zen are as much Taoist as Buddhist, and Taoism is regarded as its ancestor. Therefore, Japanese Zen is actually, in its principles and practices, the same as Chinese Tao. Like Tao, Zen is not a religion. It is a way of life or a view of life, or an example of the "way of liberation", and is similar in this respect to Taoism, Vedanta, and Yoga. Besides, the ideas advocated by Zen masters share many core elements of Taoism, such as the beliefs in immediate awakening, in naturalness, in holding that knowing is not to know, in the notion of Wu Wei, in spontaneity, in the emptiness and void of the physical world, in the value of everyday life, and in the total elusiveness and imperma- nence of the world. These beliefs also feature in a serious and emphatic manner in Lawrence's writing.

Buddhism originated in ancient India and was introduced into China when Chinese civilization was at least two thousand years old. Buddhism is a philosophy and religion based upon the teachings of Siddhartha Gautama (566-486 B. C.).[21] Among Buddhist teachings is the Middle Way—seeking moderation and avoiding extremes. According to Buddhist philosophy, the nature of reality is impermanent and interconnected. People suffer in life because of their desire to have transient things, including life and death. The way to avoid suffering is to train the mind and to act according to the laws of karma (cause and effect).

Hinduism was established in India around 1200 B. C. The two sacred texts—The Vedas and The Upanishads—are the most authorized philosophical explorations of Hinduism.[22] The metaphysical foundation of classic Hinduism, which is expressed in both the Vedas and the Upanishads, is that Reality (Brahman) is One or Absolute, changeless, perfect and eternal. The ordinary human world is an illusion, its many separate and finite things are just reflections in the mind's net of words and concepts, and they are the illusions captured by our senses. Hindu cosmology is non-dualistic. Everything that is is Brahman. "Behold but one in all things". Brahman is the eternal Now, and in eternity there is no "before" or "after", for everything is everywhere, always. In order to experience the true self and the existence of the all in one Brahman, one is encouraged to purify one's mind through meditation.[23]

Among these main Eastern religions and philosophies, the concepts and ideas I borrow most in my study are from Taoism, and the classic text *Dao De Jing* by Laozi is my main source of reference. The reason is that in Taoism I find striking affinities with nearly every aspect of Lawrence's view of nature, and *Dao De Jing* is a very useful text for its classic notions like Wu Wei, spontaneity and Yin-Yang transformation. Confucianism, on the other hand, is barely relevant to Lawrence's understanding of man's intuitive and spontaneous relationship with nature, for it only advocates rigid disciplines guiding the moral behaviour of individuals and government, the orthodoxy of relationships and social order. It is mentioned and employed in my study so that its doctrines may provide a contrast to the principles of Taoism.

While attempting to bring out the affinities, irrespective of the fact that Lawrence might or might not have been familiar with these oriental philosophies, my intention is that Lawrence's imaginative art can be appreciated, understood and assimilated better if it is analyzed through a parallel body of thought similar to his own. The parallels between Lawrence's philosophy of nature and Eastern views will, I hope, draw attention to the fact that Lawrence not only sometimes thinks in a way resembling that of Oriental traditions, but also that there is a commonality existing to a certain degree in both Eastern and Western approaches dealing with the issues of man and nature. Some of the issues and concepts concerning Lawrence's philosophy of nature as identified in Eastern thought would, on the one hand, provide unique alternative perspectives in understanding his non-Christian outlook; and on the other hand would, I hope, raise our consciousness of modern ecology.

[1] Richard Aldington, one of his friends, author of *Portrait of a Genius, But . . ..* He wrote introductions for most of Lawrence's novels.

[2] *Nation and Athenaeum,* March 29, 1930.

[3] F. R. Leavis, *D. H. Lawrence: Novelist,* p. 9.

[4] Mainly: Edwardians, Georgians, Futurists, Imagists, Vorticists, and Bloomsburians, among others. See the Introduction of *D. H. Lawrence in His Time,* p. 15-23

[5] Roger Ebbatson, *Lawrence and the Nature Tradition: A Theme in English Fiction,* Ch. 8, pp. 239-260.

[6] Ibid. p. 44.

[7] *Letters of Sri Aurobindo,* p. 315, quoted in Chaman Nahal, *D. H. Lawrence, an Eastern View,* p. 248.

[8] Aldous Huxley, in *A Conversation on D. H. Lawrence,* edited by H. Mori, p. 19, quoted in Dolores La Chapelle, *D. H. Lawrence, Future Primitive,* p. 15.

[9] D. H. Lawrence, "Morality and the Novel", *Phoenix,* p. 528.

[10] Anthony Beal, *D. H. Lawrence,* p. 123.

[11] T. S. Eliot, *After Strange Gods: A Primer in Modern Heresy,* p. 63.

[12] Anna Fernihough, "Introduction" to *The Cambridge Companion to D. H. Lawrence,* p. 7.

[13] Earl Brewster, *D. H. Lawrence: Reminiscences and Correspondence,* p. 120.

[14] J.M. Murry, quoted in Henry Miller, *The World of Lawrence,* p. 51.

[15] Earl Brewster, *D. H. Lawrence, Reminiscences and Correspondence,* p. 45.

[16] Ibid., p. 213.

[17] Ibid., p. 175.

[18] Ibid., pp. 45, 19.

[19] Alan Watts, The Way of Zen, p. 10. Alan Watts is one of the most authoritative Western writers on Eastern traditional philosophies, especially Taoism and Japanese Zen. From the large volume of Watts' works, I find that his view is largely accurate, convincing and influential.

[20] Traditional Chinese philosophy ascribes both Taoism and Confucianism to a still earlier source, the I Jing, or Book of Change, dating anywhere from 3000 to 1200 B. C.

[21] Gautama was an Indian prince who later became a wandering monk, seeking a solution to an end of suffering. Meditating under a Bodhi tree at the age of 35, Gautama (known as Buddha) reached Enlightenment, awakening to the true nature of reality, which is Nirvana (Absolute Truth).

[22] The text of the "Vedas" is the first ever written collection of Indian philosophy composed around 1200 B. C. The word "Veda" meaning "sacred knowledge" comes from the Sanskrit. Another influential text is called "The Upanishads", composed around 8th-7th century B. C.

Chapter I

Lawrence's Sensitivity to Nature

*

In 1952, on the twenty-second anniversary of Lawrence's death, a taped discussion was held in the library of the University of California. In answering the moderator's question about what sort of gifts Lawrence had, Aldous Huxley said:

> He read very widely; he could pick up extraordinarily quickly out of anything that he read, all the significant facts . . . He had something else which was obviously the core of his whole genius, which was this immediate sensitivity to the world at large. He had this capacity for being, so to speak, naked in the presence of what is actually present in the world. And I think one can trace that throughout his writings as a persistent theme. . . . And this was essentially the basis of his life and was his greatest gift, I think: this capacity to be aware of the universe in all its levels, from the inanimate and the animal and the vegetable through the human, right up to something beyond. I think he was more aware on every level than anyone I've ever known.[1]

With "this capacity to be aware of the universe in all its levels", Lawrence confronts life in the fullness of his passion and intellect. His passion for natural life, the wonder of the universe, and his "capacity for being naked" left a deep impression on both his friends and enemies. His oldest friend the Honourable Herbert

1

Asquith depicted Lawrence as "a faun" who is "receptive and alert to every sound of the fields and woods". He then recalled, "there was something sprite like, electric, elemental, in the spirit which moved this slight sensitive form . . . his power of vision was as sensitive as his power of utterance and he could see heaven in the tint of a sheet of sand".[2] Herbert's wife Lady Cynthia shared the same admiration for Lawrence:

> You couldn't possibly be out of doors with Lawrence without becoming aware of the astonishing acuteness of his senses, and realising that he belonged to an intenser existence. Yet to some degree—and this was your great debt to him—he enabled you temporarily to share that intensified existence; for his faculty for communicating to others something of his own perceptiveness made a walk with him a wonderfully enhanced experience. In fact it made me feel that hitherto I had to all intents and purposes walked the earth with my eyes blindfolded and my ears plugged.[3]

This ability to transmit the spirit of things through his life and writing was one of his great gifts, which made many people see him as an extraordinary being. When the German writer and editor Franz Schoenberner met him in September of 1927, he described Lawrence as "a sick faun who out of sheer friendliness had left his mysterious woods. . . . Only a few people whom I have met have given me this feeling of their living in a sphere of pure essentiality where everything and everyone assumes a new and higher substance".[4] Even Lawrence's Cornwall neighbour Cecil Gray, the Scottish composer who disliked him, admired his extraordinary perceptions of nature and saw him as "a faun, a child of Pan, a satyr". He comments, "In all literature there is little, if anything, to compare with the extraordinary depth and delicacy of Lawrence's perceptions of Nature in all its forms and manifestations . . . That was the essential Lawrence; there he was truly great".[5]

It has been argued that adult genius has its roots in the childhood relationship with the natural world. Edith Cobb, author of *The Ecology of Imagination in Childhood*, came to the conclusion, after a thirty year study of the biographies of three hundred creative thinkers since the sixteenth century, that "there is a special period . . . when the natural world is experienced in some highly evocative way, producing in the child a sense of some profound continuity with natural processes". There is always a particular time in early childhood when each of these creative thinkers is awoken to a certain transcendent revelation in nature, which is "basically aesthetic and infused with joy in the power to know and to be".[6] The child's "acute sensory response to the natural world" is his "ecological sense of continuity with nature",[7] which may be "extended through memory into a lifelong renewal of the early power to learn and to evolve".[8] Many poets and writers had experienced an early awakening after their encounter with the miracles of nature and later throughout their lives enjoyed an ever-fresh excitement in new discoveries. Cobb's research suggests that an adult's transcendent thinking is based on the ability to go beyond the self and reach a particular perspective, and the seed for this capacity is in the plasticity of the child's responsiveness to nature. In Lawrence's case, his childhood experiences of early natural environments provided rich soil for cultivating this capacity.

Ever since Lawrence was a small boy, he had plenty of opportunities to be exposed to the country around Eastwood. Both of his parents encouraged him to be a keen observer of nature, teaching him the names of flowers, plants and animals. At a very early age, Lawrence was able to name flowers and plants of many different species. Jessie Chambers recalls, "There seemed no flower nor even weed whose name and qualities Lawrence did not know".[9] He used to search for the first flowers of spring and was delighted to find the delicate white snowdrops. He would look for the strawberries among the bushes, and hunt "through the wet grass" for the hidden mushrooms whom "are white skinned, wonderful naked bodies crouched secretly in the green". Each year, in the old quarry near Eastwood, among the lovely flowers, he picked the first luscious blackberries of the season and proudly took them home to his mother. This early experience gave him "the joy of finding something, the joy of accepting something straight from the hand of Nature, and the joy of contributing to the family exchequer". [10]

Lawrence's father had a particular influence upon him. He showed an intense love for animals, plants and flowers, and his rich knowledge of nature was passed on to the young Lawrence. He loved his morning walks through the dewy fields to the coal-pit. The colliers, Lawrence writes, though having "no daytime ambition, and no daytime intellect", would find their happiness in the countryside whenever they could. "He (the collier) . . . roved the countryside with his dog, prowling for a rabbit, for nests, for mushrooms, anything. He loved the countryside . . . loved his garden. And very often he had a genuine love of the beauty of flowers".[11] This is actually the reminiscence of his father's simple nature-loving life, which impressed him imperceptibly, yet bred in him a strong attachment to the beauty of nature. His sister Ada's memoirs, *Young Lorenzo*, tells much of Lawrence's love of nature during his childhood. She admires Lawrence's "uncanny" observation of nature: "Not a flower, tree or bird escaped Bert's notice, and he found wonderful adventure in seeing the first celandine or early violet".[12]

Edith Cobb argues, "at the level of participation in nature during childhood, there is fusion between emotion as the energy of spirit and the spirit of place as the energy of the behaving world".[13] Lawrence loved his hometown, the coal-mining village of Eastwood between Nottingham- shire and Derbyshire, in spite of his strong opposition to industrialization of the place. He wrote in *Nottingham and the Mining Countryside* in the year of his death: "To me it seemed, and still seems, an extremely beautiful countryside, just between the red sandstone, and the oak-trees of Nottingham, and the cold limestone, the ash-trees, the stone fences of Derbyshire"[14] The old quarry beside his favorite walking path from Eastwood to Haggs Farm was his most secret childhood place. He loved the old quarry surrounded by lush greenery which "was blue with dog-violets in spring". "The quarry was a haunt of mine", he writes, for the rocks and the caves in it haunted him with their sunny and dark sides. Whenever he crept inside the cave he would feel "Now . . . for a little while I am safe and sound, and the vulgar world doesn't exist for me".[15] On his last visit to the quarry, it still fascinated him as it had in his childhood: "I felt as I had always felt, there was something there". The landscapes of his beloved valley, the brook, the old sheep bridge, the tall hawthorn hedge, the mill-dam, the woods, the pit and the old quarry in his childhood memories are dramatically visualized in his early novels, *The White Peacock, Sons and Lovers* and *The Rainbow.*

Between the ages of sixteen and nineteen years old, Lawrence visited the Chambers family on the Haggs Farm, three miles from Eastwood. These years left him with very fond memories, and later the farm became the home of Miriam and the Willey Farm of *Sons and Lovers.* The mowing field rented by the Chambers was the countryside described in "Love Among the Haystacks", where Lawrence used to help with the haymaking. The wood, near the Haggs Farm, was not only the gamekeeper's exclusive domain, but also a piece of wonderland in Lawrence's young heart. Jessie recalls, "The wood held a fascination for us. The shade, the murmur of the trees, the sense of adventure, the strong odor of the underground, the sudden startled call of a pheasant, the whir of a partridge's wings, were thrilling things".[16] With Jessie, Lawrence spent much time reading poetry, discussing novels, and walking with her across the fields to Annesley, where Byron had courted Mary Chaworth, or through the surviving fragments of Sherwood Forest. "We spent some of the most exquisite moments of our lives gathering flowers, ladysmocks and cowslips".[17] Richard Aldington points out that the young Lawrence "scarcely ever made his bicycle trip to and from the Haggs without seeing something that delighted him and was instantly preserved in his wonderful memory". And he "never took the world and his feelings about it for granted".[18] Lawrence's boyhood experience, woven with the wonders of nature, contributed immensely in bringing his early writings to the fore.

Each of the cosmic elements, the sun, the moon, the stars, the sea, the cycle of the seasons, as well as plants and animals, seems to find its own living soul in Lawrence's imaginative art, which is felt so intuitively and so constantly that it constitutes the very essence of Lawrence's writing. In the "Introduction" of *D. H. Lawrence, St. Mawr and Other Stories*, Melvyn Bragg expresses his admiration for Lawrence's "extraordinary" gift in writing about "flowers, rivers, animals, birds, the sea, the mountains, so audaciously embroidering his testaments, so earnestly reaching out to find more and more meaning". He goes on to say, "So the natural world must have flowed into Lawrence more powerfully than it flows into most of us: and he, more than all but a very few of the greatest, was well prepared to receive it, to record it, to articulate it, to wonder at it and to speculate".[19] This penetrating perception, moreover, enabled him to look deeply into the nature of human beings' lives and to see things "more than a human being ought to see". [20]

* *

Of all the plants Lawrence was most emotionally attached to trees. Whenever possible, he would sit out under a tree, writing his fictions and essays. His wife Frieda knew him best and felt that "it was as if the tree itself helped him to write his book, and poured its sap into it".[21] In a letter to Cecil Gray, Lawrence writes about the soothing quality of trees: "I find here one is soothed with trees. I never knew how soothing trees are—many trees, and patches of open sunlight, and tree presences—it is almost like having another being".[22] In another letter to Gray, he says, "There is something living and rather splendid about trees. They stand up so proud and are alive".[23] *Lady Chatterley's Lover* was written in a wood of umbrella pines near Florence. This Italian wood with its old, tall and straight pines becomes Clifford Chatterley's English forest. The big pine tree in front of his house on the Kiowa ranch in New Mexico is described in his novelette *St. Mawr* as "the guardian of the place". The pine tree is "a bristling, almost demonish guardian, from the far-off crude ages of the world. . . ."[24] The *Fantasia of the Unconscious* was written at the edge of the Black Forest in Germany. "Sitting by a grassy wood-road with a pencil and a book", he writes:

> Today only trees, and leaves, and vegetable presences. Huge, straight fir-trees, and big beech- trees sending rivers of roots into the ground . . . Their magnificent, strong, round bodies! It almost seems I can hear the slow, powerful sap drumming in their trunks. Great full-blooded trees . . . a vast individual life, and an over shadowing will. . . .

> I would like to be a tree for a while. The great lust of roots . . . He towers, and I sit and feel safe . . . I always felt them huge primeval enemies, but now they are my only shelter and strength. I lose myself among the trees. I am so glad to be with them in their silent, intent passion, and their great lust. They feel my soul.[25]

When Lawrence is lost among the trees, feeling his soul within them, he is actually approaching a stage that seems to correspond to the Buddhist awakening, in which the individual is experiencing the integration of subject and object, of himself and the whole universe. In Zen Buddhism this is known as "oneness of life and its environment", an experience genuine Buddhists strive to obtain. It is regarded as an uttermost state, as one has reached "the oneness of man and heaven" (a Taoist term called "Tian Ren He Yi" in Chinese), which can be achieved through meditation. During this transformative process, one literally feels within other beings. When Lawrence hears "the slow, powerful sap drumming in their trunks", and feels that the landscape near his ranch at Kiowa is like a living being to him, he is experiencing a free interfusion, a spiritual unity between himself, the tree and the external world at large. He writes in "Pan in America" that the blazed and lightning-scarred pine tree standing in front of his cabin,

> Vibrates its presence into my soul, and I am with Pan. . . . Something fierce and bristling is communicated. . . . I am conscious that it helps to change me, vitally. I am even conscious that shivers of energy cross my living plasma from the tree, and I become a degree more like unto the tree, more bristling and turpentiney, in Pan. And the tree gets a certain shade and alertness of my life, within itself.[26]

Lawrence's experience is a strong manifestation of his extreme sensitivity to nature. His instinctive communication with natural objects is similar to the transcendental meditation practiced by the Taoist artist who is interested in depicting the spiritual dimension of nature. His experience is a kind of intuitive inter-penetration between him and the trees. When he "suddenly looks far up and sees those wild doves there", he "realizes that the tree is asserting itself as much as I am . . . Our two lives meet and cross one another, unknowingly".[27] This realization has reached the highest state of enlightenment in Buddhism and Taoism, in which man and nature merge into oneness, and man is aware of the vital energy of nature flowing inside and around him. It is believed in Buddhism that nature and self originate from the same common ground, having the same roots and the same divine spirit. One of the living elements is probably the incarnation of the other after many life cycles, so that man's life and the tree's life could, in Lawrence's words, "meet and cross one another". This may be a main reason why it is highly recommended that a Buddhist practises through meditation the "oneness of life and its environment".

Everywhere from his first three nature novels to his last poems, we find a passionate lover of plants in Lawrence. *The White Peacock* is filled with powerful descriptions of the botanical world. The poetic hero of *Kangaroo* loiters in the wildness of Australia, exploring and feeling all kinds of things about the bush. The heroine of *St. Mawr* comes to the mountain of New Mexico and is lost in her admiration of the natural beauty. The trees and flowers draw her spirit to "soar in", making her heart beat with a desire to marry the whole place. In *Women in Love*, Birkin, after his head is struck by Hermione with a paperweight, finds comfort among the primroses and pine needles, considering this place to be "his place, his marriage places":

> This was good, this was all very good, very satisfying. Nothing else would do, nothing else would satisfy, except this coolness and subtleness of vegetation travelling into one's blood. How fortunate he was, that there was this lovely, subtle, responsive vegetation, waiting for him, as he waited for it; how fulfilled he was, how happy! . . .
> Here was his world, he wanted nobody and nothing but the lovely, subtle, responsive vegetation, and himself, his own living self.[28]

Lawrence's passion for flowers saturates every line of his narrations in *Flowery Tuscany*. His knowledge of most species of flowers in England and in Italy is illustrated in this essay with an aesthetic and scientific perception: their habits and characteristics, colours, scents, shapes, their changes along with the sun and four seasons, and the revelations he perceived from their respective beauties. Catherine Carswell is impressed by Lawrence's unusual knowledge of and affection for flowers. She writes, "Lawrence knew all about wild flowers and could name most of them."[29] David Garnett (Edward Garnett's son) recalled a mountain walking trip with Frieda and Lawrence over the Alps to Italy, during which he and Lawrence collected nearly two hundred species of wild flowers. Ford Madox Ford in *Portraits From Life* describes at length Lawrence's supernatural quality. When he took a walk with Lawrence in gardens or parks, he found a "new side of Lawrence that was not father-mother derived—that was pure D. H. It was his passion—as it were an almost super-sex-passionate—delight in the openings of flowers and leaves". Once when they were taking a walk and talking, Lawrence, on coming upon a flower, suddenly knelt down to the flower and touched it gently. Then, Ford said, he became "a half-mad, woodland creature".[30] This scenario re-appears in Lawrence's novel *The Lost Girl*. When Alvina, the heroine, "came upon a bankside all wide with lavender crocuses, "she felt like going down on her knees and bending her forehead to the earth in an oriental submission, they were so royal, so lovely, so supreme".[31] The gamekeeper decorates Lady Chatterley with forget-me-nots, oak sprays, bluebells, campions, and woodruff. The narcissus, anemone, myrtle asphodel and grape hyacinth in the Mediterranean "are the flowers that speak and are understood in the sun round the Middle Sea". The aconites in the evening "are white and excited, and there is a perfume of sweet spring that makes one almost start humming and trying to be a bee". When talking about the "extremely beautiful" young hyacinths, Lawrence said: "If we were tiny as fairies, and lived only a summer, how lovely these great trees of bells would be to us, towers of night and down-blue globes. They would rise above us thick and succulent . . . and we should see a god in them".[32] This romantic vision reflects his instinctive love of nature, or further, symbolizes his emotional affiliation with plants and flowers. Flowers to Lawrence are of great symbolic significance. Two months before his death, Lawrence, with his friend Brewster Ghiselin on the shore of the Mediterranean, watching the waves and talking about symbols, said to Brewster, "A flower is the most perfect expression of life", and went on to explain that total individuality lay hidden in the bud and came forth in the blossoming of the individual. He was referring to the lotus which grows out of the mud but blooms so beautifully in the air, and marvelling at the "oozing mud" underneath which supplies the life of the flower.[33] Each flower to Lawrence has its own individuality, and its short life span is analogy to the reality of human life. Richard Aldington summarizes his unusual passion for flowers: " . . . flowers which to him were always the loveliest symbol of the beautiful non-human world. They had meant much to him in his loneliness".[34] Frieda recalled when Lawrence first encountered the deep blue cup—the alpine gentian—lying on the ground: "I remember feeling as if he had a strange communion with it, as if the gentian yielded up its blueness, its very essence, to him. Everything he met had the newness of a creation just that moment come into being".[35]

Lawrence's supernatural insight, Ford Madox Ford remarks, is an instinctive understanding of the mysterious elements of wild objects and an existing flow of the spirit between them. Ford finds reading his work "had a feeling of disturbance", and feels he himself is "going to do something eccentric". This feeling, Ford says, "is caused by my coming in contact with his as-it-were dryad nature. As if it were the sort of disturbing emotion caused in manufacturers and bankers by seeing, in a deep woodland, the God Pan—or Priapus—peeping round beside the trunk of an ancient oak". Lawrence's writings on nature seem to Ford entirely different from others, his passages "run like fire through his books and are exciting—because of the life that comes into his writing . . . You have the sense that there really was to him a side that was supernatural . . . in tune with deep woodlands".[36]

This rare gift of being "in tune with deep woodlands" in Lawrence finds its origin in Taoist spiritual union between inner and outer worlds. During this experience one's artistic perception merges successfully with the spirit of the natural world. In Taoist terms, the interfusion of Qi (or energy in English) in nature and the Qi within the artist will result in the objectification of spirit in the artwork.[37] And the artwork will display a unique spirit reflecting the "oneness of life and its environment" in Zen Buddhist terms. The mutual influence of the subject and the objective environment lends Lawrence's writing a "disturbing" spirit. It is "disturbing" because it reveals the writer's perception of the otherness of the non-human world, which accounts for the reason why Ford feels in Lawrence's writing "something eccentric", "different", and "supernatural".

Lawrence's intuitive understanding of "the otherness" in plants seems peculiar and is met with adverse reactions. Dolores LaChapelle writes in her *Future Primitive* that "Intense feelings toward nature were not only considered aberrant in Lawrence's lifetime but have also been considered so in all the decades since".[38] It was only after Edward O. Wilson published his book *Biophilia* in 1984, and explained man's intense relationship with natural things using the word "biophilia", that people began to understand and accept it. According to Wilson, "Biophilia" is "the innately emotional affiliation of human beings to other living organisms".[39] There is a psychological need for affinity between sensitive persons and the external world. This biophilia psychology enables human beings to live their lives with a sensitive consciousness of the needs of other living things, as well as the needs for environmental protection. Lawrence's extreme sensitivity to plants and other natural things is a manifestation that he does not lose his deep primitive psyche. Seeking protection from his environment, he is happy to sit between the toes of the tree "like a pea-bug, and him (the tree) noiselessly overreaching me . . . he towers, and I sit and feel safe". This is the same emotional attachment to nature he experienced as a young boy when he was inside the cave of the quarry in his hometown. [40]

To a biophilic person, as Lawrence is, everything in nature is "shimmering" with wonder and "the mystery of creation". It is blissful for him to find that the "wonder and fascination of creation shimmers in every leaf and stone, in every thorn and bud, in the fangs of the rattlesnake, and in the soft eyes of a fawn".[41] Aldous Huxley was deeply impressed by Lawrence's transcendental knowledge of the vital spirit hidden inside all the natural elements around him:

> To be with Lawrence was a kind of adventure, a voyage of discovery into newness and otherness . . . He looked at things with the eyes, so it seemed, of a man

> who had been at the brink of death and to whom, as he
> emerges from the darkness, the world reveals itself as
> unfathomably beautiful and mysterious . . . He seemed
> to know, by personal experience, what it was like to be a
> tree or a daisy or a breaking wave or even the mysterious
> moon itself. He could get inside the skin of an animal and
> tell you in the most convincing detail how it felt and how,
> dimly, inhumanly, it thought.[42]

His ability to enter into the "skin" of other living things and to register the uniqueness of each individual being is illustrated in the volume of poems called "Birds, Beasts and Flowers". In this series of poems, birds and beasts claim as much of his love as vegetation.

* * *

E. Neumann says in his book *The Origin and History of Consciousness*:

> Man's original fusion with the world, with its landscape
> and its fauna, has its best known anthropological
> expression in totemism, which regards a certain animal
> as an ancestor, a friend, or some kind of powerful and
> providential being . . . there is no doubt that early man's
> magical view of the world rests on identity relationships
> of this kind.[43]

With the same "identity relationship", Lawrence feels a close affinity with certain animals. With them, "he felt connected and heard the voice of the Holy Ghost".[44] His pretty cat, Miss Timsy, his cow Susan, his brown hen and little black bitch Bibbles, his white cock Moses in New Mexico and many more, are to him perfect beings, each of which epitomized its own living universe. Lawrence is fascinated by their mysterious "otherness" in the unknown world and he believes there exists in them a more natural flow to the sun and the whole cosmos than in human beings.

The birds, he writes, " . . . are the life of the skies, and when they fly, they reveal the thoughts of the skies".[45] Birds to him are active primeval creatures that bridge the heaven and the earth. The "blood-thirsty" eagle in Mexico fronted the sun "so obstinately", as if he owed the sun "an old, old grudge . . . or an old, old allegiance". The kangaroo "watches with insatiable wistfulness. / Untold centuries of watching for something to come, / For a new signal from life, in that silent lost land of the South".[46] The poem "Fish" is probably most illuminating, in which the poet attempts to imagine the alien life-experience of fishes:

> . . . soundless, and out of contact.
> They exchange no word, no spasm, not even anger.
> Not one touch.
> Many suspended together, forever apart,
> Each one alone with the waters, upon one wave with the rest.[47]

He was wondering who was the god of the fish. When he caught a fish in Germany, he immediately regretted it, at seeing the "horror-tilted eye": "And my heart accused itself /thinking: I am not the measure of creation", because, "This is beyond me, this fish / His God stands outside my God".[48] His depiction of the fish reveals an absolute otherness of the fish kingdom.

Love and equality between all living creatures are essential elements of the Buddhist nature. In the Hinayana texts of Buddhism there is a non-killing principle: Kill no living creature, and give living creatures life, freedom and happiness consistent with your own existence. Lawrence's sympathy for the fish suggests he has a Buddha heart—a Buddha heart is supposed to be lenient, clean and free of any earthly desires—in the sense that he loves those non- human living things, and is aware of an equality with them. Lawrence always feels regret after he has killed or injured some animals. There is in Lawrence sometimes a conflicting feeling of both love and fear towards certain animals such as the porcupine and the snake. In "Snake", for example, he is at first delighted at coming across a golden snake: "he had come like a guest in quiet, to drink at my water-trough / and depart peaceful, pacified, and thankless/ into the burning bowels of this earth". But being aware of its venomous nature, he throws a log at it and it "writhed like lightning, and was gone". He immediately regrets, hating violently his "mean act", and "accursed human education", because the snake "seemed to me again like a king", and he "missed my chance with one of the lords of life".[49]

The horse triggers Lawrence's imagination greatly. To him, the horse symbolizes an unknown world from which he perceives a mysterious linkage between the otherness of the animal kingdom and his human heroes. The horse in the story *St. Mawr* exerts a weird sensation on Lawrence's female characters. Both mother and daughter are enchanted by the dark power of the stallion St. Mawr. Lou, the American lady, worships the splendid demon-like stallion, in whose eyes and body she and her mother could see the other world of the "fallen Pan". In his neighing, Lou "seemed to hear the echoes of another, darker, more spacious, more dangerous, more splendid world than ours, that was beyond her. And there she wanted to go".[50] Mellors, the gamekeeper in *Lady Chatterley's Lover*, is not only interested in pheasants and flowers but also in the four-footed creatures. He says to Lady Chatterley that the horses and cows have a soothing effect on him, and being with them he feels "very solaced". This is very much the same feeling Lawrence experienced when he was with his cow at Taos. In his back yard, Lawrence had a black cow named Susan, whom he would milk every morning and evening. Susan was not just his life companion; she was to him "a religious object and a symbol of life and salvation".[51] "How can I equilibrate myself with my black cow Susan"? he asked. "There *is* a sort of relation between us. And this relation is part of the mystery of love . . ..The queer cowy mystery of her is her changeless cowy desirableness".[52] Later when he left his Kiowa Ranch, he wrote in a letter: "It grieves me to leave my horse, and my cow Susan, and . . . the white cock, Moses—and the place".[53]

Lawrence not only feels a connection with his animals, but also gains revelations and power from their unknown world. His fascination with the otherness of the non-human world enables him to draw most intimate associations between the human world and the animal kingdom. "The dolphin", he writes in "Etruscan Places", "is like the phallus carrying the fiery spark of procreation down into the wet darkness of the womb". And the duck becomes "to man, the symbol of that part of himself which delights in the waters, and dives in, and rises up and shakes its wings. It is the symbol of a man's own phallus and phallic life".[54] His intimate and joyful depictions of dolphins and tortoises, as well as St. Mawr, draw us into the proposition that, in effect, they are superior to human beings. Lawrence's poems of "Birds, Beasts and Flowers" not only registers his most sympathetic feelings towards animals, but also invites us to think of our own world. The picture of the animal kingdom is beautiful yet cruel. It is full of unpredicted terror and is in a way similar to the human world.

Lawrence's love of animals and his desire to "equilibrate myself with my black cow Susan" is in line with the Buddhist concept that animals play a vital role in the formation of natural lives. It is a Buddhist belief of incarnation that man and animal can be incarnated into each other's flesh after certain cycles of birth. From this point of view, a familiar link may be assumed: "Being connected with the process of taking birth, one is kin to all wild and domestic animals, birds, and beings born from the womb".[55] Accordingly, repeated births of man, animals and other beings generate an interconnected web of life. Human beings are thus required to observe the Buddhist precepts of harmlessness and kindness towards all animals. For Lawrence, his loving feelings toward animals are in line with his instinctive acknowledgement of man's affinity to animals. In describing birds, fish and animals, Lawrence seems to be part of them, which is seen in Taoism as an accomplished balancing process between subject and object. Alan Watts writes that this balancing process comes into full effect only when the feeling of being the subject becomes "itself part of the stream of experience and does not stand outside it in a controlling position". As for observing things, he further explains, the subject should be treated as "the inseparable pole or term of a subject-object identity".[56] The same notion is expounded in the work of Zhuangzi, one of the founders of Taoism:

> Only the truly intelligent understand this principle of the identity of all things. They do not view things as apprehended by themselves, subjectively, but transfer themselves into the position of the things viewed. And viewing them thus they are able to comprehend them, nay, to master them.[57]

The way Lawrence presents animal life suggests he has transferred himself "into the position of the things viewed" when observing the animals. Being part of the observing experience, he, the subject, has achieved an understanding of "mutual distinction". And "mutual distinction of . . . subject and object" reveals their "inner identity".[58] With this "inner identity", Lawrence feels a living connection between himself and his cow. Because of the same "inner identity", the mysterious St. Mawr is more equilibrate with the grooms than with its master Rico.

* * * *

In Lawrence's work there are abundant references reflecting his intense lifetime awareness of the beauty and power of the land. While in Cornwall, Lawrence wrote *Studies in Classic American Literature* (which was entirely rewritten when he was in America). In his introductory essay "The Spirit of Place", he writes:

> Every continent has its own great spirit of place. Every people is polarized in some particular locality, which is home, the homeland. Different places on the face of the earth have different vital effluence, different vibration, different chemical exhalation, different polarity with different stars: call it what you like. But the spirit of place is a great reality.[59]

In Lawrence's notion of "the spirit of place", we find an extension of the same idea in Aldo Leopold's theory of the land: "Land, then, is not merely soil; it is a fountain of energy flowing through a circuit of soils, plants, and animals . . .."[60] Is this "fountain of energy" not "the spirit of place" in Lawrence's words? This spirit is referred to as "Qi" in traditional Chinese philosophy (Qi is the source of all beings and the eternal flow of nature, upon which the cosmos and the living world are constructed). Paralleling Aldo Leopold's view, the Chinese vision of the land is seen as a single living organism created out of the interfusion of numerous streams of vital force which together establish the wholeness and continuity of nature.

Lawrence's later life was in a constant state of travelling with the purpose of "running away from the horror of one's conflict"[61] and escaping from the horrible society, as well as the need to improve his poor health and to find new revelation and stimulation for his imaginative art. Since he first left England in

1919, Lawrence, with his wife Frieda, travelled all over the world. After his visit to Germany, he settled for a significant time in Sicily, Taormina and some other places in Italy until 1922. Later he moved on to Ceylon, to Australia and then from the Pacific he came to the Southwest of America. After his fruitful time in New Mexico, he finally went back to Europe, where he died in the south of France in 1930. During this period Lawrence was encountering completely new and often exotic scenes and the spirit of exotic lands contributes a great deal to Lawrence's creative works. Just the first four years between his departure and his first return visit to England promised a large portion of his creative production, such as *Aaron's Rod, Kangaroo, The Lost Girl*; his best travel book, *Sea and Sardinia*, "The Fox" and some other short stories; his best single volume of poetry, *Birds, Beasts and Flowers*; and the collected essays, *Studies in Classic American Literature* which has since often considered to be the most influential piece of criticism written on the subject.

In 1922, Lawrence and Frieda stayed in Australia for three months. During this short space of time, Frieda felt that "it was as if through a sixth sense something came to him of the country itself, of the place itself".[62] W. Siebenhaar, who lived most of his life in Australia, expressed his admiration for the power of Lawrence's vision in capturing the magic of the place: " . . . in so short a space of time, and at so unpropitious a stage of the year, Lawrence succeeded in obtaining an estimate of the magic of the scene".[63] Before he went to Taos of New Mexico, Lawrence wrote to Catherine Carswell about the old spirit of Australia:

> But also there seems to be no inside life of any sort: just a long lapse and drift. A rather fascinating indifference, a *physical* indifference to what we call soul or spirit . . . As you get used to it, it seems so *old*, as if it had missed all this Semite Egyptian-Indo-European vast era of history, and was coal age, the age of great ferns and mosses. . . . A strange effect it has on one. Often I hate it like poison, then again it fascinates me, and the spell of its indifference gets me. I can't quite explain it: as if one resolved back almost to the plant kingdom, before souls, spirits and minds were grown at all: only quite a live, energetic body with a weird face.[64]

Somers in *Kangaroo* loves the wild spiritual beauty of Australia. Whenever caught up in the rush of worldly business, his feeling of agony would be soothed by the overwhelming "indifference" of this ancient world.

Lawrence was always quick to grasp the transcen- dental power of each place wherever he went; nothing trivial seems to have escaped his observant eyes. His strong feelings towards each place have been recorded in his travel books such as *Sea and Sardinia, Mornings in Mexico and Etruscan Places*. He writes in "New Mexico" of the exquisite beauty of Sicily, Tuscany, and Australia: "How lovely is Sicily, with Calabria across the sea like an opal, and Etna with her snow in a world above and beyond! How lovely is Tuscany, with little red tulips wild among the corn".[65] But when he came to New Mexico he was completely intoxicated by its magnificent landscape. Nothing, he writes, could be compared with the beauty of New Mexico:

> But the moment I saw the brilliant, proud morning shine high up over the deserts of Santa Fe, something stood still in my soul, and I started to attend. . . . In the magnificent fierce morning of New Mexico one sprang awake, a new part of the soul woke up suddenly and the old world gave way to a new.[66]

This passage has been frequently quoted but often derided as the "hyperbole of a neurotic man". However, in Buddhism the effect of a stunning landscape on human psychology has been recognized and justified. The release of feelings while immersed in one's surroundings—either laughing suddenly or bursting into tears or any other emotional expressions—suggests that one is experiencing a complete unity with one's environment. Lawrence understands the beauty of nature more deeply than most people. A sensitive biophilia as he is, how could he not be touched when facing the absolute and "almost unbearable" beauty of the mountain landscape? To Lawrence this landscape of Taos is "way beyond mere aesthetic appreciation". It strikes him as "undauntedly religious", which he says is a genuine religious feeling he has been searching for elsewhere for years.[67] The fact that one can achieve religious revelation from a landscape has long been recognized since the medieval period in Japanese history.

According to Steve Odin's explanation, "The natural environment is seen as laden not only with aesthetic but also religious values so that it becomes the ultimate ground and source of salvation itself".[68]

Lawrence's worship of the landscape and his lifetime sensitive awareness of the power of the land are not strange to us. He was influenced by the Western traditions of nature, which he read about in various works. We could draw a conclusion that much of his views of nature have their roots in the Romantic Movement beginning from Rousseau, through Goethe and the Romantic poets such as Blake, Wordsworth, Coleridge, Shelley, and in the Transcendentalist writers such as Whitman, Emerson and Thoreau, as well as in the fiction of Meredith, Hardy and Jefferies. They all show the same enthusiasm in their appreciation for the beauty of the land. Their emotional attachment to the landscape has been studied by Aldo Leopold in his *A Sand County Almanac*. Leopold calls it "land aesthetic". In Leopold's view, it is the beauty or aesthetic value intrinsic to nature that arises our awareness of the symbiotic relation between humans and land, and therefore suggests the importance of establishing an ecological harmony between people and their natural environment of soil, plants, and animals. According to Steve Odin, "our moral love and respect for nature is based on an aesthetic appreciation of the beauty and value of the land", which is the foundation for a land ethic, and "is one of the deepest insights into the human/nature relation developed in the ecological worldviews both East and West". [69]

In Lawrence there is an intrinsic attachment to a non-human world, a world of "Birds, Beasts and Flowers", and, most of all, a world with primitive environments. This kind of place reveals to man the true spirit of nature, in which man would put his social identity aside and see his humble place in the whole living system. It is wildly acknowledged that a most effective wild place for an artist is perhaps a wild mountain. The sacred potential and the transcendental power of mountains could make human beings think and see differently. Lawrence needed a good environment for his health and inspiration. During the last years of his life, he lived in the Villa Mirenda near Florence. Here he lived "against an immense landscape", with a view of Monte Morello and the peaks of the Apennines.[70] His very understanding friend Catherine Carswell described the wild mountain: "The spring came beautifully at the Mirenda, with sky-staring daisies and earth-gazing violets, with blonde narcissi and dark anemones, both trembling, and 'under the olives all the pale-gold bubbles of winter aconites'".[71]

After his trip to Australia, Lawrence went to live in Taos, New Mexico in the fall of 1922. He was delighted at living on a small Kiowa Ranch given to him by his American sponsor Mabel Luhan. The ranch was situated at a hundred and sixty acres high in the skirts of the mountains, untouched by humans, with "unbroken spaces" and splendid scenes around him. Deeply moved by the spirit of the place, Lawrence wrote in the letter:

> . . . so lovely, the wild plum everywhere white with snow, the cotton-wood trees all tender plumy green, like happy ghosts, . . . But I do like having the big unbroken spaces round me. There is something savage unbreakable in the spirit of place out here. [72]

Enjoying the absolute beauty of the changing land and sky, Lawrence was so comfortable with this silent, spacious and untamed mountain landscape. Brett remembered the magic evenings when she, Lawrence and his wife went to have dinner with the Indians around the big fire: "It is one of those magical evenings: a clear sky, a very young moon. No sound, not a twig moves".[73] Taos' magnificent circling landscape was later written in *St. Mawr* as "the landscape lived, and lived as the world of the gods, unsullied and unconcerned". In December of the same year, Lawrence came to live on the Del Monte ranch, some three miles away from Kiowa Ranch, which was among the pine trees at the foot of the Rockies and with spectacular views of the desert and the range of distance peaks. The landscape of the Rocky Mountain regions "crystallized all his previous glimpses into the power of the land itself".[74]

For ancient Chinese sages and artists, retreating to the mountains was a search for grandeur and awesomeness in nature. When he was talking about Chinese painting, Lin Yutang, the world-renowned Chinese philosopher, explained that if an artist went to a grand surrounding of mountains, it was inevitable that he should obtain an elevation of the spirit as well as a physical elevation. Life always looks different from an altitude of five thousand feet. He mentions that people fond of horseback riding always say that the moment one goes up on horseback one obtains a different view of the world. Thus from his god-like height an artist surveys the world with a calm expansion of the spirit, and this spirit goes into his painting.[75] He pointed out that people retreating to the mountains also means "a search for moral elevation". Being immersed in the tranquil mountain surroundings one tends to receive a spiritual and moral uplift. It is said that in the mountain there prevails a vital source of Qi, or "Shan Lin Qi" (literally it means the spirit of the mountain and the forest in Chinese), which suggests a spiritual mixture of calm, harmony, wisdom and health. This "moral elevation" is what Lawrence was searching for. Qi, in traditional Taoism, belongs to both natural objects and to human beings as aforementioned. The merging of the two Qis will have its aesthetic manifestation in one's artwork, in poems or paintings. And in Lawrence's case, of course, it will bring him health, wisdom and a spiritual uplift.

* * * * *

Lawrence's extraordinary sensitivity to nature leads him to feel deeply man's affinity to all things in the universe. For him, the sun, the moon and the sea together with human beings are all members of the same cosmic family. In his vision the sun is not only his father, but also the symbol of democracy, freedom, power, decency and nobility. It is often associated with integrity, glory and truth. He takes pride in being a "sun-man": "I feel aristocratic, noble, when I feel a pulse (sent from the sun) go through me".[76] He wants people to "draw your nobility directly from the sun" and "be an aristocrat of the sun". To him, sun aristocrats are in opposition to those "dead people, money-slaves, and social worms". Lawrence criticizes the narrowness of the middle-classes in that they "have utterly no reference to the sun"; instead "they have only two measures: mankind and money". He writes:

No sun, no earth,
nothing that transcends the bourgeois middlingness,
the middle class are more meaningless
than paper money when the bank is broke.

Lawrence's message is that man's "sun-awareness" is linked with his life principle, thus whoever denies the sun, is denying life and is immoral.[77] The short story "Sun" dramatizes the sun's mysterious effects on human body and mind. Lying naked in the sun, Juliet "could feel the sun penetrating even into her bones; nay, farther, even into her emotions and her thoughts. The dark tension of her emotion began to give way, the cold dark clots of her thoughts began to dissolve."[78] Bathing in the hot sun without clothes, she has a feeling "of detachment from people"; the sun has changed her worldly attitude towards life and sex.[79] This story reflects Lawrence's vision of the power and nobility of the "Father Sun", which is no doubt associated with pagan civilization and the cosmic consciousness of the primitive American Indians. To them the sun is the living source of everything human and non-human on earth. The Indians in Taos and Hopi, like the tribes of Africa and ancient Egypt, perform religious ceremonies to welcome the sun, gesturing their adoration of the sun when waiting for their god, the "Father Sun", to rise and to set. Lawrence's New Mexico experience enhances his understanding of why the Aztecs would sacrifice the hearts of men to the sun. "For the sun is not merely hot or scorching, not at all. It is of a brilliant and unchallengeable purity and haughty serenity . . ."[80] In *Apocalypse*, Lawrence criticises modern man's scientific interpretation of the sun as different from "the cosmic sun of the ancients":

> Don't let us imagine we see the sun as the old civilizations saw it. All we see is a scientific little luminary, dwindled to a ball of blazing gas. In the centuries before Ezekiel and John, the sun was still a magnificent reality, men grew forth from him strength and splendour, and give him back homage and lust and thanks. But in us the connection is broken, the responsive centres are dead. Our sun is a quite different thing from the cosmic sun of the ancients, so much more trivial.[81]

The moon, to Lawrence, is also of particular importance. His unusual sensitivity to the mysterious power of the full moon has been reflected in both his own life and his fictions. Jessie Chambers recollects several times when Lawrence was deeply distressed by the full moon. Once when they were walking along the beach before the moon rose, she found that,

> Gradually some dark power seemed to take possession of Lawrence, and when the final beauty broke upon us, something seemed to explode inside him . . . his words were wild, and he appeared to be in great distress of mind, and possibly also of body.

Another time in the moonlight, Lawrence frightened Jessie by leaping "from one white boulder to another in the vast amphitheatre of the bay until I could have doubted whether he was indeed a human being".[82] The similar scenes of "dehumanised" moon experience are repeated in *The White Peacock, The Trespasser, Sons and Lovers,* and *The Rainbow.* Paul Morel and Miriam, on holiday by the ocean, experience the extraordinary impact of the moon. When Paul suddenly sees "an enormous orange moon . . . staring at them from the rim of the sandhills", he is so excited that "the whole of his blood seemed to burst into flame, and he could scarcely breathe".[83] The moon has always stirred a sense of absurdity and terror in Lawrence's characters. In the chapter "First Love" of *The Rainbow*, towards the end of the party, when "a great white moon is looking at her over the hill", Ursula opened her breast to it:

> She was cleaved like a transparent jewel to its light. She stood filled with the full moon, offering herself. Her two breasts opened to make way for it, her body opened wide like a quivering anemone, a soft, dilated invitation touched by moon. She wanted the moon to fill in to her, she wanted more, more communion with the moon, consumma- tion.[84]

Later Ursula and Skrebensky come to the stack yard. Ursula seems to be transformed by "the overwhelming luminosity of the moon. She seemed a beam of gleaming power. She was afraid of what she was." Looking at the shadow of Skrebensky, she feels he is "unreal", and then "a sudden lust seized her": she wants to "lay hold of him and tear him and make him into nothing".[85] But Anna of *The Rainbow* experiences ecstasy in the bright moonlight, as she responds physically and spiritually to a large golden moon when she and Will Brangwen set up the oat sheaves. Many moon scenes in Lawrence novels suggest the moon's enormous influence upon man's life. Immersed in the moonlit landscape, walking, dancing, picking flowers, working in the fields or making love in the open, his main characters feel as if they have gone through something which is like a "joyous, serene, powerful, life-filled ritual".[86]

The moon is not just a dead satellite reflecting the light of the sun, as seen by scientists. It brings us ecstasy and blesses our lives. In his *Last Poems*, Lawrence, at this point a very sick man, writes a passionate poem to the "great glorious lady" moon, begging her "to be good" to him, to "set me again on moon-remembering feet / a healed, whole man".[87] According to Lawrence, moonlight has a special influence on love and sex. The moon scenarios, as LaChapelle points out, seem to convey a message that, when man and woman are in the full moon, they must follow their natural response, and fully enter into moonlit experiences with both body and mind. Then they will arrive at a perfect and blessed occasion. Otherwise, "if a person cannot be fully present because of interference from the conscious mind, then it becomes a negative thing, a tragedy".[88] Such tragedy happens to Paul and Miriam, for Paul shrinks from giving "physical love" to Miriam under the full moon.[89] The bright moonlight also witnesses the tragic ending of Ursula and Skrebensky's love. It is because their sexual activity in the moonlight is unnatural, is forced or driven by mind instead of body. Their lovemaking on the moonlit slope is like a "fight", an "ordeal", and "the struggle for consummation was terrible". The tragedy is a result from want of complete body and mind balance between the two and the male balance with the moon.[90] In criticizing modern man's ignorance of the "mother" moon, Lawrence wrote metaphorically about the vital connection of the moon with our "nerves" and "moist flesh":

> And we have lost the moon, the cool, bright ever-varying moon. It is she who would caress our nerves, smooth them with the silky hand of her glowing, soothe them into serenity again with their cool presence. For the moon is the mistress and mother of our watery bodies, the pale body of our nervous consciousness and our moist flesh. Oh, the moon could soothe us and heal us like a cool great Artemis between her arms. But we have lost her, in our stupidity we ignore her, and angry she stares down on us and whips us with nervous whips. [91]

Many of his poems suggest the magic influence of the moon upon our earthly psyche:

> When the moon falls on a man's blood
> white and slippery, as on the black water in a port
> shaking asunder, and flicking at his ribs—
> then the noisy, dirty day-world
> exists no more, nor ever truly existed . . . [92]

Lawrence's moon complex is not without any scientific reason. Lachapelle points out in her *Future Primitive* that there are some links between the moon and mental illness because of "phases of the moon" that "bring about modulations in the earth's electric and magnetic fields". Dr. Leonard J. Ravitz of the Virginia Department of Health and Education, during his research about seasonal and lunar changes in mental patients, found that the moon's effect on the ratio of terrestrial electromagnetic forces could precipitate disorders in persons whose mental balance was precarious or who were unusually sensitive.[93] Dr. William Petersen of Chicago points out the full moon has a strong influence upon those who are ill with tuberculosis, and the deaths caused by tuberculosis are most frequent eleven to seven days before the full moon.[94] Lawrence's lifelong battle with tuberculosis serves as another source for his intense sensitivity to the impact of the full moon. Lawrence himself is conscious of the moon's impact upon his weak body. He is also aware of the conditions of those who are similarly influenced by the moon's effect. Rhys Davies, the Welsh novelist who lived near him in France in early 1929, recalls Lawrence's unique explanation of his conditions:

> What the Celts have to learn and cherish in themselves is the sense of mysterious magic that is born with them . . . the dark magic that comes with the night especially, when the moon is due, so that they start and quiver, seeing her rise over their hills, and get her magic into their blood.[95]

Lawrence's knowledge of mythology, primitive cultures and ancient philosophies enhances his romantic vision of the "unseparatedness" between human beings and the sun, the moon and other aspects of nature. He condemns Christianity for breaking man's old living connection with the cosmos. To modern man, the landscape and the sky become only a "delicious background of our personal background, and no more", but to the pagan, "the cosmos was a very real thing. A man lived with the cosmos, and knew it greater than himself". Modern man's lack of cosmic consciousness is to Lawrence a "tragedy": "We have lost the cosmos, by coming out of responsive connection with it, and this is our chief tragedy".[96] The tragic absence of a cosmic connection accounts for modern man's obsession with rationalism, intellectualism, as well as science and machinery. In *Apocalypse* we hear his metaphorical vision of man's dependence upon the vital "cosmic law" of the sun and the moon:

> We and the cosmos are one. The cosmos is a vast living body, of which we are still parts. The sun is a great heat whose tremors run through our smallest veins. The moon is a great leaning nerve- centre from which we quiver forever . . . He who is not with me is against me!—that is a cosmic law.[97]

At the end of *Apocalypse*, Lawrence writes: all we want is to "re-establish the living organic connections, with the cosmos, the sun and the earth . . . Start with the sun, and the rest will slowly, slowly happen".[98]

Lawrence's cosmic mentality is in a way a portrayal of that of Taoism and Zen. A genuine Taoist is supposed to feel completely at home in this universe and to see human beings as an integral part of his environment. The ancient Taoists view nature as a member of the whole organism: "heaven and earth are alike members of this organism, and nature is as much our father as our mother".[99] In his essay "The Spinner and the Monks", Lawrence expresses a similar cosmic perception: "All are alike members of this organism", the sun is our father, the moon or sea is the mother, and the morning star the "gleaming clue" to bridge the light and the night. Each of these eternal elements is forever "alone" and "partial", yet when they unite, it is perfect. He ends the essay by presenting a cosmic picture of organic oneness:

> Where is the supreme ecstasy in mankind, which makes day a delight and night a delight, purpose an ecstasy and a concourse in ecstasy, and single abandon of the single body and soul also an ecstasy under the moon? Where is the transcendent knowledge in our hearts, uniting sun and darkness, day and night, spirit and senses? Why do we not know that the two in consummation are one; that each is only part; partial and alone for ever; but that the two in consummation are perfect, beyond the range of loneliness or solitude?[100]

It is emphasized by Lawrence that man's existence as a part of nature has its significance only when he achieves a living wholeness with the universe. Two and a half years before his death, he wrote to Dr. Trigant Burrow:

> And I do think that man is related to the universe in some "religious" way, even prior to his relation to his fellow man . . . . There is a principle in the universe, towards which man turns religiously—a life of the universe itself. And the hero is he who touches and transmits the life of the universe.[101]

Lawrence, a religious man, believes in the intrinsic relations of man with the universe and in turn "transmits the life of the universe" into the life of his characters in his creative world. From a Taoist perspective, the man who feels a pre-human relation to the universe, as Lawrence did, must possess positive elements that are called by Zhuangzi "pre-social qing" ("qing" means "affections, feelings, or emotions" in this context). This pre-social qing is one's "true nature" which is regarded by Taoists as an inherent, presocialized identity—an original, natural qing that exists prior to any Shi-Fei (pro-and-con) judgments. People who possess this original qing are free from the influences of society, and are thus capable of following the guide of Tao in nature. He who feels a pre-human relation to the universe will live a spontaneous life, and share with nature the same characteristics. He who feels a pre-human relation to nature will live a harmonious life along side it without imposing artificial restrictions and divisions on it. The issue of the relationship between man and nature, as well as their mutual identity, will be further discussed in the next chapter "Man and Nature".

[1] Aldous Huxley, in H. Mori, *A Conversation on D. H. Lawrence*, pp. 18-19, quoted in Dolores LaChapelle, *D. H. Lawrence, Future Primitive*, p. 15.

[2] Herbert Asquith, *Moments of Memory*, p. 189.

[3] Cynthia Asquith, *Remember and Be Glad*, p. 133.

[4] Franz Schoenberner, "When D.H. Lawrence was Shocked", in book by the same title *When D.H. Lawrence was Shocked*, quoted in Dolores LaChapelle, *D. H. Lawrence, Future Primitive*, p. 22.

[5] Cecil Gray, *Musical Chairs*, p. 141.

[6] Edith Cobb, *The Ecology of Imagination in Childhood*, p. 23.

[7] Ibid., p.30.

[8] Edith Cobb, "The Ecology of Imagination in Childhood", quoted in Dolores LaChapelle, *D. H. Lawrence, Future Primitive*, p. 12.

[9] Jessie Chambers, *D. H. Lawrence: A Personal Record*, p. 34.

[10] D. H. Lawrence, *Sons and Lovers*, Ch. 4, pp. 87-8.

[11] D. H. Lawrence, "Nottingham and the Mining Countryside", *Phoenix*,

p. 137.

[12] *D. H. Lawrence: A Composite Biography*, Edward Nehls, ed., Vol. II, p. 14.

[13] Edith Cobb, *The Ecology of Imagination in Childhood*, p. 32.

[14] D. H. Lawrence, "Nottingham and the Mining Countryside", *Phoenix*, p. 133.

[15] D. H. Lawrence, "Autobiographical Fragment", *Phoenix*, p. 825.

[16] Jessie Chambers, *D. H. Lawrence: A Personal Record*, p. 33.

[17] Ibid., p. 111.

[18] Richard Aldington, *Portrait of a Genius, But . . .*, p. 79.

[19] Melvyn Bragg, "Introduction" to *D. H. Lawrence, St. Mawr and Other Stories*, pp. x-xi.

[20] Ford Madox Ford, *Portraits From Life*, p. 75.

[21] Frieda Lawrence, *Not I, But the Wind . . .*, p. 94.

[22] *The Letters of D. H. Lawrence*, Aldous Huxley, ed., p. 435.

[23] Ibid., p. 428.

[24] D. H. Lawrence, *St. Mawr* in *St. Mawr and Other Stories*, p. 184.

[25] D. H. Lawrence, *Fantasia of the Unconscious and Psychoanalysis and the Unconscious*, pp. 38-9.

[26] D. H. Lawrence, "Pan in America", *Phoenix*, p. 25.

[27] Ibid., p. 25.

[28] D. H. Lawrence, *Women in Love*, Ch. 8, p. 107.

[29] Catherine Carswell, *The Savage Pilgrimage*, p. 202.

[30] Ford Madox Ford, *Portraits from Life*, pp. 78-9.

[31] D. H. Lawrence, *The Lost Girl*, Ch. 16, p. 392.

[32] D. H. Lawrence, "The Flowery Tuscany", *Phoenix*, pp. 45-51.

[33] Brewster Ghiselin, quoted in Dolores LaChapelle, *D. H. Lawrence, Future Primitive*, p. 44.

[34] Richard Aldington, *Portrait of a Genius, But . . .*, p. 134.

[35] Ibid., p. 35.

[36] Ford Madox Ford, *Portraits from Life*, pp. 78-9.

[37] Ben Willis, *The Tao of Art*, p. 72.

[38] Dolores LaChapelle, *D. H. Lawrence, Future Primitive*, p.45.

[39] Edward O. Wilson, *The Diversity of Life*, quoted in Dolores LaChapelle, *D. H. Lawrence, Future Primitive*, p. 45.

[40] D. H. Lawrence, "Autobiographical Fragment", *Phoenix*, p. 823.

[41] D. H. Lawrence, "Indians and Entertainment", in *Mornings in Mexico and Etruscan Places*, p. 61.

[42] *D. H. Lawrence, A Composite Biography*, Edward Nehls, ed., Vol. III, pp. 172-3.

[43] E Neumann, *The Origin and History of Consciousness*, quoted in Alan Watts, *Nature, Man and Woman*, p. 30.

[44] William Y. Tindall, *D. H. Lawrence & Susan His Cow*, p. 82.

[45] *The Complete Poems of D. H. Lawrence*, Vivian de Sola Pinto, ed., p. 368.

[46] Ibid., pp. 374, 394.

[47] Ibid., p. 339.

[48] Ibid., p. 339.

[49] Ibid., p. 351.

[50] D. H. Lawrence, *St. Mawr*, in *St. Mawr and Other Stories*, p. 50.

[51] William Y. Tindall, *D. H. Lawrence & Susan His Cow*, p. vii.

[52] D. H. Lawrence, "Love Was Once a Little Boy", in *Reflections on the Death of a Porcupine and Other Essays*, p. 334.

[53] *The Collected Letters of D. H. Lawrence*, Harry T. Moore, ed., Vol. I, p. 343.

[54] D. H. Lawrence, "The Painted Tombs of Tarquinia", in *Mornings in Mexico and Etruscan Places*, p. 151.

[55] *The Lankavatara Sutra,* quoted in Mary E. Tucker, ed., *Buddhism and Ecology*, p. 143.

[56] Alan Watts, *Nature, Man and Woman*, p. 93.

[57] *Zhuangzi*, quoted in Alan Watts, *Nature, Man and Woman*, p. 93.

[58] Alan Watts, *Nature, Man and Woman*, pp. 93-4.

[59] D. H. Lawrence, "The Spirit of Place", *Studies in Classic American Literature*, p. 12.

[60] Leopold, *A Sand County Almanac*, p. 253. Aldo Leopold: wildlife biologist of the 1930s and 1940s. His classic essay: " The Land Ethic".

[61] Henry Miller, *The World of Lawrence: A Passionate Approach*, p. 161

[62] H. Mori, *A Conversation on D. H. Lawrence*, p. 24, quoted in Dolores LaChapelle, *D. H. Lawrence, Future Primitive*, p. 19.

[63] W. Siebenhaar, *Reminiscences of D. H. Lawrence*, quoted in Dolores LaChapelle, *D. H. Lawrence, Future Primitive*, p. 19.

[64] *The Letters of D. H. Lawrence*, Aldous Huxley, ed., p. 549.

[65] D. H. Lawrence, "New Mexico", *Phoenix*, p. 142.

[66] Ibid., p. 142.

[67] Ibid., p. 143.

[68] Steve Odin, "The Japanese Concept of Nature in Relation to the environmental Ethics and Conservation Aesthetics of Aldo Leopold", quoted in Mary E. Tucker, ed., Buddhism and Ecology, p. 99.

[69] Ibid., p. 92.

[70] *D. H. Lawrence: A Composite Biography*, Edward Nehls, ed., Vol. III, p. 107.

[71] Catherine Carswall: *Savage Pilgrimage*, p. 265.

[72] Ibid., p. 231.

[73] Dorothy Brett, *Lawrence and Brett*, p. 71

[74] Dolores LaChapelle, *D. H. Lawrence, Future Primitive*, p. 101

[75] Lin Yutang, *My Country and My People*, p. 273.

[76] *The Complete Poems of D. H. Lawrence*, Vivian de Sola Pinto, ed., p. 525.

[77] Ibid., pp. 526-7.

[78] *The Collected Short Stories of D. H. Lawrence*, p. 495.

[79] Ibid., p. 497.

[80] D. H. Lawrence, "New Mexico", *Phoenix*, p. 142.

[81] D. H. Lawrence, *Apocalypse*, pp. 41-2.

[82] Jessie Chambers, *D. H. Lawrence: A Personal Record*, pp. 127-8.

[83] D. H. Lawrence, *Sons and Lovers*, Ch. 7, p. 220.

[84] D. H. Lawrence, *The Rainbow*, Ch. 11, p. 296.

85 Ibid., p. 298.

86 Dolores LaChapelle, *D. H. Lawrence, Future Primitive*, p. 30.

87 *The Complete Poems of D. H. Lawrence*, Vivian de Sola Pinto, ed., pp. 695-6.

88 Dolores LaChapelle, *D. H. Lawrence, Future Primitive*, p. 30.

89 D. H. Lawrence, *Sons and Lovers*, Ch. 7, p. 221.

90 D. H. Lawrence, *The Rainbow*, Ch. 15, pp. 444.

91 D. H. Lawrence, *Apocalypse*, p. 43.

92 *The Complete Poems of D. H. Lawrence*, Vivian de Sola Pinto, ed., p. 453.

93 Michel Gauquelin, *The Cosmic Clocks*, p. 150, quoted in Dolores LaChapelle, *D. H. Lawrence, Future Primitive*, p. 31.

94 Dolores LaChapelle, *D. H. Lawrence, Future Primitive*, p. 31.

95 Rhys Davies, "D. H. Lawrence in Bandol", quoted in Dolores LaChapelle, *D. H. Lawrence, Future Primitive*, p. 32.

96 D. H. Lawrence, *Apocalypse*, pp. 41, 42.

97 Ibid., p. 45.

98 Ibid., p. 200.

99 Alan Wats, *The Way of Zen*, p. 175.

100 D. H. Latwrence, "The Spinner and the Monks", in *Twilight in Italy*, p. 37.

101 *The Letters of D. H. Lawrence*, Aldous Huxley, ed., p. 688.

Chapter II

Man and Nature

*

The thirteenth-century Japanese Zen master Dogen says: "Delusion is seeing all things from the perspective of the self. Enlightenment is seeing the self from the perspective of the myriad things of the universe".[1] The former is egotistical and anthropocentric, a western way of thinking, which is "inspired by the conceited notion that man, or human reason, or the human distinction between good and evil, is the centre and pivot of the universe".[2] The latter is a more humble vision of man with more reverence of the cosmos in the traditional oriental belief, which "allow you . . . to take yourselves simply, humbly, for what you are, and to salute the wild, indifferent, non-censorious infinity of nature".[3] Nature not only humbles human beings or enhances our spirit; it also serves as a standard model for human beings to follow. Nature in Taoism is seen as the ultimate reality. "The only true reference point for Taoists that is not twisted or distorted by social influences is *nature*",[4] so untwisted human nature finds true references in the natural world. The best way of acting, for the Taoists, always expresses itself as action inspired by the natural processes of the earth: "Be still like a mountain and flow like a great river", as the traditional Taoist teaching says. Since natural processes reflect the principles of Tao, nature is then regarded as the constant that Taoists use to model behaviour. Man's standard behaviour, in Taoism, should be as spontaneous, harmonious and detached as the mountains and rivers. In other words, if a person follows the Tao, his everyday life will be natural and resemble the characteristics of nature itself, as Zhuangzi puts it:

> To the man who does not reside in himself, the identity of all forms becomes clear. He passes about like water, shows a reflection as though he were a mirror, and answers as though he were an echo. He is so light as to seem to vanish altogether. He is placid and clear as a calm lake. His interactions with others are utterly harmonious, regardless of whether he gains or loses something. He does not bustle forward in front of people, but rather follows them.[5]

The Taoist notion of judging man's standard action by natural law contains the same notion as Lawrence's deep correspondence between natural man and natural world. Lawrence views man's true self in plants, flowers and beasts, in mountains and rivers. After his visit to the Etruscan tombs, he writes in the essay "Etruscan Places": "All things corresponded in the ancient world, and man's bosom mirrored itself in the bosom of the sky, or *vice versa*".[6] In other words, the sky and the myriad things of the universe mirror man and correspond to man's understanding of himself. Martin Heidegger expresses the same mirror concept: "The appropriating mirror-play of the simple fourfold of earth and sky, divinities and mortals, we call the world".[7] Earth and sky, god and man, each mirrors in its own way the presence of the others. This reciprocal picture of the cosmic standard is similarly depicted by Laozi:

> Man models himself on earth,
> The earth models itself on heaven,
> Heaven models itself on the Tao,
> And the Tao on naturalness (*ziran*).[8]

The natural motions of both the sky and the earth are examples of "constancy", which will forever serve as a constant model for human beings. In "Etruscan Places", we have Lawrence's interpretation of mirror-identity: " . . . if you live by the cosmos, you look in the cosmos for your clue. . . . All it depends on is the amount of *true*, sincere, religious concentration you can bring to bear on your object". He then clarifies: "It is the same with the study of stars, or the sky of stars, whatever object will bring the consciousness into a state of pure attention, in a time of perplexity, will also give back an answer to the perplexity".[9] For Lawrence, he can always find clues in flowers and plants, in birds and animals, in the landscapes of his hometown, and registers the truth in his imaginative art. Nature's beauty and cruelty, its indifferent and disturbing effects echo the stories of human play.

In his Australian novel *Kangaroo*, Lawrence writes of the influence of the sea, and the moral standard it provides. When Somers with his wife "walked along the sands, watching the blue sky mirror purple and the white clouds mirror warm on the wet send", he feels that the simplicity of the sea has brought back his "inward peace" and "a quiet stillness in his soul". At the same time, he realizes it is ridiculous that he should desire to learn shooting "with a rifle and a revolver". The peaceful and indifferent sea gives him a certain enlightenment on the "unconscious faith" of "his own inward soul":

> Some men must live by this unremitting inwardness, no matter what the rest of the world does. They must not let the rush of the world's 'outwardness' sweep them away: or if they are swept away, they must struggle back. . . . back again like a creature into the sea. The sea of his own inward soul, his own unconscious faith, over which his will had no exercise.[10]

"Myriad things of the universe" serve as models for Lawrence to visualize human life and social problems. Here is Ursula's vision of the hopeful future manifested by the non-censorious rainbow:

> And the rainbow stood on the earth. She knew that the sordid people who crept hard-scaled and separate on the face of the world's corruption were living still, that the rainbow was arched in their blood and would quiver to life in their spirit, that they would cast off their horny covering of disintegration, that new, clean, naked bodies would issue to a new germination, to a new growth, rising to the light and the wind and the clean rain of heaven. She saw in the rainbow the earth's new architecture, the

old, brittle corruption of houses and factories swept away, the world built up in a living fabric of Truth, fitting to the over-arching heaven.[11]

David Cavitch points out that Ursula's vision of the rainbow indicates "the correlation between the natural scene and individual subjectivity", which is "the dominant and thematic metaphor of the fiction".[12] Just as the natural scene corresponds to individual subjectivity, human psychic events mirror themselves in the wild, indifferent, non-censorious nature. In *St. Mawr*, Lou's mother Mrs Witt has a "tall red-brick Georgian house looking straight on to the churchyard, and the dark, looming, big church". She takes great pleasure in watching the funeral ceremonies in the churchyard under her window, longing for her own morbid way of death. The gloomy graveyard in turn reveals the peculiar, decadent nature of Mrs Witt.[13] In his analyses of the "vague metaphors of vegetative growth" of the three Brangwen generations in *The Rainbow*, David Cavitch concludes: "The landscape glows or fades throughout the novel as the major characters gain or lose a capacity for symbolic vision that relates their objective circumstances to their purely psychological realities".[14] Cavitch remarks, the characters' "perceptions create the symbols, and the reader witnesses what they see in their heightened emotional states". In this case, the landscape of the physical world would serve as "schemata indicating psychic events".[15] There are many symbols in *The Trespasser*. The sun, the moon and the sea all correspond to his characters' psyche. In *The White Peacock*, for example, Annable hates woman and sees the white peacock dirtying the graveyard stone as "a screeching devil" and "the very soul of a lady".[16] Mountains in Lawrence's three Mexican tales (*St. Mawr*, and the two novelettes, "The Woman Who Rode Away" and "The Princess") serve as "constant" references for the characteristic human world. Lawrence has found in them clues of both male potency, illustrated by the mountain landscape such as in *St. Mawr*, and barren sexuality for its unconscious wildness, such as in "The Woman Who Rode Away". Prior to these three mountain tales, the snow mountain image in *Women in Love* symbolizes both a barren sexuality and death and destruction.

Lawrence sees original human nature from the primitive, uninhabited landscapes, and from the landscapes he refines his vision of the natural, spontaneous character of man. In his second novel *The Trespasser*, there are many descriptive passages of the Isle of Wight. The white, sunny and salty landscape does not just provide a romantic background for Siegmund's and Helena's love affairs, the uninhibited landscape represents their original spontaneous nature, and in a way "conditions and flavours" their whole relationship.[17] From the close association between man's life and the universe comes a Taoist view that the very struggle between men, or man and woman is not just "personal", and the struggle for man's growth and achievement is not solely his own business, they are actually a manifestation of the cosmic struggle—the struggle between creation and destruction, life and death, love and hate. Man's healthy desires, to Lawrence, could achieve fulfilment only through his primal spontaneous relationship with the whole universe.

* *

In spite of the concept that nature always contains a symbolic meaning for sensitive men to perceive themselves, nature is on the whole indifferent to the little moral play of human beings. The human world is full of struggles and tragedies, but there is no mourning in nature. Life goes on, nothing in nature will express any sympathy or excitement for human stories. Chaman Nahal in *D. H. Lawrence: An Eastern View* points out that "the cosmos is vibrant as ever, thronging not merely with life . . . but with 'life-which- is-bliss-in-itself'".[18] The bliss is in life itself, it has nothing to do with human standards of happiness. Whatever exists exists in reality, and exists in delight, in spite of human knowledge of success or failure, birth or death. Regarding this point of view, *The White Peacock* is again a good example. Graham Hough concludes in the *Dark Sun*, "Annable asserts his manhood, scorns idealism and society, and is killed. George fails to assert his, and sinks into a sodden wreck. Cyril has none to assert, and ends as ineffectual as he began. Emily remains elusive and Lettie unsatisfied". Though none of the characters seems to be living a successful life and no one achieves fulfilment, the overall impression the book leaves behind is "one of tenderness, freshness and young growth".[19] The reason for this seeming contradiction is that Lawrence's interest in writing this novel is not in the human and social destiny of his characters. Rather, as Lawrence puts it, somehow "that which is physical—non-human in humanity, is more interesting to me than the old fashioned human element".[20] Hough holds that the centre of this novel is "displaced", so that,

> The circumference of the book includes, not only the characters and their personal fates, but the whole life of nature which surrounds and flows through them. The characters are only forms into which this universal *mana* transitorily flows, and it is *mana* that is Lawrence's real subject.[21]

Thus, in spite of the failures of the characters in *The White Peacock*, we can still feel the vibrant natural beauty and recognize the *mana* of the life-flow behind the human play. The "omnipresent natural vitality" in *The White Peacock* as in many of his early poems, in Hough's view, "is habitual and pervasive, almost independent of particular occasions".[22] Here is a much-quoted passage about Annable—the gamekeeper's funeral day:

> It was a magnificent morning in early spring when I watched among the trees to see the procession come down the hillside. The upper air was woven with the music of the larks, and my whole world thrilled with the conception of summer. The young pale wind-flowers had arisen by the wood-gate, and under the hazels, when perchance the hot sun pushed his way, new little suns dawned, and blazed with real light. There was a certain thrill and quickening everywhere . . .Birds called and flashed on every hand; they made off exultant with streaming strands of grass, or wisps of fleece, plunging into the dark spaces of the wood, and out again into the blue. [23]

The evocation of Annable's funeral day serves as a complementary vision of Darwinian views of nature and the good spirit of nature existence. Annable was killed and was to be buried. This is life, this is existential reality. There is no mention of a conventional sadness in man's death. The life force is still flowing with its particular "delicate vitality" in the air. Hough comments:

> Coming on the heels of the gamekeeper's horrible death, it suggests that the life of a man is in itself a small thing: it is only an expression of a force that is everywhere, quick, tender and strong. Human life is only significant so far as it perceives and participates in this; and it is more complex only because it has so many opportunities of turning away from and denying the authentic life that is everywhere.[24]

Hough in this passage has grasped Lawrence's point that human life is small yet significant within an overall "universal *mana*". George fails because he is "turning away from . . . the authentic life". Had he lived a spontaneous life, being brave enough to follow his own impetus or desire and ignoring his conscious will, he would have had a happy life. His situation is purely man made, and could be avoided if he was more aware of man's shared life force with nature. Lawrence makes this point clear in his Hardy essays. Those who are submissively experiencing their share with the cosmic life-flow will naturally receive benevolence from nature. In Annable's case, there are, as I have observed, at least two revelations.

The first is what we have just discussed. Annable is dead, but the cosmos is vibrantly moving on as ever, swarming with life, with a universal "Existence- Consciousness-Bliss". This is for Hindus, as Nahal puts it, the "is-ness of things—things as they are, regardless of how we would like them to be".[25] In Taoism this reality of existence in itself is called "Suchness" (tathata), a name vaguely meaning ultimate reality. This absolute reality allows no conventional reasoning. Death and birth, sad or happy, bad or good, whatever it is, it does not affect nature at all. It is nothing but "suchness". Annable's death is a natural cycle or a completion of life, the same as any other creature's life process. The "suchness" of reality is non-human, and nature in its indifferent manner urges the other lives on earth to move on ceaselessly.

The second revelation this Annable episode tells us of is nature's immorality and indifference. According to the traditional Chinese view, the universe is essentially a sinless organism. It is not only sinless, but also totally empty of any ethics and morality in man's judgement. Man's ethical laws are often in conflict with the needs of the rest of life in the cosmos. Nature is as it is, never deliberately kind or deliberately unkind. It would not show its sympathy for Annable's death. Regardless of human tragedy, the birds go on singing and the golden sun rays shoot through the woods. Neither would nature be sweeter because of man's intellectual exertion. Lawrence argues: "This Nature- sweet-and-pure business is only another effect of intellectualizing. Just an attempt to make all nature succumb to a few laws of the human mind. The sweet-and-pure sort of laws".[26] Baruch Hochman in *Another Ego* expresses his deep impression of a strong "sense of nature's life" pervading in *The White Peacock*, and says that this "is alternatively felt to be a tender mother and a cruelly indifferent stepmother".[27] The Indian thinker Sri Aurobindo points out that man's ethical laws do not apply to sinless nature. "We have to recognise", he says, "if we thus view the whole, not limiting ourselves to the human difficulty and the human standpoint, that we do not live in an ethical world". It is because:

> Material Nature is not ethical; the law which governs it is a coordination of fixed habits which take no cognisance of good and evil, but only of force that creates, force that arranges and preserves, force that disturbs and destroys impartially, non-ethically, according to the secret Will in it, according to the mute satisfaction of that Will in its own self-formations and self- dissolutions.[28]

Therefore, man's destination in this vast universe, living or dying, is determined without purpose by the secret will of nature. Nature's destructive force as one of its "fixed habits" is indifferent to man's fate. This theory reminds us of Richard Jefferies' similar perception. Having spoken lovingly of the grass, the bees, and the yellow wheat, he suddenly feels, "All nature . . . has no concern with man", and "there is nothing human in nature or the universe". He characterises the secret will of nature as "force without a mind", claiming, "All nature, all the universe we can see, is absolutely indifferent to us. The trees care nothing for us".[29] Nature has no mind. Lawrence, a devoted reader of Jefferies' work, shares with him the same view of the characteristic indifference of nature. He says in the "Study of Thomas Hardy":

> What matters if some are drowned or dead, and others preaching or married . . .what matters, any more than the withering heath, the reddening berries . . .? The Heath persists. Its body is strong and fecund, it will bear many more crops besides this. Here is the sombre, latent power that will go on producing, no matter what happens to the product.[30]

It is because, to borrow an ancient Chinese saying, "Heaven and earth are not benevolent". They are "not benevolent" because they have no mind. Man will die, his mind and will, his preaching will not at all affect the workings of the eternal productive power of nature. The great Tao will never be touched or changed by any mechanical force originated from human beings. In Lawrence's words, though the will of man would "destroy the blossom yet in bud, over and over again", the "primal impulsive body" or nature's powerful fecundity of Egdon Heath will not be affected. It will "go on producing all that was to be produced, eternally".[31] To Hardy and Lawrence, if human beings are aware of their place in nature, they will realize the futility of attempting to exert man's will and any mechanical force upon it. They will not be swept away by nature, if they live intuitively and spontaneously according to the principles of natural laws.

*   *   *

Lawrence, contrary to the Western anthropocentric view, insists that "we are not the authors of the universe",[32] as man is only "one year's accidental crop".[33] So man is bound to have his life and fate intermingled with nature as he writes in his *Love Poems*:

> . . . I see the valley
> Fleshed all like me
> With feelings that change and quiver:
> And all things seem to tally
> With something in me. . . .[34]

In *Psychoanalysis and the Unconscious* and *Fantasia of the Unconscious*, Lawrence raises the point time and again that man is embedded in the matrix of nature and is living in the rhythm of the cosmic life. Lawrence realizes that in some deep way woman, sex and nature are connected. In *Lady Chatterley's Lover*, Lawrence presents a particular tender and warm scene in which the spring flowers, the new-born pheasant chicks and the deep woods suggest a sympathetic yet mysterious background to Connie's love affair with Mellors. In the short story "Love Among the Haystacks", Maurice, the young brother, stays alone at the hayfield before going to meet Paula there. Having washed in a stone basin, he feels his soul is full of the wonder of nature. "The flowers, the meadow-sweet particularly haunted him . . . Things never had looked so personal and full of beauty, he had never known the wonder in himself before".[35] In *Sons and Lovers*, Paul Morel, when his consciousness returns after his first love with Clara Dawes by a canal, feels "the grass, and the peewit" and the "warmth" of "Clara's breathing" all wonderfully connected in the darkness. The natural world around them "was all so much bigger than themselves that he was hushed. They had met, and included in their meeting the thrust of the manifold grass stems, the cry of the peewit, the wheel of the stars".[36] Paul is at that moment acutely aware of the blessing of nature's potent life force upon his small life.

Baruch Hochman writes in *Another Ego* that, "The sense of the consubstantiality of man and nature and of the intertwinedness of man's life and that of the cosmos" is strongly felt in Lawrence's early poems and novels.[37] In the first chapter of *The Rainbow*, Lawrence describes the life of the Brangwens as closely "associated with the fields and the horizontal land", Keith Sagar remarks. "Their moods correspond to the changes in the weather. Their lives are directed by the rhythm of the seasons".[38] There is so much "interchange" between the Brangwens' life and the natural world:

> So much warmth and generating and pain and death did they know in their blood, earth and sky and beast and green plants, so much exchange and interchange they had with these, that they lived full and surcharged, their senses full fed, their faces always turned to the heat of the blood, staring into the sun, dazed with looking towards the source of generation, unable to turn round.[39]

In this "interchange", man's life becomes part of the life of the cosmos. And man's innermost experiences, his psychic development, are closely linked with the natural process of the external world. The sheaf-gathering scene in the chapter "Girlhood of Anna Brangwen" is a demonstration of the connection between psychological and natural rhythms. Will approaches Anna, bearing his load of corn stalks:

> Into the rhythm of his work there came a pulse and a steadied purpose. He stooped, he lifted the weight, he heaved it towards her, setting it as in her, under the moonlit space. And he went back for more. Ever with increasing closeness he lifted the sheaves and swung striding to the centre with them, ever he drove her more nearly to the meeting, ever he did his share, and drew towards her, overtaking her. There was only the moving to and fro in the moonlight, engrossed, the swinging in the silence, that was marked only by the splash of sheaves, and silence, and a splash of sheaves. [40]

This passage suggests that man's instinct and passion are reflected in the rhythm of work which is synchronized with the rhythm of nature. The repetition of physical actions suggests an underlying coital pattern and indicates "a continual recurrence of love and strife" between the lovers,[41] as Scott Sanders' puts it in *D. H. Lawrence: The World of Major Novels*. Man's life shares with nature its cycles of up and down.

Lydia, equally influenced by the workings of nature, restores her desire for living and for Tom's courtship after a period of depression and withdrawal from the world:

> ... there was a strange insistence of light from the sea, to which she must attend. Primroses glimmered around, many of them, and she stooped to the disturbing influence near her feet. .... the light came off the sea, constantly, constantly, without refusal, till it seemed to bear her away, and the noise of the sea created a drowsiness in her, a relaxation like sleep. Her automatic consciousness gave way a little ... She went past the gorse bushes shrinking from their presence, she stepped into the heather as into a quickening bath that almost hurt. ....one morning there

was a light from the yellow jasmine caught her, and after that, morning and evening, the persistent ringing of thrushes from the shrubbery, till her heart, beaten upon, was forced to lift up its voice in rivalry and answer . . . she would wake in the morning one day and feel her blood running, feel herself lying open like a flower unsheathed in the sun, insistent and potent with demand.[42]

Lydia is reawakening from the "quickening bath" as she is literally immersed in the "influences" and "presences" of nature. Her reaction to urge of the natural world has developed along with the process of diminishing her "automatic consciousness", and of her gradual yielding to the unconscious and to the potent life forces within her and around her. Lydia's awakening "is likened to the growth and blossoming of a flower", Sanders comments. By thus depicting psychological processes in terms of natural ones, Lawrence demonstrates "not just a metaphorical resemblance between the two, but an actual, fundamental connection".[43] The much-quoted text in the opening chapter of *The Rainbow* serves as a most eloquent example of Lawrence's romantic vision of nature's unleashed force and its potent influence in determining the Brangwens' lives:

> But heaven and earth was teeming around them, and how should this cease? They felt the rush of the sap in spring, they knew the wave which cannot halt, but every year throws forward the seed to begetting, and, falling back, leaves the young-born on the earth. They know the intercourse between heaven and earth, sunshine drawn into the breast and bowels, the rain sucked up in the daytime, nakedness that comes under the wind in autumn, showing the birds' nests no longer worth hiding. Their life and interrelations were such; feeling the pulse and body of the soil, that opened to their furrow for the grain. . . .[44]

This heavily sexualised description speaks itself for Lawrence's vision of the wonder of nature and the interrelationship between man's life and nature's power. Heaven and earth and the seasons generate life ceaselessly and profoundly. The imagery of the "intercourse" between them presents a constant model for human beings to follow. The ever-lasting life of the cosmos flows into the blood of the Brangwens and gives much hope to the people farming the land.

Sanders points out:

> When Lawrence's ideas are treated as a coherent system . . . it becomes apparent that his world-view is constructed from a fundamental opposition between nature and culture. All of the more familiar dichotomies in his work—mind/body, social self/natural self, instinct/idea—are reducible to this radical conflict between the demands of culture and the demands of nature.[45]

In this "radical conflict", nature is regarded as "the divine milieu" that enables the natural self to live "much more freely and finely and peacefully than their present society permitted".[46] In Lawrence's novels there are always two parallel worlds presented: nature and society. In general, the societal sphere is identified with early twentieth- century industrial England, a world he is bitterly disappointed with because of its "evil" forces which hinder individuals from developing freely their integral humanity. Nature, the primordial source of all life, is identified with the pre-social and instinctive aspects of the self. The close ties between environment and psyche he depicts in the novels show that "man is governed by culture" but "is freed by nature".[47]

The industrial world Lawrence describes in his novels is represented by the canal, the colliery, the advancing railway and the ugly mining town with smoking pitheads. This mechanical world is contrasted with the green, organic world of nature characterized by the immemorial farm life described in the opening pages of *The Rainbow*. Industrialism in *Lady Chatterley's Lover* is depicted as a mechanical force which has degraded human beings and the landscape. The gamekeeper Mellors resents the world outside his green wood. For him, that is the world of the "greedy mechanism . . .sparkling with lights and gushing hot metal and roaring with traffic, there lay the vast evil thing, ready to destroy whatever did not conform. Soon it would destroy the wood, and the bluebells would spring no more".[48] Man's submission to the machine and dedication to economic profits inevitably become a destructive force to both man's integrated life and the natural world. In *Sons and Lovers*, the poor miners for instance, are prisoners of industrialism, all the spontaneity and sensual nature in them bound to be lost in constant struggles against the threats from merciless economic forces and from a hostile community. Constantly living in her fears of both the authority and the masses, Ursula of *The Rainbow* seems bitterly disillusioned with the human world. Her problems are the problems of Lawrence himself. Apart from the dehumanised industrial force, the war—the manifestation of collective insanity—only confirms and deepens Lawrence's suspicion of man-made society, and drives him deeper still into the natural, nonhuman world.

In Sanders' view, nature invariably dwarfs society: "The natural inevitably appears more powerful and more appealing than the social".[49] Nature, therefore, is often used as an antidote to society for its life-renewing power and its silent acknowledgement of the holiness of man's instincts. Lawrence's characters are in constant flight into the non-human natural world from society, from the much-hated masses, from war, and from the ugly urban-industrial environment, which becomes a regular pattern in Lawrence's novels. Their retreat into nature is sympathized by their desires to seek nature's response to their instinctive body and to their souls' consolation. Husbands, fathers, mine-owners and vicars in his novels generally serve as representatives of the mind and the industrial world. Their wives and daughters attempt to escape from that world, and are finally freed by the aid of grooms, gamekeepers and gypsies, who have powerful intuitions and despise mechanical pursuance. Lady Chatterley escapes from her deteriorated husband into the warm arms of the gamekeeper and the green woods. Lou in *St. Mawr* escapes from the cardboard-like unreal society of England, and decides to live in the mountains of New Mexico. The contemporary society described in *Women in Love* is full of human problems. In Sanders' words, it is "so irrational and destructive" that "it must be escaped altogether if the individual . . . is to survive".[50] However, most of Lawrence's characters can only retreat to the pastoral world depicted in the *White Peacock* and *Sons and Lovers*, or Lady Chatterley's reserved woods. By Lawrence's time, the unspoilt natural retreats in his novels were in reality fast diminishing and under threat from the industrial world.

Lawrence on the other hand is also clearly aware of the fact that it is no good for one to simply escape into the natural world and be totally cut off from one's people and society. In a letter to Dr. Trigant Burrow, he congratulates his getting over the "cutoffness", and then tells him,

> Myself, I suffer badly from being so cut off. But what is one to do? One cannot link up with the social unconsciousness. At times, one is *forced* to be essentially a hermit, I don't want to be . . .. One has no human relations—that is so devastating.[51]

Lawrence writes of the destructive consequences of isolating oneself from the world of man in the story "The Man Who Loved Islands". The man who lives a hermit life on the island cuts himself off from society and finally meets his death in a snowstorm. Mellors the gamekeeper of *Lady Chatterley's Lover* realizes that his hermit life is bound to be broken up not only by his involvement with the woman, but also more inevitably by "the world of mechanical greedy": "A man could no longer be private and withdrawn. The world allows no hermits".[52]

One of the ways to relieve oneself from the pressure of society, according to Lawrence, is to retreat into one's soul, to seek temporary consolation from one's inner world. Lawrence writes: "I think one must for the moment withdraw from the world, away towards the inner realities that ARE real; and return, maybe, to the world later, when one is quiet and sure".[53] This retreat into one's inner self is in principle the same as meditation in Taoism and Buddhism. Oriental meditation requires the self to "withdraw from the world" completely, free of any anxiety, so that the self achieves enlightenment through one's "inner realities".

Modern society and the natural world represent two antagonistic forces, which in turn represent the natural and social aspects of human beings. The social self, bearing community consciousness and playing social roles, is often for Lawrence false and pernicious, such as those morbid characters in *Women in Love*. Whereas the natural self, spontaneous and creative, is able to survive the evil of industrial society by transcending community. According to

Lawrence the self is naturally consanguineous with nature, and when the self is unfolding in spontaneity and intuition, he shares the same qualities and divinity with the universe. By then man is in nature and nature in man. Lawrence illustrates this belief in his description of man's physical and emotional experiences in a natural context. The individual characters, particularly in his early novels, are integrated into an encompassing natural process that is opposed to society. Human passion and enlightenment within the sympathetic embrace of a natural landscape facilitate Lawrence's vision of man's intrinsic affinity with nature, as well as man's instinctive repellence from society. The vision of nature's powerful impact is vividly illustrated in episodes such as Tom's courtship of Lydia, the sheaf-gathering scene, Will and Anna's silent love in the moonlight, and the passionate love-affair between Ursula and Skrebensky. Men are embraced by nature and feel new and stronger after gaining access to its immense power.

Ursula and Skrebensky's love experience is an example. Being immersed in this natural power, they feel reluctant to return to society:

> He came to her finally in a superb consummation. It was very dark, and again a windy, heavy night. They had come down the lane towards Beldover, down to the valley. . . .
>
> They would soon come out of the darkness into the lights. It was like turning back. It was unfulfilment. Two quivering, unwilling creatures, they lingered on the edge of the darkness, peering out at the lights and the machine-glimmer beyond. They could not turn back to the world—they could not. . . .
>
> . . . And in the roaring circle under the tree, that was almost invisible yet whose powerful presence received them, they lay a moment looking at the twinkling lights on the darkness opposite, saw the sweeping brand of a train past the edge of their darkened field.
>
> . . . She was caught up, entangled in the powerful vibration of the night. . . . She passed away as on a dark wind, far, far away, into the pristine darkness of paradise, into the original immortality. She entered the dark fields of immortality.

Her soul was sure and indifferent of the opinion of the world of artificial light. As they went up the steps of the footbridge over the railway, and met the train-passengers, she felt herself belonging to another world, she walked past them immune, a whole darkness dividing her from them . . . Her everyday self was just the same. She merely had another, stronger self that knew the darkness.

This curious separate strength, that exists in darkness and pride of night, never forsook her. She had never been more herself. It could not occur to her that anybody, not even the young man of the world, Skrebensky, should have anything at all to do with her permanent self. As for her temporal, social self, she let it look after itself.[54]

Ursula's socially conscious self, like the adept of Zen Buddhism, is thus extinguished by nature. Through sexuality she is replaced by a new stronger self—a natural self—who "knew the darkness" of the unknown, and feels herself as an agent of a great force of this larger ordering. The heavy darkness envelops everything, swallowing the railways and the meaningless sound of society. Ursula's "permanent self" in the darkness separates from her "temporal, social self" in the lighted world, and there is no longer from her any respect paid to "the opinion of the world of artificial light". Her psychic world, having merged into the natural environment, is completely divorced from society. The glimmering mechanical world both Ursula and Skrebensky dread to return to is for them an alien order, regulated under science and technologies, and is bound to mislead or suppress man's natural self. It is the same moral theme centred in the story of *Lady Chatterley's Lover.*

* * * *

Sanders points out, "Not only are most of Lawrence's love-encounters transferred physically to another environment—to woods, moors, rivers, clearings and beaches—they are also transferred ethically into another framework of values".[55] Immersed mentally and physically in the natural environment, Lawrence's characters inevitably revolt against the old framework of values and use nature as a standard by which to judge their human activities. As Sanders observes, "Nature and society represent wholly different systems of value, and offer wholly different grounds for identity". According to this viewpoint, we do not consider Ursula and Skrebensky's case to be simply "the breaking of sexual taboos", but rather we regard their behaviour as something with a different set of natural values.[56] The social self is defined by the ethical conventions of society, but the natural self—associated with the green world—is grounded in the experiences that trespass those conventions. The sexual experiences of Lawrence's characters show us a perfect picture of nature's response to human beings' passion and their instinctive nature, which in turn suggest man's intrinsic connection to the greater life of the external world.

Lawrence's views on sex have aroused more suspicion and criticism than any other issues. The misunderstanding of his pronouncements on this subject has brought the greatest harm to his reputation by critics and the public. He himself did not realize the exact reason why there was hostility from the public until after *Lady Chatterley's Lover* was published in 1928. Until then he is surprised to notice the misinterpretation of the innocent word "sex":

> So that at last I began to see the point of my critics' abuse of my exalting of sex. They only know one form of sex: in fact, to them there *is* only one form of sex: the nervous, personal, disintegrative sort, the "white" sex. And this, of course, is something to be flowery and false about, but nothing to be very hopeful about. I quite agree. And I quite agree, we can have no hope of the regeneration of England from such sort of sex.[57]

Then what does he mean by sex? He elaborates on this in *A Propos of Lady Chatterley's Lover*, and in other essays such as "Love", "Pornography and Obscenity", "We Need One Another", "Sex Versus Loveliness", and "Nobody Loves me". He explains in *A Propos of Lady Chatterley's Lover*:

> It is a mistake I have made, talking of sex I have always inferred that sex meant blood-sympathy and blood-contact. . . . But as a matter of fact, nearly all modern sex is a pure matter of nerves, cold and bloodless. This

49

is personal sex. And this white, cold, nervous, "poetic" personal sex, which is practically all the sex that moderns know, has a very peculiar physiological effect, as well as psychological.[58]

He then comments on the falsity of the whole situation, emphasizing "the current sort of sex is just what I *don't* mean and *don't* want".[59] He only wants the "warm blood-desire" type of sex. Sex for him is synonymous with life, is similar to any genuine feeling flowing between man and woman. "And what is sex, after all, but the symbol of relation of man and woman, woman to man? . . . It consists in infinite different flows between the two beings, different, even apparently contrary".[60] According to Lawrence, sex, marriage and man's whole life must constantly keep in time with the rhythms of the year and the universe. "Sex", he writes, "is the balance of male and female in the universe, the attraction, the repulsion, the transit of neutrality . . . always different, always new". It "goes through the rhythm of the year . . .ceaselessly changing", which he sees as "the rhythm of the sun in his relation to the earth". He thus warns that it would be a great "catastrophe" if sex and love were cut off "from the rhythm of the year, from his unison with the sun and the earth".[61] Marriage is the same. He emphasises: "Marriage is no marriage that is not basically permanently phallic, and that is not linked with the sun and the earth, the moon and the fixed stars and the planets, in the rhythm of days . . . and of centuries". So marriage too must be set "in relationship to the rhythmic cosmos", and "the rhythm of the cosmos is something we cannot get away from, without bitterly impoverishing our lives". On the other hand, "the oneness of the blood-stream of man and woman in marriage completes the universe, as far as humanity is concerned, completes the streaming of the sun and the flowing of the stars".[62] The significance of sex, according to Lawrence, lies in the fact that it is primary for man. Man's very existence is the result of a sexual encounter, and through the sexual encounter he returns to his origins and achieves complete fulfilment. The reason people claim that their sexual experiences do not bring them complete fulfilment and satisfaction is, as Lawrence holds, due to a radical perversion of human nature which has been going on for over two thousand years. This is a deep-rooted social and cultural problem which he has studied in his essays profoundly. Graham Hough in *The Dark Sun* speaks of Lawrence's mind on the fundamental significance of sex :

> All the great pagan cults, before the advert of the "higher religions", were cults of fertility and generation, and it is the genial influence of the phallus that alone can produce active and happy forms of human society. If sex is not our primary fulfilment, it is due to a cultural failure in which we are nearly all involved.[63]

Zen Buddhism holds the same views regarding sex and sexual love. In Alan Watts' explanation, it is "the most vivid of man's customary expressions of his organic spontaneity, the most positive and creative occasion of his being transported by something beyond his conscious will".[64] Sex is brought about by intuitive passion, and the spontaneous relationship between man and his world. It is a pleasure, and pleasure is a grace, which should not be obedient to the commands of the will. And "There is obviously nothing degrading in sensuous pleasure which comes 'of itself'. . . ."[65] Lawrence, sharing the same Eastern perception of love and sex, often reminds us that genuine sexual love is beautiful because it comes along intuitively and spontaneously. Sex, Lawrence writes in his poem, is not "a thing to be afraid of, / a threatening, torturing, phallic Moloch". It is not something "ashamed, and shameful, and vicious". When sex "comes upon us . . .we must learn to satisfy with pure, real satisfaction".[66] The word "pure" suggests sex should be free of any social or conventional consciousness, and should act upon its "pure" instinctive desire. The intuition, whether it is in love or in sex or in marriage, is to complete "soul's impulse", and to satisfy the urges of the body. Along with other urges of the body, Lawrence places great importance on the sexual urge, because he regards it as a hunger. In the poem "Look! We Have Come Through" he writes: "The hunger for the woman, Alas,/ it is so deep a Moloch, ruthless and strong,/ 'tis lie the unutterable name of the dread Lord,/ not to be spoken aloud. / Yet there it is, the hunger which comes upon us,/ which we must to learn to satisfy with pure, real satisfaction; / or perish, there is no alternative." It is a hunger "more frightening, more profound / than stomach or throat or even the mind".[67] He writes to Morris L. Ernest, urging modern men to embrace "the emotions and passions of sex, and the deep effects of human physical contact".[68] It is because they are the crucial part of an instinctive, spontaneous life, and an instinctive, spontaneous life is the way to experience the wonder of the cosmos and to achieve the body's innocence and integrity. With regard to this view, the sexual union of Birkin and Ursula is portrayed as a proud recovery of human original sensuality, which is a healthy desire instead of corruption, because they respect and follow the instinctive life-flow of both man and the universe. In *The Plumed Serpent*, Kate is longing for an extra-individual wholeness with the living cosmos through sex, which is "the greater, not the lesser sex":

> The waters over the earth wheeling upon the waters under the earth . . .. She felt her sex and her womanhood caught up and identified in the slowly revolving ocean of nascent life . . .. How strange to be merged in desire beyond desire, to be gone in the body beyond the individualism of the body, with the spark of contact lingering like a morning star between her and the man. . . . [69]

Later on the religious leader—her supposed husband—Cipriano fulfils her desire through the ancient sexual rituals, during which Kate feels in his body a powerful cosmic force. It links her with the vital cosmos and transports her beyond her prison-like individuality into the "morning star". Kate's experience comes from her submissive relationship with the unknown universe, in which man's "self-will" is in unity with the whole cosmos.

Lawrence asserts in *A Propos of Lady Chatterley's Lover*: "the real point of this book" is that "I want men and women to be able to think sex, fully, completely, honestly and cleanly. Even if we cannot act sexually to our complete satisfaction, let us at least think sexually, complete and clear".[70] Shaman Nahal argues that Lawrence has never advocated that the pure satisfaction of the hunger of sex is the only aim of a person's life. On the contrary, he strongly holds that a sexual union is not to be indulged in unless it comes from the innermost desires of both souls. The attitude he adopts reflects "restraint rather than licentiousness".[71] In "The State of Funk", Lawrence further clarifies his views on sex:

> If there is one thing I don't like it is cheap and promiscuous sex. If there is one thing I insist on it is that sex is a delicate, vulnerable, vital thing that you mustn't fool with. If there is one thing I deplore it is heartless sex. Sex must be a real flow, a real flow of sympathy, generous and warm, and not a trick thing, or a moment's excitation, or a mere bit of bulling.[72]

What Lawrence emphasizes in this passage is that since sex is a "delicate, vulnerable" yet "vital" thing, it must be highly respected instead of being treated frivolously. On the other hand, sex, being an instinctive urge of the body, is a living spontaneous flow. It is pure and sacred and beautiful and must be accepted without fear.

Lawrence's view is in violation of the doctrines of Christianity, which aim to acquire spiritual power and renounce the urges of the body. In Christian cultures, as there is a strong sense of man's separation from nature, sexuality is not a thing to be glorified, or to be spoken of if possible. It is only allowed to stay in the mind, "sex-in- the-head", in Lawrence's words. So he is strongly against spiritual love as advocated in the Christian religion for its denial of the body, and instead encourages people to accept "living sex":

> The whole trouble with sex is that we daren't speak of it and think of it naturally. We are not secretly sexual villains. We are not secretly depraved. We are just human beings with living sex. We are all right, if we had not this unaccountable and disastrous *fear* of sex.[73]

Lawrence then recalls how he was ashamed of his sexual thoughts and desires when he was a boy. This "fear of sex" is a painful experience resulting from conflict between mind and body. After a long struggle he came to accept his sexuality freely. He was happy to ignore his "social mental" self: the boy having these "feelings with such fear, shame and rage was the social mental me", while "The boy that had excited sexual thought and feelings was the living, warm-hearted, passionate me". Living naturally in his warm sexual flow, he felt, "it is wonderful how much deeper and more real the human sympathy flowers". He is hence no longer afraid of sex: "My sex is me as my mind is me, and nobody will make me feel shame about it".[74]

Lawrence regards *Lady Chatterley's Lover* as "obviously a book written in defiance of convention".[75] As for the use of the taboo words, he argues that "the so-called obscene words . . . are the natural part of the mind's consciousness of the body. Obscenity only comes in when the mind despises and fears the body, and the body hates and resists the mind". Lawrence shows his contempt of "the poor, nervous counterfeit phallus of modern 'nervous' love", and eulogizes "the warm blood-sex that establishes the living and vitalizing connexion between man and woman".[76] He is trying to bring the phallus to its divine status as most Eastern traditions do. Fear of sex and the body, he believes, leads to cold and politically oriented relationships between people, which has become a disturbing disease infecting certain Western cultures. "We suppress the instincts", Lawrence comments, "we cut off our intuitional awareness from one another and from the world. Now we know one another only as ideal or social or political entities, fleshless, bloodless, and cold . . .Intuitively we are dead to one another, we have all gone cold".[77] With a hope to save people from cold sexlessness, Lawrence writes books about the sexual relations of men and women, such as *Lady Chatterley's Lover*. He says in "The State of Funk":

> It is not because I want all men and women to begin having indiscriminate lovers and love affairs, off the reel. All this horrid scramble of love affaires and prostitution is only part of the funk . . . is just as unpleasant and hurtful as repression, just as much a sign of secret fear.[78]

It is because he wants the readers to "Accept sex in the consciousness, and let the normal physical awareness come back". "Conquer the fear of sex", he writes towards the end of the essay, "and restore the natural flow. Restore even the so-called obscene words".[79]

Sexuality, according to Lawrence's cosmic vision, has a much wider meaning than in its conventional sense. It should not only be restricted to the flesh; instead, it pervades the whole universe and engenders everything that exists. Lawrence points out that there exist two basic modes, a masculine one and a feminine one, within the integral, unconscious self, as well as in the whole universe. He writes in the "Study of Thomas Hardy":

> Why do we consider the male stream and the female stream as being only in the flesh? It is something other than physical. The physical, what we call in its narrowest meaning, the sex, is only a definite indication of the great male and female duality and unity. It is that part which is settled into an almost mechanized system of detaining some of the life which otherwise sweeps on and is lost in the full adventure.[80]

He further explains that female and male do not necessarily exist in the flesh of a woman and a man; they exist in everything within the cosmos. They are in "my poppy plant . . . It is part of the great twin river, eternally each branch resistant to the other, eternally running each to meet the other". In this text, female is defined as the principle of things that enclose and contain; male is that which struggles to break out of containment. The essential quality of the two principles is conveyed in an elaborate metaphor for the sexual relationships of men and women: "The male exists in doing, the female in being. The male lives in the satisfaction of some purpose achieved, the female in the satisfaction of some purpose contained".[81] Hochman points out that, according to Lawrence's cosmic sexuality, "The universe, like the self, is made up of the push-and-pull of masculinity and femininity". Furthermore, in his arts the shared sexuality between man and universe is implicitly projected "as a rainbow that spans the two oceans, or as the foam that spumes at the clashing of the waves where the two oceans meet". The iris and the rose of "The Crown" are much like the rose and the poppy of his "Hardy study". They are the images of that mysterious sex: abundant, erotic, beautiful, flamboyant, fragile and transient.[82] The message of this text not only suggests a homological correspondence between cosmos and human beings, but also depicts a vision of the universe in perpetual creative motion and with sexual vitality.

Earl Brewster, Lawrence's Buddhist friend who spent much time living with Lawrence and knew him well, wanted to do Lawrence justice with regard to the public misunderstanding of his proposition of sexuality. He writes: "To those who did not know Lawrence personally, and to his readers who may not have discovered the real man in his books, I must bear witness of the Lawrence I knew". The following passage provides a picture of the real Puritan in Lawrence. Let it be the conclusion of this chapter.

> He was a puritan—a term I often heard applied to him in his presence, and one which he accepted and admitted. Those who read praise of licentiousness into his works, should know the disgust with which he regarded that quality. Nature he worshipped, and *natural* impulses he deeply respected, but that pathological condition when the *mind* is absorbed in sex he abhorred. It is true that Lawrence himself was possessed by the subject of sex— but in what a different way! His possession was like that of the doctor who wishes to heal. He deserves our efforts to understand him whether he succeeds fully or not, or whether we can agree with him. It is clear that he believed mental life and sex should be more separate—even as our other organic life is more separate from the mental consciousness. To-day most of us deny and repress sex, or indulge ourselves in it without respect for its significance. He did neither, but tried to show that sensuality like sentimentality is false, while sensuousness free of mental tempering—is part of the divine life. . . .
>
> My first impression of Lawrence as the Botanist, deeply loving nature, still seems to me to contain the essential truth of his character. I think of him as close to those Hindu worshippers of *Shakti*,—life, vitality, power. . . .
>
> Never during my years of intimacy with him—gay and free as were our hours together—believing as he did that what a man feels and thinks should be expressed—have I ever known him to tell a vulgar story, nor to joke and speak lightly of sex, never have I known him to treat or regard one human being with less dignity or less delicacy than another. Indeed he was the Puritan.[83]

Indeed, what once seemed so scandalous in Lawrence's time now seems quite innocent. The sexual freedom which he espoused has been extended far beyond anything he himself advocated. Had Lawrence lived today, he would be horrified by the commercialist use to which sex is put in modern societies.

[1] Genjō kōan Dōgen, *Shōbōgenzō*, p.77, quoted in Mary E. Tucker, ed., *Buddhism and Ecology*, p. 170.

[2] Philosopher George Santayana's speech given at the University of California in 1911, quoted in Dolores LaChapelle, *D. H. Lawrence, Future Primitive,* p. 102.

[3] Ibid., p. 102.

[4] The Centre of Traditional Taoist studies, www.tao.org.

[5] Brandon Toropov, ed., *The Complete Idiot's Guide to Taoism*, p. 138.

[6] D. H. Lawrence, "The Painted Tombs of Tarquinia", in *Mornings in Mexico and Etruscan Places*, p. 152.

[7] Martin Heidegger, *The Thing*, quoted in Dolores LaChapelle, *D. H. Lawrence, Future Primitive*, p. 131.

[8] Laozi, *Dao De Jing*, Ch. 25, p. 48, Chinese Version .

[9] D. H. Lawrence, "The Painted Tombs of Tarquinia", in *Mornings in Mexico and Etruscan Places*, pp. 152-3.

[10] D. H. Lawrence, *Kangaroo*, Ch. 8, pp. 172-3.

[11] D. H. Lawrence, *The Rainbow*, Ch. 16, pp. 458-9.

[12] David Cavitch, *D. H. Lawrence and the New World*, p. 55.

[13] D. H. Lawrence, *St. Mawr* in *St. Mawr and Other Stories*, p. 50.

[14] David Cavitch, *D. H. Lawrence and the New World*, pp. 54-5.

[15] Ibid., p. 55.

[16] D. H. Lawrence, *The White Peacock*, Ch. 2, p. 175.

[17] Graham Hough, *The Dark Sun*, p. 34.

[18] Chaman Nahal, *D. H. Lawrence: An Eastern View*, p. 64.

[19] Graham Hough, *The Dark Sun*, p. 31.

[20] *The Letters of D. H. Lawrence*, Aldous Huxley, ed., p. 197.

[21] Graham Hough, *The Dark Sun*, pp. 31-2.

[22] Ibid., pp. 193-4.

[23] D. H. Lawrence, *The White Peacock*, Ch. 2, p. 182.

[24] Graham Hough, *The Dark Sun*, p. 32.

[25] Chaman Nahal, *D. H. Lawrence: An Eastern View*, p. 62.

[26] D. H. Lawrence, *Study in Classic American Literature*, p. 31.

[27] Baruch Hochman, *Another Ego*, p. 28.

[28] Sri Aurobindo, *The Life Divine*, p. 90, quoted in Chaman Nahal, *D. H. Lawrence: An Eastern View*, p. 74.

[29] Richard Jefferies, *The Story of My Heart*, pp. 52, 54-5.

[30] *Lawrence on Hardy and Painting*, J. V. Davies, ed., p. 27.

[31] Ibid., p. 30.

[32] D. H. Lawrence, "Reflections on the Death of a Porcupine", in *D. H. Lawrence, A Selection from Phoenix*, p. 451.

[33] *Lawrence on Hardy and Painting*, J. V. Davies, ed., p. 27.

[34] D. H. Lawrence, *Love Poems*, pp. xxxiii-xxxiv.

[35] D. H. Lawrence, "Love Among the Haystacks", in *Love Among the Haystacks and Other Stories*, p. 28.

[36] D. H. Lawrence, *Sons and Lovers*, Ch. 13, p. 430.

[37] Baruch Hochman, *Another Ego*, p. 42.

[38] Keith Sagar, *The Art of D. H. Lawrence*, p. 45.

[39] D. H. Lawrence, *The Rainbow*, Ch. 1, pp.10-11.

[40] Ibid., Ch. 4, p. 161.

[41] Scott Sanders, *D. H. Lawrence: The World of the Major Novels*, p. 78.

[42] D. H. Lawrence, *The Rainbow*, Ch. 2, pp. 51-4.

[43] Scott Sanders, *D. H. Lawrence: The World of the Major Novels*. p. 79.

[44] D. H. Lawrence, *The Rainbow*, Ch. 1, pp. 9-10.

[45] Scott Sanders, *D. H. Lawrence: The World of the Major Novels*, p. 13.

[46] Ibid., p. 84.

[47] Ibid., p. 207.

[48] D. H. Lawrence, *Lady Chatterley's Lover*, Ch. 10, p. 124.

[49] Scott Sanders, *D. H. Lawrence: The World of the Major Novels*, p. 88.

[50] Ibid., p. 208.

[51] *The Letters of D. H. Lawrence*, Aldous Huxley, ed., p. 687.

[52] D. H. Lawrence, *Lady Chatterley's Lover*, Ch. 10, p. 124 .

[53] *The Letters of D. H. Lawrence*, Aldous Huxley, ed., p. 687.

[54] D. H. Lawrence, *The Rainbow*, Ch. 15, p. 418.

[55] Scott Sanders, *D. H. Lawrence, The World of Major Novels*, p. 64.

[56] Ibid., p. 64.

[57] D. H. Lawrence, *A Propos of Lady Chatterley's Lover*, in *D. H. Lawrence, A Selection from Phoenix*, p. 352.

[58] Ibid., pp. 351-2.

[59] Ibid., p. 352.

[60] D. H. Lawrence, "We Need One another", *Phoenix*, p. 193.

[61] D. H. Lawrence, *A Propos of Lady Chatterley's Lover*, in *D. H. Lawrence, A Selection from Phoenix*, p. 348.

[62] Ibid., pp. 349, 350.

[63] Graham Hough, *The Dark Sun*, p. 231.

[64] Alan Watts, "Introduction", *Nature, Man and Woman*, p. 11.

[65] Alan Watts, *Nature, Man and Woman*, p. 188.

[66] *The Complete Poems of D. H. Lawrence*, Vivian de Sola Pinto, ed., p. 264.

[67] Ibid., 264.

68 *The Collected Letters of D. H. Lawrence*, Harry T. Moore, ed., Vol. II, p. 1099.

69 D. H. Lawrence, *The Plumed Serpent*, Ch. 7, pp. 140-1.

70 D. H. Lawrence, *A Propos of Lady Chatterley's Lover*, in *D. H. Lawrence, A Selection from Phoenix*, p. 330.

71 Chaman Nahal, *D. H. Lawrence: An Eastern View*, p. 110.

72 D. H. Lawrence, "The State of Funk", in *D. H. Lawrence, A Selection from Phoenix*, p. 370.

73 Ibid., p. 368.

74 Ibid., pp. 368-9.

75 D. H. Lawrence, *A Propos of Lady Chatterley's Lover*, in *D. H. Lawrence, A Selection from Phoenix*, p. 360.

76 Ibid., pp. 331, 353.

77 *Lawrence on Hardy and Painting*, J. V. Davies, ed., p. 130.

78 D. H. Lawrence, "The State of Funk", in *D. H. Lawrence, A Selection from Phoenix*, p. 370.

79 Ibid., p. 371.

80 *Lawrence on Hardy and Painting*, J. V. Davies, ed., p. 55.

81 Ibid., pp. 55, 443.

82 Baruch Hochman, *Another Ego*, pp. 52-3.

83 Earl Brewster, *D. H. Lawrence: Reminiscences and Correspondence*, pp. 121-2.

Chapter III

Enigma of Nature

*

In the previous chapters, we have examined Lawrence's intense sensitivity to nature and his view of the inseparable relationship between man and nature. In this chapter we are going to examine Lawrence's world outlook regarding the enigma of nature, the power of the unknown, and his understanding of god and evolution.

Lawrence, ever since his school days, was fascinated by the eternal creative mystery of the universe. Jessie Chambers in her reminiscence writes that Lawrence was always "interested in the enigma of life", "trying to find the hidden reality behind the appearance of things".[1] To Lawrence, the nature of the universe is ultimately unknowable and inscrutable. "In my opinion, one can never know: and never—never understand", he writes to Trigant Burrow.[2] Aldous Huxley points out that Lawrence's "special and characteristic gift was an extra-ordinary sensitiveness to what Wordsworth called 'unknown modes of being'", and goes on:

> He was always intensely aware of the mystery of the world, and the mystery was always for him a *numen*, divine. Lawrence could never forget, as most of us almost continuously forget, the dark presence of the otherness that lies beyond the boundaries of man's conscious mind.[3]

His perspective on this mysterious "otherness" is somewhat like a central thread running through his writing. Man is a product of an "eternal creative mystery", a small part of a greater organism, and man's little moral play has its significance only when the play develops in accordance with the unfathomable force of nature, or only when his pulse is "beating direct from mystery". In *Women in Love*, Lawrence through Birkin expresses a profound respect for the "creative mystery" of the universe that decides human destiny: "Whatever the mystery which has brought forth man and the universe, it is a non-human mystery, it has its own great ends, man is not the criterion". Though he is sad about Gerald's sudden death, he is aware of the "creative mystery" which he believes exerts a decisive influence upon man's life:

> The eternal creative mystery could dispose of man, and replace him with a finer created being: just as the horse has taken the place of the mastodon . . . To be man was as nothing compared to the possibilities of the creative mystery . . .To have one's pulse's beating direct from mystery, this was perfection, unutterable satisfaction.[4]

Years earlier Lawrence expresses the same worldview in the "Study of Thomas Hardy". Having analysed the cause of the tragedy of Hardy's characters, he talks with admiration about the "revelation" Hardy's novels present to us:

> There exists a great background, vital and vivid, which matters more than the people who move upon it. Against the background of dark, passionate Egdon . . . of the unfathomed stars, is drawn the lesser scheme of lives . . . Upon the vast, incomprehensible pattern of some primal morality greater than ever the human mind can grasp, is drawn the little, pathetic pattern of man's moral life and struggle, pathetic, almost ridiculous.[5]

It is "ridiculous" because man's "little fold of law and order" is like a "walled city" that is "too small" for man to "defend himself from the vast enormity of nature". "The unfathomed moral forces", or "unknown morality" of the universe, are unexplored by human moral consciousness. Instead it is the "primal morality" of the universe that has brought forth human beings' life:

> The vast, unexplored morality of life itself, what we called immorality of nature, surrounds us in its eternal incomprehensibility, and in its midst goes on the little human morality play, with its queer frame of morality and its mechanized movement.[6]

Lawrence regards this revelation as the "wonder" and "quality" of Hardy's work, which he considers to be the very quality Hardy shares with the great writers such as Shakespeare, Sophocles and Tolstoy. There are two categories of moralities. One is "a small system of morality, the one grasped and formulated by the human consciousness"; the other is "the vast, uncomprehended and incomprehensible morality of nature or of life itself". As the latter is "surpassing human consciousness", the former is destined to be within the latter.[7] Huxley grasps Lawrence's point in his "Introduction" to *The Letters of D. H. Lawrence* that both man's system of morality and the powerful sciences are false understandings of reality:

> Most men live in a little puddle of light thrown by the gig-lamps of habit and their immediate interest; but there is also the pure and powerful illumination of the disinterested scientific intellect. To Lawrence, both lights were suspect, both seemed to falsify what was, for him, the immediately apprehended reality—the darkness of mystery.[8]

Lawrence's view of the inexplicability of the mystery of reality parallels an essential concept of Eastern philosophy. In the light of Zen, "the darkness of mystery" exists all around and within us, which needs not be invoked nor sought after, it spontaneously appears only when our vision is clear enough to see it. The wonder and glory of the universe is incomprehensible, wordless, unimaginable, and will always lead to awe. Life itself as a natural process is an organic mysticism. It is not a function of cultivation, examination, manipulation, or adaptation; it rejects unnatural things, including man's morality and science, for they are false and unable to explain the reality. Ernst Haeckel, whose books Lawrence had read and known well in his university days, holds that the essence of nature is beyond human conscious knowledge, it "becomes more mysterious and enigmatic the deeper we penetrate into the knowledge of its attributes".[9]

The ancient Taoist sage Laozi describes the indescri- bability of nature in the first chapter of *Dao De Jing*:

> Nature can never be completely described, for such a description of Nature would have to duplicate Nature.
> No name can fully express what it represents.
> It is nature itself . . ., which is the ultimate source of all that happens, all that comes and goes, begins and ends, is and is not.[10]

Nature to Laozi is utterly beyond human comprehension. "What is ultimate in Nature" is "invisible", "inaudible", and "intangible". "But even all three of these together cannot adequately describe it".[11]

> If we cannot describe it intelligibly, this is because it is beyond our understanding.
> Nature is the formless source of all forms, and yet it remains unaffected by its forms.
> Thus it appears to us as if mysterious.[12]

In Taoist theory, there are no words to describe the indescribable, as "Nature is inexpressible, he who desires to know Nature as it is in itself will not try to express it in words".[13] Nature is self-sufficient, it needs no explanation and cannot be captured in words; it is free from form and colour, and is not an object of the senses. It is firm, difficult to comprehend, and totally inexplicable. Nature is self-perfected. There is no point trying to understand intellectually the imperceptible nature. For those who accept nature's way or can identify with the universe do not fear the mystery. Their understanding of the mysteries of nature is in terms of describing the existential phenomena, which is the visible, not the invisible. It is the visible that is the unknown mystery. In a Zen poem, the inexpressible mystery is expressed eloquently by the natural pictures:

Wind subsiding, the flowers still fall;
Bird crying, the mountain silence deepens.[14]

The wonder of the enigma of nature and human life is a characteristic feature in many of Lawrence's novels and essays. The incidents Lawrence draws from real life often serve as background information with the purpose of presenting the mystery of man's life, as well as nature's elusiveness and the greater morality behind it. Tom Brangwen, with his wife Lydia on his way to Anna and Will's wedding, experiences a sense of the nothingness of human beings and the eternity of the "roaring vast space":

> He felt himself tiny, a little upright figure on a plain circled round with the immense, roaring sky: he and his wife, two little, upright figures walking across this plain, whilst the heavens shimmered and roared about them. When did it come to an end? In which direction was it finished? There was no end, no finish, only this roaring vast space . . . What was sure but the endless sky? But that was so sure, so boundless. . . . [15]

Being circled with the shimmering and roaring space, Tom couldn't help wondering about the "boundless" and "endless" universe, from which comes man's short life, miraculous yet insignificant. Human beings are born and die; they come from dirt and return to dirt, they are like, in Lawrence's words, "one year's accidental crop" of the fecund land.[16] Ursula of *The Rainbow* experienced a feeling of frightening helplessness when faced with nature's huge power: "Vaguely she knew the huge powers of the world rolling and crashing together, darkly, clumsily, stupidly, yet colossal, so that one was brushed along almost as dust. Helpless, helpless, swirling like dust"![17] Kate Leslie of *The Plumed Serpent*, after reading the long Hymn of Quetzalcoatl, realizes the humbleness of human beings:

> Man only like green-fly clustering on the tender tips, an aberration there. So monstrous the rolling and unfolding of the life of the cosmos, as if even iron could grow like lichen deep in the earth, and cease growing, and prepare to perish. . . . And man are less than the green-fly sucking the stems of the bush, so long as they live by business and bread alone. Parasites on the face of the earth.[18]

Against the background of the unknown power of nature, human beings would naturally have a sense of helplessness and humility. For, as he writes in the essay "Blessed Are the Powerful", this unknown power is "the first and greatest of all mysteries. It is the mystery that is behind all our being, even behind all our existence".[19] In his early essay "Art and the Individual", Lawrence claims that the "incomprehensible purposes" of nature make man feel less self-awareness and self-importance, and this is to him "a most useful" revelation:

> When it (religious sympathy) reverentially recognizes the vast scope of the laws of nature, and discovers something of intelligibility and consistent purpose working through the whole natural world and human consciousness, the religious interest is developed and the individual loses for a time the sense of his own and his day's importance, feels the wonder and terror of eternity with its incomprehensible purposes. This, I hold it, is a most useful and fruitful state. [20]

Paul in *Sons and Lovers*, after making love with Clara, experiences a sense of the "nothingness" of the human being overwhelmed by the "magnificent power" of the wheeling universe, and thus feels "a sort of peace":

> To know their own nothingness, to know the tremendous living flood which carried them always, gave them rest within themselves. If so great a magnificent power could overwhelm them, identify them altogether with itself, so that they knew they were only grains in the tremendous heave that lifted every grass blade its little height, and every tree, and living thing, then why fret about themselves? They could let themselves be carried by life, and they felt a sort of peace each in the other.[21]

Compared with the divine mystery of nature, "man's moral life and struggle" is nothing. Paul and Clara's experience illustrates Lawrence's vision of human life's position in this unknown universe.

* *

Although he shows great reverence to the mysterious universe, Lawrence does not believe in a personal god, neither does he believe in evolution. The reason he criticizes evolution is that he hates the enigma of nature being broken up by any scientific explanation. Science and intelligence are associated with man's intellectual mind, and have developed according to the laws of the human world, which in his opinion are all false (see the chapter of Mind and Body). For him only the mysterious moral laws of nature, instead of evolutionary science, should be employed to explain the existence of the universe. The perception of no first cause "pleases my fancy" Lawrence admits.[22] For him, there is no god, no first cause in the formation of the universe, only an unknown force that accounts for the whole history of creation.

Laozi says, "Nature did not originate in beginnings, and will not reach its goal in endings . . . No matter how closely we scrutinize its coming toward us, we cannot discover a beginning. No matter how long we pursue it, we never find its end".[23] Likewise, Lawrence believes the origin or cause of the universe is utterly unknowable. Here is his poem "Let There Be Light":

> If ever there was a beginning
> There was no god in it
> There was no Verb
> No Voice
> No Word.
> There was nothing to say:
> Let there be light!
> All that story of Mr. God switching on day
> Is just conceit.
>
> . . .
>
> All we can honestly imagine in the beginning
> is the incomprehensible plasm of life, of creation struggling
> and *becoming* light.[24]

Lawrence's rejection of the first cause suggests his Eastern understanding of the origins of life and the universe. Chaman Nahal, talking about the first cause of the universe in her book *D. H. Lawrence, An East View*, points out that in Hinduism, according to Veda (the most ancient Hindu scriptures) there is no such thing as first creation. There are only endless cycles.

Nothing exists at the present; nothing has ever existed or will exist, except "Braham" which is always there.[25] The "Braham" of Hinduism is exactly equivalent to the Tao of Taoism. Both of them are believed to have been in existence before the universe came into being. *Dao De Jing* describes the essence of Tao as: "Deep, it is like the ancestor of the myriad creatures"[26] and it is "born before heaven and earth, silent and void . . . It is capable of being the mother of the world".[27] Nahal explains that the Hindus, owing to man's inability of ever achieving the precise knowledge of how the universe was first created, express the first creation in one word "Om" in Vedas. Om is not a word, it is only a sound, a mystic sound, which indicates that everything is created out of Om and at the same time is part of Om. According to Hindu philosophy, "All this world is the syllable Om. Its further explanation is this: the past, the present, the future—everything is just Om. And whatever transcends the three division of time—that, too is just Om".[28] Incidentally, Lawrence is also fascinated by this word. He says in "On Being Religious": "Of course, nobody can define it (the God). And a word nobody can define isn't a word at all. It's just a noise and a shape, like Pop! Or Ra or Om".[29] He also uses this word to explain his view that there is no God, neither is there a "First Cause" of the universe:

> But it is tiring to go to any more tea parties with the Origin, or the Cause, or even the Lord. Let us pronounce the mystic Om, from the pit of the stomach, and proceed.
> There is not a shadow of doubt about it, the First Cause is just unknowable to us, and we'd be sorry if it wasn't. Whether it's God or the Atom. All I say is Om![30]

All is Om, it is useless for man to make a scientific quest for the first cause of nature and human life. "In the beginning—there never was any beginning, but let it pass", as Lawrence writes in *Fantasia of the Unconscious.* [31]

However, considering everything should have a start, Lawrence advances an assumption that our world is created by a little living creature: "In the very beginning of all things, time and space and cosmos and being, in the beginning of all these was a little living creature . . . Its palms quivering and its life-pulse throbbing". It died "before it had had young ones . . . And that was the beginning of the cosmos". Constant life and death cycles finally generate the whole universe. He writes: "Out of living creatures the material cosmos was made: out of the death of living creatures when their little living bodies fell dead and fell asunder into all sorts of matter and forces and energies, sun and moon(s), stars and worlds. So you got the universe".[32] From a very little cell comes a world. This semi- evolutionary concept reminds us of Laozi's creative theory:

> From the Tao, one is created;
> From the one, two;
> From the two, three;
> From the three, ten thousand things.[33]

The numbers used here simply indicate a creative process, which includes the process of both affirmation and negation—the living thrives upon the dead. Lawrence imagines that the active cosmos is made out of both "living creatures" and "the death of living creatures". His understanding resembles the eastern view of life cycles: no first cause, but endless life upon death. As to "where you got the living creature from, that first one, don't ask me", Lawrence says, "He was just there . . . He wasn't life with a capital L". [34]

To Lawrence the first living creature is not a Western god, that is for certain, it is a life force existing everywhere and sustaining the universe forever. Lawrence's view of living creatures is similar to the essential principle of Tao and Braham in that they are "just there", no beginning, no end. Lawrence rejects the theory of evolution and dislikes the suggestion of a "First Cause" being the start of the universe. But he is happy to imagine a possible big bang:

> Myself, I don't believe in evolution, like a long string hooked on to a First Cause, and being slowly twisted in unbroken continuity through the ages. I prefer to believe in what the Aztecs called Suns: that is, worlds successively created and destroyed. The sun itself convulses, and the worlds go out like so many candles when some body coughs in the middle of them. Then subtly, mysteriously,

the sun convulses again, and a new set of worlds begins to flicker alight.

This pleases my fancy better than the long and weary twisting of the rope of Time and Evolution, hitched on to the revolving hook of a First Cause. I like to think of the whole showing going bust, *bang!*—and nothing but bits of chaos flying about. Then out of the dark, new little twinklings reviving from nowhere, nohow. [35]

The Aztec legend provides a more receptive vision of world creation for Lawrence's imagination. He would rather believe in a big bang than the slow, weary evolution. Because he would not believe things that he could not "feel" by "intuition". He rejects any scientific explanation of the first cause of the created world, because he does not "feel" intuitively there are "the laws of evolution" that could explain for him the enigma of nature.

After years of acceptance of the 'laws' of evolution— rather desultory or humble acceptance—now I realise that my vital imagination makes great reservations. I find I can't feel it, with the best will in the world, believe that the species have 'evolved' from one common life-form. I just can't feel it, I have to violate my intuitive and instinctive awareness of something else, to make myself believe it. [36]

Something like the creativity of the universe simply has nothing to do with any mechanical law. The theory of evolution does not please his "vital imagination", for it also violates his deep belief in life and in the integrity of the individual. The scientific teaching of cause and effect, for him, not only fails to explain the incomprehensible formation of the universe, but also fails to explain the incomparable uniqueness of an individual. He argues in *Psychoanalysis and the Unconscious*, "this causeless created nature of the individual being is the same as the old mystery of the divine nature of the soul". Moreover, "the origin" of "specific individual nature cannot be found in any cause-and-effect process whatever", and "Cause-and-effect will not explain even the individuality of a single dandelion". Because "There is no assignable cause, and no logical reason, for individuality. On the contrary, individuality appears in defiance of all scientific law, in radiance of even reason".[37] Just as there is no beginning or end to the cosmos, there is no cause or effect in the creation of individuality. The mysterious creative power is the only response to the timeless and spaceless existence of the universe, as well as the lives of living creatures within it.

However, as Ebbatson points out: "Lawrence's work centres upon the clash between the rationalist-materialist reading of the Universe expounded by Darwinism and the transcendental-vitalist reading of the Romantic Nature tradition".[38] In Lawrence's work there are traces of influences from both scientific and romantic writers. At an early age, as Jessie Chambers records, he was deeply impressed by Darwin's *The Origin of Species*, Huxley's *Man's Place in Nature*, and Haeckel's *The Riddle of the Universe*. The stress of evolution upon the organic interrelatedness of the whole of nature is characteristically manifested in Lawrence's "Reflection on the Death of a Porcupine": "In nature, one creature devours another, and this is an essential part of all existence and of all being".[39] He further explains, "The primary way, in our existence, to get vitality, is to absorb it from living creatures lower than ourselves. It is thus transformed into a new and higher creation".[40]

Darwin's theory of "the survival of the fittest" is reflected in many of his tales, in which the image of the struggle goes on in all organic life with a pattern of survival and extinction. In *The White Peacock,* when the unknown father is discovered asleep on a log, "Suddenly through the gloom of the twilight-haunted woods came the scream of a rabbit caught by a weasel". Lettie notices "the cruel pitiful crying of a hedgehog caught in a gin . . . the traps for the fierce little murderers . . . and baited with the guts of a killed rabbit".[41] These ruthless struggles between animals mirror the cruel reality of the survival of the fittest in the human world. George Saxton's deterioration in *The White Peacock*, the death of the miner in the story "Odour of Chrysanthemums", Gerald Crich's snow-mountain tragedy in *Women in Love* and so on all illuminate a Darwinian struggle for existence in both natural and human worlds.

In order to satisfy his emotional needs, Lawrence has only partially accepted the theory of evolution by way of reconciling causal evolution with Romantic nature mysticism, as Ebbatson suggests. Romantic and imaginative by nature, Lawrence necessarily feels more congenial to the Romantic tradition for its exploration of a mode of spiritual transcendence, and rejects scientific determinism. Ebbatson has expounded how Lawrence's nature philosophy is vitally shaped by the transcendental-vitalist readings of the Romantic, particularly the influences of the work of Meredith, Hardy, Hale White and Richard Jefferies, as well as that of such sages as Carlyle, Ruskin, Schopenhauer, and Edward Carpenter.[42] Jefferies, for instance, whose philosophy of nature was transmitted directly to Lawrence, holds that in man's passionate realization of his relationship with nature, man experiences a mystical sense of transcendence. During man's sensual communion with the sun, the moon and the earth, the personal relationship withers or is broken up, and is replaced by something larger and more universal. In the eleventh and twelfth chapters of *The Trespasser*, Lawrence depicts a world that reflects the natural world in Jefferies' *The Story of My Heart* and *Greene Fern Farm*. In that world, there is no division between man's life and nature's life, all are sacred, all are mysterious and beyond scientific explanation. Jefferies' understanding of nature is purely romantic, which leaves no room for the ideas of the first cause and evolution. "Nothing is evolved, no evolution takes place, there is no record of such an event; it is pure assertion", Jefferies claims. He believes there is no "inherent necessity for a first cause", because "There is no evolution any more than there is any design in nature". He goes on "By standing face to face with nature . . . I have convinced myself that there is no design and no evolution".[43] For Jefferies, "there is an immense range of thought quite unknown to us yet", but the limitations of man's mind have hindered him in his imagination of the alternatives to extinction and immortality. He proclaims, "There may be something else, more wonderful than immortality, and far beyond and above that idea".[44] Haeckel holds the same viewpoint in his belief that man may not be at the highest evolutionary point; there may be some other planets containing "higher beings" who may "far transcend us earthly men in intelligence".[45] This vision of neo-Darwinism pleases Lawrence and is repeated in *Women in Love*. Birkin feels "consoling" when thinking: "The eternal creative mystery could dispose of man, and replace him with a finer created being". He is trying to put aside his sadness upon Gerald's death by assuring himself: "If humanity ran into a cul de sac, and expended itself, the timeless creative mystery would bring forth some other being, finer, more wonderful, some new, more lovely race, to carry on the embodiment of creation".[46] Lawrence's most natural character, the gamekeeper Mellors in *Lady Chatterley's Lover*, finds great satisfaction in contemplating the rise of some other species following the extermination of human beings. He is assuring Connie: "To contemplate the extermination of the human species and the long pause that follows before some other species crops up, it calms you more than anything else". [47]

In his essay "Love", Lawrence talks at length about man's unalterable fate influenced by the unknown creative power: "There is the unknown and the unknowable which propounds all creation . . . we can only accept it as a term of our own limitation and ratification".[48] He writes to Lady Ottoline Morrell in 1915 and mentions the fate: "But one can't run away from fate. The thought of fate makes me grin in my soul with pleasure: I am so glad it is inevitable, even if it bites off my nose". *The Rainbow* is for him something enables him to embark upon "the voyage of discovery towards the real and eternal and unknown".[49] What is the unknown? The unknown to him are the mysterious laws or forces of nature. It can find its closest and best explanations in the Tao of Taoism. In Taoism, there is the order of Tao functioning in the universe, it is invisible and formless, no laws and no end, yet it penetrates everywhere and operates an orderly world. Alan Watts writes of the characteristic of Tao in *Nature, Man and Woman*, "the Tao is always anonymous and unknown, and the incessant changefulness and flowing impermanence of nature is seen as a symbol of the fact that the Tao can never be grasped or conceived in any fixed form".[50] Ben Willis elaborates the same nature of Tao. Tao, he says, involves both fundamental reality and spirituality. It governs all truth and universal beings; it works in cyclic rhythms of constant transformation and change; it pervades every form of organic and inorganic life. This Tao is the base of all existence, of all real being, which includes, of course, our human beings.[51] Tao is full of unknown mystery, yet it creates everything. Creativity is an essential feature of Tao. Willis expounds nature's "creative process":

> The fact is that the seasonal, evolutionary, physical and biological changes and stages of the natural world are a rich creative process, and that all of the universe is in a constant state of creative renewal . . . Cyclic ebb and flow as found in nature and human life is . . . a living, growing, changing, harmonizing state of infinite creative activity and infinite quiescence.[52]

The force of creation is described by Lawrence in *Mornings in Mexico* as "a great flood, forever flowing, in lovely and terrible waves". He admires deeply the creative force: "In everything, the shimmer of creation, and never the finality of the created. Never the distinction between God and God's creation, or between Spirit and Matter".[53] *Women in Love* expresses the same admiration and wonder at the creative power of nature through Birkin's Alpine reflection:

> The mystery of creation was fathomless, infallible, inexhaustible, forever. Races came and went, species passed away, but ever new species arose, more lovely, more equally lovely, always surpassing wonder. The fountain-head was incorruptible and unsearchable. It had no limits. It could bring forth miracles, create utterly new races and new species in its own hour, new forms of consciousness, new forms of body, new units of being.[54]

Lawrence's essay "Life" elaborates at length about the unknown progress of all life creation:

> We issue from the primal unknown. Behold my hands and feet, where I end upon the created universe! But who can see the quick, the well-head, where I have egress from the primordial creativity? Yet at every moment . . . between the fecund darkness of the first unknown and the final darkness of the afterlife, wherein is all that is created and finished.[55]

He asks us to yield ourselves "to the unknown, only to the unknown, the Holy Ghost".[56] His Holy Ghost is not the Christian God. It represents an unknown creative force like Tao and Braham in a traditional Eastern sense. The "primordial creativity" of the earth is vividly illustrated in his essay "The study of Thomas Hardy": "Where in the unfathomable womb (of the body of Egdon Heath) was begot and conceived all that would ever come forth". The land of Egdon is "the powerful, eternal origin seething with production". It is "the dark, powerful source whence all things rise into being, whence they will always continue to rise, to struggle forward to further being". This land "is the primitive, primal earth, where the instinctive life heaves up", and "out of the body of this crude earth" are born Eustacia, Wildeve and all the others.[57]

In every created being, there is an inborn, natural urge for the creation of life. The fulfilment of that urge is the wonder of creation itself, which is beyond man's morality and sensibility. Its process sometimes contains a negative element:

> Everything, everything is the wonderful shimmer of creation, it may be a deadly shimmer like lightning or the anger in the little eyes of the bear, it may be the beautiful shimmer of the moving deer, or the pine-boughs softly swaying under snow. Creation contains the unspeakably terrifying enemy, the unspeakably lovely friend, as the maiden who brings us our food in dead of winter, by her passion of tender wistfulness. Yet even this tender wistfulness is the fearful danger of the wild creatures, deer and bear and buffalo, which find their death in it. [58]

Nature is pure and powerful. It accepts everything and creates new things endlessly, no matter whether the creative process undergoes wonderful shimmering or fearful danger. This text contains a dialectical principle of creation which involves both life and death. In Taoism, a vital life force generated from Tao is seen as the creativity of transformation in its most primal and elemental form. Tao vitalizes and constructs all forms of life; and so do all things created flow back into it again ceaselessly. This is the nature of Tao, which, in Laozi's words, "involves initiation of growth, initiation of growth involves completion of growth, and completion of growth involves returning to that whence it came".[59]

It is suggested in Taoism that the final purpose of this transformational process or the cyclic rhythms of the cosmos "is to bring about an all-encompassing harmony designed for the good of every living thing".[60] This principle bears a close affinity to Lawrence's above text concerning the creative process of nature. For Lawrence, whether it be a "beautiful shimmer" or a "deadly shimmer", it is all part of "the wonderful shimmer of creation", life and death construct a harmonious natural world. Further more, each part, good or bad in man's moral judgement, is to him a necessary and inseparable link in the whole creative wonder. In traditional Chinese understanding, the Tao of nature possesses a positive, beneficent and constructive good will. It is because nature never fails in the regularity of its cyclic rhythms of the cosmos. Nature's Yin-Yang mode brings forth everything into life. In this sense, the law of nature should not be regarded as merely a physical law; it is ethical. And nature is the result of this ethical alternation and is said to be "good", and thus nature's law is considered to be moral. Dolores LaChapelle, when discussing Lawrence's "phallic vision", also mentions the goodness of nature in Taoist view: "since human beings were produced by nature, nature must be good in the larger sense and therefore nature is to be trusted".[61]

* * *

There are two types of laws according to Taoism. One is the law of nature, which does not need to be known in order to be followed and which, being violated, will bring punishment spontaneously. The other is the law of man, which is artificial and has to be enforced with effort. Laozi says:

> Whenever a regulation is imposed from above, it is not willingly obeyed.
> Then effort is used to enforce it. . . .
> But when law is enforced, spontaneous and sincere loyalty declines, and disintegration of the harmonious society sets in.
> Thus valuing law as an end in itself results in minimizing fidelity to Nature itself.
> Knowledge of law appears at once as a flowering of nature's way and as the source of the error.[62]

Any effort to know and to make law is in opposition to "nature's way", and is thus regarded as "the source of the error".

Laozi's notions of the law of man and the law of nature correspond to Lawrence's theories of ideal and desire. Ideal, Lawrence maintains, "is superimposed from above, from the mind; it is a fixed, arbitrary thing, like a machine control". Whereas, a desire "proceeds from within, from the unknown, spontaneous soul or self", hence it is instinctive, and is likened to the natural law.[63] When an ideal or a law "is enforced", the "spontaneous and sincere loyalty declines". Laozi wants people to "be intelligent and follow Nature itself. / let us not stray./ Nature's way is simple and easy, but men prefer the intricate and artificial".[64] Lawrence likewise wants modern people to take a lesson "to learn to break all the fixed ideals, to allow the soul's own deep desires to come direct, spontaneous into consciousness".[65] Desire, unlike the arbitrary and mechanical ideal, helps man to establish an integrity and freedom in his being. Lawrence explains:

> Desire itself is a pure thing, like sunshine, or fire, or rain. It is desire that makes the whole world living to me, keeps me in the flow connected. It is my flow of desire that makes me move as the birds and animals move through the sunshine and the night, in a kind of accomplished innocence.[66]

Therefore, Mellors and Lady Chatterley's desire makes the whole world live to them, because of their desire it "flows from me and consummates me with the other unknown".[67] The fulfilment of consummation they have achieved is the fulfilment of "the greater morality" of nature. Man achieves happiness through his "accomplished innocence" under the laws of nature. Compared with the "simple" law of nature, the law of mankind is unbearable. Through Connie, Lawrence expresses his revulsion toward the "complicated" human laws:

> She thought again of Clifford's dictum: "Nature is a settled routine of crude old laws. One has to go beyond nature, break beyond. And that is one's destiny that makes one break beyond the settled, arbitrary laws of nature".

> She herself saw it differently. She couldn't feel the laws of nature so arbitrary. It was the laws of man that bothered her. She couldn't feel anything very arbitrary about the tossing daffodils, dipping now in shade. If only one could be simple! Men were so complicated and full of laws. [68]

Man's artificial laws hinder individuals from acknowledging their spontaneous self, from being "thyself", "pure", and "desirable". Lawrence explains, "Be thyself does not mean *Assert thy ego!* It means, be true to your own integrity, as man, as woman: let your heart stay open, to receive the mysterious inflow from the unknown . . ."[69] So that man's deep desire is to Lawrence "a wish for pure, unadulterated relationship with the universe". He writes in a letter to Catherine Carswell (16 July 1916) expressing this belief:

> What we want is the fulfilment of our desires, down to the deepest and most spiritual desire. The body is immediate, the spirit is beyond: first the leaves and then the flower: but the plant is an integral whole: therefore *every* desire, to the very deepest. And I shall find my deepest desire to be a wish for pure, unadulterated relationship with the universe, for truth in being.
>
> It is this establishing of pure relationships which makes heaven, wherein we are immortal, like the angels, and mortal, like men, both. And the way to immortality is in the fulfilment of desire.[70]

For Lawrence, man's desires are the desires of nature, of the unknown. He says in "Love": "we can only know that from the unknown, profound desires enter in upon us, and that the fulfilling of these desires is the fulfilling of creation".[71] This insight again bears an affinity to Taoism. In Taoism, as discussed in the previous chapter, it is believed that man's nature reflects the nature of the cosmos, and man's freedom consists in conformity with nature. So man's fulfilment of his desires is nature's will manifested in man. In Laozi's words, "All aiming is Nature's aiming, and is Nature's way of being itself".[72] Happiness means to accept the natural law of the universe, living one's life and having one's desire realized along the right track of the universe. Archie

J. Bahm, one of the translators of *Dao De Jing*, explains this point of view as the following:

> He who trusts Nature's way as best for him can feel assured that the fulfilment of the life which Nature has provided for him is all he needs and all he should desire. He may, . . . appreciate the fact that his own nature realizing itself is Nature's way of realizing itself through him, and that thus he is a genuine expression of an everlasting process.[73]

Hence we have Laozi's teaching, "Submit to Nature if you would reach your goal./ For, whoever deviates from Nature's way, Nature forces back again".[74] Lawrence holds the similar view. He says in "The Reality of Peace" that man's "great desire of creation and the great desire of dissolution" are ultimately the great desires of nature. Man's desires "must submit" to the power from the unknown, so that he can keep his true self and be forever new:

> I remain myself only by the grace of the powers that enter me, from the unseen, and make me forever newly myself. I am myself, also, by the grace of the desire that flows from me and consummates me with the other unknown, the invisible, tangible creation.[75]

The "tangible creation" is the fulfilment of nature in man, which involves "death with life and life with death". Man's consummation with the unknown is the achievement of what Lawrence calls the ultimate "immortality".[76]

Lawrence maintains a submissive attitude towards the unknown force of nature. He writes in a letter: "Behind in all are the tremendous unknown forces of life, coming unseen and unperceived as out of the desert to the Egyptians, and driving us, forcing us, destroying us if we do not submit to be swept away".[77] The "unknown forces of life" are the greater morality of nature that "can be dodged for sometime, but not opposed".[78] If man's little moral play goes against the "moral forces of nature", if he does "deviate from Nature", he will inevitably meet with failure or death, like all those failed characters in his novels, as well as in Hardy's. Lawrence in his Hardy essay expounds how

Hardy's heroes in *The Return of the Native* met their calamities. According to his point of view, Clym, whom Eustacia married, is "utterly blind to the tremendous movement carrying and producing the surface. He did not know that the great part of every life is underground, like roots in the dark in contact with the beyond". Instead, he "calculated a moral chart from the surface of life", and thus he binds himself to the code and system of human morality. His heart is beating far away from the "dark, powerful source" of nature and is finally swept away by it.[79] His own hero Birkin arrives at a more or less satisfactory destination because he keeps to the principle of not competing with nature.

Then, is it necessary and possible for an individual to face his fate and survive the harsh social existence? According to Lawrence, one should face the storm of the outside world, and accept it come what may. He wrote to Tietjens in 1917: "You see it is impious for us to assert so flatly what *should be*, in face of what *is*. It is our responsibility to know how to accept and live through that which *is*".[80] For him, once an individual squarely faces what *is*, and goes through his fate submissively, he will get over it and achieve a true understanding of life. Lawrence writes about this principle of life in the preface to his play *Touch and Go*, advocating a submissive attitude to face one's fate: "And the whole business of life, at the great critical periods of mankind, is that men should accept and be one with their tragedy".[81] This notion of accepting one's fate is not utterly pessimistic in a conventional sense, as Lawrence's final aim is to get over the "critical" moments without risking too much unnecessary trouble. Laozi's preaching in *Dao De Jing* has drawn our attention to its affinity with Lawrence's submissive attitude towards one's fate:

> Submit to Nature if you would reach your goal.
> For, whoever deviates from Nature's way,
> Nature forces back again.
> Whoever gives up his desire to improve upon Nature will find Nature satisfying all his needs.
> Whoever finds his desires extinguished will find more desires arising of their own accord.
> Whoever desires little is easily satisfied.
> Whoever desires much suffers frustration.

> Therefore the intelligent person is at one with Nature, and so serves as a model for others.[82]

Submitting to nature is an essential feature of Wu Wei in Taoism (Wu Wei means Non-action in Chinese, Wu: 'no or not'; Wei: 'action'). "Wu Wei" or non-action is a means to resolve any tragedy, conflict or discord. It does not mean purely passivity or doing nothing. It means not pushing anything to its extreme limit, but acting in accordance with the laws of the endurance of nature:

> Wu Wei is the habit and discipline of stilling the mind so that intuition, the voice of spirit, will penetrate our consciousness and supply a creative or spiritual solution to every problem of life. Such solutions can include a judicious doing nothing about the problem, and it is often extraordinary how things have a way of righting themselves if left alone. [83]

When Lawrence says, "men should accept and be one with their tragedy", he possibly means the same as "a judicious doing nothing about the problem", but waiting to see what will be the correct way to solve the problem. According to Lawrence, it was necessary to have "patience, always patience",[84] because the problems that happen "are beyond one's will and one's control",[85] and "One can only wait and let the crisis come and go".[86] "Active punishment" can only worsen the whole situation, and it is no good to allow oneself to be "dragged down";[87] "One should have courage, and stand clear".[88] With the same attitude of Wu Wei, Lawrence wishes that Anna, Eustacia or Tess would not be "at war with society"; and Oedipus, Hamlet, Macbeth would not go to extremes to punish their enemies.

Wu Wei reveals that it is much easier to go with nature than against it, and by doing so we shall accomplish our purpose far more efficiently. If one could be "patient and wait", his creative intuition would provide him some alternative way, and then by taking some right action, he could finally solve the problem. The positive effect of this Wu Wei philosophy manifests itself in all aspects of life and in every kind of human relationship. It is because at the centre of all existence, the spirit or Tao "can always restrain imbalance or excess, and so can't fail to be positively creative and renewing".[89] Thinking in the same way as Wu Wei, Lawrence points out that "had Oedipus, Hamlet and Macbeth been weaker, less full of real potent life, they would have been made no tragedy".[90] For it could be expected that something positively balancing would come to their help and renew their life. According to Wu Wei, nothing should be excessive, as nature itself is never excessive but always balanced. Any excessive expenditure of energy is an indication of imbalance, which is against the flow of spirit and will result in destroying the harmony of Yin and Yang. In the last chapter of *Women in Love*, when Birkin is mourning the loss of his only friend Gerald, thinking about his death and his own future, he decides to give up the struggle for a better world and deliver himself to a transcendent order: "(Birkin) turned away. Either the heart would break or cease to care. Best cease to care. . . .. Best leave it all to the vast, creative, nonhuman mystery. Best strive with oneself only, not with the universe".[91] Lawrence leaves Birkin's problem to the transcendental power of the mysterious universe, which is the attitude of Wu Wei. Willis points out, if this Wu Wei concept is difficult for modern people to understand, it is because we have lost our spiritual touch with nature and been away from our inner selves. People today tend to sink into "the destructive extremes of abused energy, ego obsession and excessive rationalism", which easily creates tensions and problems.[92] The submissive attitude towards social conflict Lawrence proposes in his Hardy essay is an effective art of living. The Wu Wei spirit will enable us to get out of a world exclusively worshipping man's intellectual and rational capability, and to follow the unwritten moral law of nature "voluntarily and spontaneously".[93]

* * * *

As early as 1907, Lawrence was seriously thinking about Christianity. He questioned the existence of a personal god in a letter to Reverend Robert Reid: "Cosmic harmony there is—a Cosmic God I can therefore believe in. But where is the human harmony, where the balance, the order, the 'indestructibility of matter' in humanity? And where is the *personal, human* God"?[94]

In the same year as this letter, Lawrence read Spencer and Haeckel. Both of them had argued that from the point of view of the modern scientist, "God must be viewed as an immanent force that manifests itself in all parts of nature".[95] This "immanent force" is Lawrence's cosmic god, or as he sometimes calls it "the Unknown", the "Holy ghost", the "Holy Spirit", or the "will". In a letter to his sister Lawrence talks about god and nature's concern for the species:

> There still remains a God, but not personal god: a vast shimmering impulse which waves onwards towards some end, and I don't know what—taking no regard of the little individual, but taking regard for humanity. When we die, like rain-drops falling back again into the sea, we fall back into the big, shimmering sea of unorganized life which we call God. We are lost as individuals, yet we count in the whole.[96]

God for him is an immanent power with an active presence in man and in the universe; it is manifested in the fundamental rhythms of the cosmos and in human life. Lawrence writes:

> There is no god
> apart from poppies and the flying fish,
> Men singing songs, and women brushing their hair
> in the sun.
> The lovely things are god that has come to pass, like Jesus
> came . . .[97]

God does not exist separately beyond us, he penetrates everywhere. He inhabits or is embodied in human life and in all physical things: in light, in "cold shadow", "water", "rock", "foam", in "every molecule of creation", and "There is no end to the birth of God".[98] In the poem "God is Born", he points out that god must be viewed and comprehended both in "the history of the cosmos" and "in the history of the struggle of becoming". "What are the gods, then, what are the gods?" Lawrence is seeking the meaning and form of gods:

> The gods are nameless and imageless
> yet looking in a great full lime-tree of summer
> I suddenly saw deep into the eyes of god:
> it is enough.[99]

Lawrence associates god with the wonder and mystery of creation. The god's existence signifies a continuous living experience as manifested in the process of everyday life. He further explains, "There is no God looking on. The only god there is, is involved all the time in the dramatic wonder and inconsistency of creation. God is immersed, as it were, in creation, not to be separated or distinguished. There can be no Ideal God".[100] Or there is no god "in our sense of the word", Lawrence stresses, he is only "the mystery of creation, the wonder and fascination of creation" that exists everywhere in the universe, and is forever working through all natural process, which is the god in his real sense.[101]

Whatever god is, he is not thought of by Lawrence in any intellectual or rational terms, neither has he moralistic and personalized attributes. In this sense, Lawrence's god is identical with Braham in Hinduism, Dharmakaya in Buddhism, and Tao in Taoism. His god, though perhaps not regarded as an exact equivalent to those Eastern "gods", in many respects encompasses the same essential qualities and principles. I am tempted to compare Lawrence's god with the Tao:

> The great Tao flows everywhere,
> to the left and to the right.
> All things depend upon it to exist,
> and it does not abandon them.
> To its accomplishments it lays no claim.
> It loves and nourishes all things,
> But does not lord it over them.
> The Tao, without doing anything (Wu Wei),
> leaves nothing undone.[102]

During Lawrence's last months, however, his vision of god changed. In his conversations with Brewster, he expressed a wish to establish a relationship with God: "I intend to find God: I wish to realize my relation with Him. I do not any longer object to the word God. My attitude regarding this has changed. I must establish a conscious relation with God".[103] Whether he finally accepted a Christian god after a lifetime detour or looked to seek god's recognition in order to give his soul a peaceful rest after this earthly life we do not know. However, the enigma of nature and the quest for god in its real sense haunted him all his life and become a notable feature of his writings.

[1] Jessie Chambers, *D. H. Lawrence: A Personal Record*, p. 59.

[2] *The Letters of D. H. Lawrence*, James T. Boulton, ed., Vol. II, p. 643.

[3] Aldous Huxley, *"Introduction" to The Letters of D. H. Lawrence,* Aldous Huxley, ed., pp. xi-xii.

[4] D. H. Lawrence, *Women in Love*, Ch. 31. pp. 478-9.

[5] *Lawrence on Hardy and Painting*, J. V. Davies, ed., p. 31.

[6] Ibid., p. 31.

[7] Ibid., p. 31.

[8] Aldous Huxley, "Introduction" to *The Letters of D. H. Lawrence*, Aldous Huxley, ed., p. xiv.

[9] Ernst Haeckel, *The Riddle of the Universe*, quoted in Roger Ebbatson, *Lawrence and the Nature Tradition: A Theme in English Fiction*, pp. 37-8.

[10] Laozi, *Dao De Jing*, Archie J. Bahm, ed., Ch. 1, p. 11.

[11] Ibid., Ch. 14, pp. 20-1.

[12] Ibid., p. 21.

[13] Ibid., Ch.1, p. 11.

[14] Quoted in Alan Watts, *The Way of Zen*, p. 188.

[15] D. H. Lawrence, *The Rainbow*, Ch. 5, p. 126.

[16] *Lawrence on Hardy and Painting*, J. V. Davies, ed., p. 27.

[17] D. H. Lawrence, *The Rainbow*, Ch. 11, p. 304.

[18] D. H. Lawrence, *The Plumed Serpent*, Ch. 16, p. 256.

[19] D. H. Lawrence, "Blessed Are the Powerful", *Phoenix* II, p. 442.

[20] D. H. Lawrence, "Art and the Individual", *Phoenix II*, p. 222.

[21] D. H. Lawrence, *Sons and Lovers*, Ch. 13, p. 430-1.

[22] D. H. Lawrence, "Corasmin and the Parrots", *Selected Essays*, p. 206.

[23] Laozi, *Dao De Jing*, Archie J. Bahm, ed., Ch. 14. p. 21.

[24] *The Complete Poems of D. H. Lawrence*, Vivian de Sola Pinto, ed., p. 681.

[25] Chaman Nahal, *D. H. Lawrence: An Eastern View*, p. 52.

[26] Laozi, *Tao De Jing*, Betty Radice, ed., Ch. 4, p. 8.

[27] Ibid., Ch. 25, p. 30.

[28] Upanishad, 3, 1, quoted in Chaman Nahal, *D. H. Lawrence: An Eastern View*, p. 52.

[29] D. H. Lawrence, "On Being Religious", *Phoenix*, p. 724 .

[30] D. H. Lawrence, *Fantasia of the Unconscious and Psychoanalysis of the Unconscious*, p. 14.

[31] Ibid., p. 15.

[32] Ibid., pp. 15, 16.

[33] Laozi, *Dao De Jing*, Chinese version, Ch. 42, p. 81.

[34] D. H. La6wrence, *Fantasia of the Unconscious and Psychoanalysis of the Unconscious*, p. 16.

[35] D. H. Lawrence, "Corasmin and the Parrots", *Selected Essays*, p. 206.

[36] D. H. Lawrence, "Introduction to his Paintings", *Selected Essays*, p. 335.

[37] D. H. Lawrence, *Fantasia of the Unconscious and Psychoanalysis of the Unconscious*, p. 210.

[38] Roger Ebbatson, *Lawrence and the Nature Tradition: A Theme in English Fiction*, p. 258.

[39] D. H. Lawrence, "Reflections on the Death of a Porcupine", in *D. H. Lawrence, A Selection from Phoenix*, p. 451.

[40] Ibid., p. 454.

[41] D. H. Lawrence, *The White Peacock*, Ch. 5, p. 59.

[42] Roger Ebbatson, *Lawrence and the Nature Tradition: A Theme in English Fiction*, Ch. 8, pp. 239-260.

[43] Richard Jefferies, *The Story of My Heart*, p. 91.

[44] Ibid., pp. 94-5.

[45] E. Haeckel, *The Riddle of the Universe*, p. 303, quoted in Roger Ebbatson, *Lawrence and the Nature Tradition: A Theme in English Fiction*, p. 36.

[46] D. H. Lawrence, *Women in Love*, Ch. 31, p. 479.

[47] D. H. Lawrence, *Lady Chatterley's Lover*, Ch. 15, p. 227.

[48] D. H. Lawrence, "Love", *Phoenix*, p. 156.

[49] *The Letters of D. H. Lawrence*, Aldous Huxley, ed., p. 240.

[50] Alan Watts, *Nature, Man and Woman*, p. 39.

[51] Ben Willis, *The Tao of Art*, Ch. 2, pp.16-30.

[52] Ibid., p. 19.

[53] D. H. Lawrence, "Indians and Entertainment", in *Mornings in Mexico and Etruscan Places*, p. 61.

[54] D. H. Lawrence, *Women in Love*, Ch. 31, p. 479.

[55] D. H. Lawrence, "Life", *Phoenix*, pp. 695-6.

[56] Ibid., p. 698.

[57] *Lawrence on Hardy and Painting*, J. V. Davies, ed., p. 30.

[58] D. H. Lawrence, "Indians and Entertainment", in *Mornings in Mexico and Etruscan Places*, p. 61.

[59] Laozi, *Dao De Jing*, Archie J. Bahm, ed., Ch. 25, p. 30.

[60] Ben Willis, *Tao of Art*, p. 19.

[61] Dolores LaChapelle, *D. H. Lawrence, Future Primitive*, p. 169.

[62] Laozi, *Dao De Jing*, Archie J. Bahm, ed., Ch. 38, p. 39.

[63] D. H. Lawrence, "Democracy", *Phoenix*, p. 713.

[64] Laozi, *Dao De Jing*, Archie J. Bahm, ed., Ch. 53, p. 49.

[65] D. H. Lawrence, "Democracy", *Phoenix*, p. 713.

[66] D. H. Lawrence, " . . .Love was Once a Little Boy", *Phoenix II*, p. 455.

[67] Ibid., p. 457.

[68] D. H. Lawrence, *First Lady Chatterley*, p. 42.

[69] D. H. Lawrence, " . . .Love was Once a Little Boy", *Phoenix II*, p. 457.

[70] *The Letters of D. H. Lawrence*, Aldous Huxley, ed., p. 360.

[71] D. H. Lawrence, "Love", *Phoenix*, p. 156.

[72] Laozi, *Dao De Jing*, Archie J. Bahm, ed., Ch. 25, p. 30.

[73] Archie J. Bahm, "About the Author and His Work", in *Dao De Jing*, p. 79.

[74] Laozi, *Dao De Jing*, Archie J. Bahm, ed., Ch. 22, p. 27.

[75] D. H. Lawrence, "The Reality of Peace", *Phoenix*, p. 678.

[76] Ibid., p. 681.

[77] *The Collected Letters of D. H. Lawrence*, Harry T. Moore, ed., Vol. I, p. 291.

[78] *Lawrence on Hardy and Painting*, J. V. Davies, ed., p. 32.

[79] Ibid., p. 30.

[80] Unpublished letter from D. H. Lawrence to Miss E. Tietjens, dated July 27, 1917. University Library, Nottingham.

[81] *The Plays of D. H. Lawrence*, p. 90.

[82] Laozi, *Dao De Jing*, Archie J. Bahm, ed., Ch. 22, p. 27.

[83] Ben Willis, *The Tao of Art*, p. 76.

[84] *The Letters of D. H. Lawrence*, James T. Boulton ed., Vol. III, p. 58.

[85] Ibid., Vol. II, p. 662.

[86] Ibid., Vol. III, p. 125.

[87] *Lawrence on Hardy and Painting*, J. V. Davies, ed., p. 32.

[88] *The Letters of D. H. Lawrence*, James T. Boulton, ed., Vol. III, p. 71.

[89] Ben Willis, *The Tao of Art*, p. 76.

[90] *Lawrence on Hardy and Painting*, J. V. Davies, ed., p. 32.

[91] D. H. Lawrence, *Women in Love*, p. 478.

[92] Ben Willis, *The Tao of Art*, p. 77.

[93] Ibid. p. 77.

[94] *The Letters of D. H. Lawrence*, James T. Boulton, ed., Vol. I, p. 41.

[95] Daniel J. Schneider, *The Consciousness of D. H. Lawrence: An Intellectual Biography*, p. 49.

[96] *The Letters of D. H. Lawrence*, James T. Boulton, ed., Vol. I, p. 256.

[97] *The Complete Poems of D. H. Lawrence*, Vivian de Sola Pinto, ed., p. 691.

[98] Ibid. pp. 682-3.

[99] Ibid., p. 650.

[100] D. H. Lawrence, "Indians and Entertainment", in *Mornings in Mexico and Etruscan Places*, p. 62.

[101] Ibid., p. 61.

[102] Laozi, *Dao De Jing*, Chinese version. Ch. 34, p. 64.

[103] Earl Brewster, *D. H. Lawrence: Reminiscences and Correspondence*, p. 224.

Chapter IV

Interrelationship and Individuality

*

Lawrence's life principle, as we have discussed in the previous chapters, is to achieve and preserve "a vivid relatedness between the man and the living universe".[1] In his opinion, all things, whether sentient or insentient, assert their own lives to each other and influence each other. He writes at the beginning of "Aristocracy": "Everything in the world is relative to everything else. And every living thing is related to every other living thing".[2] In "We Need One Another", he emphasises that since everything in this world is a part of the "living wholeness", so "everything, even individuality itself, depends on relationship".[3]

The interrelatedness between man's life and all other creatures become one of the major concepts relating to his view of nature. He writes in the essay "Aristocracy":

> In the great ages, man has vital relation with man, with woman, and beyond that, with the cow, the lion, the bull, the cat, the eagle, the beetle, the serpent. And beyond these, with narcissus and anemone, mistletoe and oak-tree, myrtle, olive, and lotus. And beyond these, with humus and slanting water, cloud-towers and rainbow and the sweeping sun-limbs. And beyond that, with sun and moon, the living night and the living day. [4]

The primeval country life of the Brangwens in *The Rainbow* depicts the "exchange and interchange" of man's life with the universe:

> So much warmth and generating and pain and death did they know in their blood, earth and sky and beast and green plants, so much exchange and interchange they had with these, that they lived full and surcharged, their senses full fed, their faces always turned to the heat of the blood, staring into the sun, . . . looking towards the source of generation, unable to turn around.[5]

Lawrence's vital relationship with the great pine tree in front of his ranch cabin, as mentioned in the first chapter, is a revealing example of the mutual influence man shares with his environment: "It gives out life, as I give out life. Our two lives meet and cross one another, unknowingly: the tree's life penetrates my life, and my life the tree's. We cannot live near one another, as we do, without affecting one another". He writes a few lines later:

> I have become conscious of the tree, and of its interpenetration into my life . . . I am even conscious that shivers of energy cross my living plasm, from the tree, and I become a degree more like unto the tree, more bristling and turpentiney, in Pan. And the tree gets a certain shade and alertness of my life, within itself.[6]

The reciprocal relations between man and other living things also suggest a vital relationship between man's innermost world and the unknown force of nature. Hence, Ursula of *The Rainbow* sees in the rainbow the hope of mankind. Somers of *Kangaroo*, when he "saw the rainbow fume beyond the sea", establishes "a pledge of unbroken faith, between the universe and the innermost".[7] Later when Lawrence is immersed in the magnificent glory of the natural beauty of Taos, his insight of living unity has developed towards an understanding of what we call "ecology" today. LaChapelle points out in *Future Primitive* that Lawrence is well advanced in putting forward this theory, as in the early nineteen twenties the word ecology did not exist even in the circles of naturalists and biologists. The ecological consciousness is explained by Eddith Cobb:

> Ecology as a science permits us to evaluate reciprocal relations of living organisms with their total environment and with one another as living interdependent systems. This reciprocity . . . extends into a counterpoint between universe and geographical place. Plants, animals, and humans must now be thought of as living in ecosystems, in a web of related, interacting, dynamic energy systems.[8]

More than eighty years ago, Lawrence saw the same web system in nature, which is expressed in many of his essays, such as "Aristocracy", "We Need One Another", "Reflections on the Death of a Porcupine", and so on. Lawrence's own life sets a good example in this mutual relatedness. He has established an equal relationship in everyday life with his Cow Susan, his cat and dog, and a recognized "bond" with flowers and trees, snakes, rocks, and the sun, the moon and the stars. "To me", Frieda said in 1944, "his relationship, his bond with everything in creation was so amazing, no preconceived ideas, just a meeting between him and a creature, a tree, a cloud, anything".[9] The building of this "relatedness" is to him the whole business of life, as he writes in "Pan in America": "What can a man do with his life but live it? And what does life consist in, save a vivid relatedness between the man and the living universe that surrounds him"?[10] So he stresses that the purpose of life is to "re-establish the living organic connection, with the cosmos, the sun and earth".[11] His understanding of "relatedness" bears a close affinity with Taoist theory. In Taoism, not only is man's fate closely linked with the universe, but everything and every event is linked with each other, and exerts influence upon each other. The interrelatedness between everything in this world is the nature of reality, the way things really are. Alan Watts writes in *Man and Woman and Nature*: we are living in a world "in which all events seem to be mutually interdependent—an immense complexity of subtly balanced relationships which, like an endless knot, has no loose end from which it can be untangled and put in supposed order".[12] Such a world is a seamless unity, in which man himself is a loop in the endless knot. Watts is talking about the famous metaphor of "Indra's net", which is found in the Avatamsaka school of Buddhism ("Hua-yen" in Chinese and "Kegon" in Japanese). It presents a cosmic web of dynamic causal interrelationships:

> The universe is considered to be a vast web of many-sided and highly polished jewels, each one acting as a multiple mirror. In one sense each jewel is a single entity. But when we look at a jewel, we see nothing but the reflections of other jewels, and so on in an endless system of mirroring. Thus in each jewel is the image of the entire net.[13]

The mirror image reflects the interdependencies of everything in nature's web. Francis H. Cook sees this "Indra's net" as a symbol of cosmos, "in which there is an infinitely repeated interrelationship among all the members of the cosmos. This relationship is said to be one of simultaneous mutual identity and mutual intercausality".[14] According to Cook, this relationship is not simply biological and economic, a matter of causal relationships of bees and blossoms; it is a more pervasive and complicated interdependency than we have so far imagined. A Buddhist, or a Taoist, would find no problem in understanding this theory due to their ecological consciousness:

> Each individual is at once the cause for the whole and is caused by the whole, and what is called existence is a vast body made up of an infinity of individuals all sustaining each other and defining each other. The cosmos is, in short, a self-creating, self-maintaining, and self-defining organism.[15]

In this vast Indra's net, "if one strand is disturbed, the whole web is shaken".[16] This ecological consciousness is imagined as a picture of naturalistic monism, for a Buddhist or a Taoist is used to visualizing an organic continuity of the universe. Zhuangzi's classic butterfly metaphor signifies a characteristic monism: the butterfly, by flapping its wings in Beijing, causes a blizzard in New York. Cook presents a similar vision: "Thus in a universe which is pure fluidity, or process, no act can but have an effect on the whole, just as a pebble tossed into a pool sends waves out to the farthest shore and stirs the very bottom".[17] According to this traditional Chinese view of the continuum of the human world and nature, man's actions, big or small, will causally ripple throughout the universe.

For Lawrence, there is no gulf between the ego and the external world. Subject and object, oneself and the circumambient universe are a united oneness. His perception of oneness is dramatized in his novels, poems and essays. In *The Trespasser*, for example, Siegmund deeply realizes the relationship between himself and the universe, "Whatever I have or haven't from now on, the darkness is a sort of mother, and the moon a sister, and the stars children, and sometimes the sea is a brother and there's a family in one house".[18] In his last work *Apocalypse*, Lawrence writes: "I am part of the sun as my eye is part of me. That I am part of the earth my feet know perfectly, and my blood is part of the sea". This text is often quoted as an example of Lawrence's vision of oneness, and further as his environmental consciousness expressed through his imaginative art.

The Chinese sage Zhuangzi depicts a similar perception of a global oneness: "Heaven and earth and I live together, /And therein all things and I are one". This oneness can be achieved only through one's spontaneous daily life. Every small job done, every ritual performed and every relationship established is in Taoism the way to the eternal life of the whole universe. Lawrence holds a similar view, seeing the achievement of oneness as the nexus of man's daily life. He writes in *Apocalypse*:

> If we think about it, we find that our life consists in this achieving of a pure relationship between ourselves and the living universe about us. This is how I 'save my soul' by accomplishing a pure relationship between me and another person, me and other people, me and a nation, me and a race of men, me and the animals, me and the trees or flowers, me and the earth, me and the skies and sun and stars, me and the moon: an infinity of pure relations, big and little, like the stars of the sky: that makes our eternity, for each one of us, me and the timber I am sawing, the lines of force I follow; me and the dough I knead for bread, me and the very motion with which I write, me and the bit of gold I have got. This, if we knew it,

> is our life and our eternity: the subtle, perfected relation
> between me and my whole circumambient universe.[19]

This "subtle, perfected relation" is not obtained through meditation, but through everyday activities. Whatever you are doing, even though it is just a moment, if you are aware of your relations to the circumambient universe, it is to Lawrence a true life and is eternal. In Taoist tradition, it is seen as the return to the natural. "Living at the moment" has also become a much approved way of living in modern times. Every action and thing itself is enough to be affirmed in its own right; each moment can be responded to naturally and spontaneously as sufficient in itself. This everyday moment is seen as a culminating state, and is the natural function of Tao.

Paul O. Ingram summaries a principal Buddhist worldview that reality is constituted by the "Six Great Elements in ceaselessly interdependent and interpenetrating interaction: earth, water, fire, wind, space, and consciousness or 'mind'", so that "all sentient and non-sentient beings, all material 'worlds' are 'created' by the ceaseless interaction of the Six Great Elements".[20] In order to "train ourselves to experience this eternal cosmic harmony and attune ourselves to it as it occurs", the practice of meditation is suggested, for it will bring us the integration of "our body, speech and mind . . . with the eternal harmony of Dainichi (Buddha)'s body, speech, and mind". In this sense, Ingram explains, meditation is "a process of imitation of Dainichi's enlightened harmony with nature through ritual performance" of body, speech and mind.[21]

In Buddhism, there are many kinds of "ritual performance" in seeking harmony with nature, for example, meditation, chanting, drumming, rituals of eating and drinking, and of looking after the dead. Lawrence, though he does not believe in meditation, advocates everyday performance as a means to arrive at a "perfected relation": "the way is through daily ritual, and the re-awakening". He writes in *A Propos of Lady Chatterley's Lover*:

> We *must* get back into relation, vivid and nourishing relation to the cosmos and the universe. The way is through daily ritual, and the re-awakening. We *must* once more practice the ritual of dawn and noon and sunset, the ritual of the kindling fire and pouring water, the ritual

of the first breath, and the last. This is an affair of the individual and the household, a ritual of day.[22]

For him, the practice of rituals will help us to recover "the great sources of our inward nourishment and renewal, sources which flow eternally in the universe". In order to "plant ourselves again in the universe", Lawrence says we must return to these ancient rituals or create the forms to meet our needs.[23]

There is a famous saying in Taoism, "Heaven, earth and I have the same Li". "Li" means "holy ritual" or "sacred ceremony", it can also be translated as "pattern", or in the larger sense as the principle of nature. The underlying Li behind everything makes man and nature closely interrelated. The practice of sacred ceremonial action is the pursuance of the coordination of the practical, the intellectual and the spiritual in one act. Yen Yuan, a seventeen-century Neo-Confucian, writes:

> The ancients taught men to do house work, and while doing housework to practice reverence. They taught the proper ways of dealing with people, and in these to practice reverence. They taught rituals, music, archery, riding and mathematics, but in arranging the order of the rituals . . . there was nothing without the practice of reverence.[24]

The old Chinese sages would make any action into a sacred ceremony, such as serving tea or having a meal. Lawrence follows the same precepts in his daily life to a considerable extent. Whether making tea, dinner or doing housework, he would turn these small jobs into a kind of ritual ceremony. The reverence he shows to everyday chores impresses the people around him. William Gerhardi recalls:

> Mrs. Lawrence dislikes housework; her husband excels in it. Lawrence, a beam on his face, which like a halo, brought in the dishes out of the kitchen, with the pride of a first-class chef in his unrivalled creations: no, as if cooking and serving your guests were a sacrament, a holy rite.[25]

Apart from daily life, Lawrence's novels also tell us of his interest in rituals and ceremonies. In *The Plumed Serpent*, for example, ancient rituals are introduced into many scenes, such as beating drums, singing hymns, weaving fabric, and dressing in different costumes according to character and occasion. To him, the practice of rituals is the way to recover a "vivid and nourishing relation to the cosmos and the universe", which is the same as to achieve Buddha's "enlightened harmony with nature".

Another interpretation of the practice of rituals in Taoism is that it suggests the return to Pooh (or Pu, which means simplicity in Chinese), or to a status as simple as an uncarved block. In Zhuangzi's opinion, the man who has the quality of the uncarved block will not lose his original nature, so that he is closely related to his circumambient universe. With the quality of simplicity, we see the free movement of nature, the truth of nature within man himself. There is a famous poem in ancient China:

> When the sun rises I work in the field.
> When the sun sets I have my rest.
> I dig a well and I drink.
> I till the soil and I eat.
> What has the imperial power to do with me?

The author of this poem is unknown, but the rituals of his everyday life indicate he is the man living with nature most harmoniously. Things with him are just as natural as the water murmuring in the stream and the autumn leaves dropping by the window. The first Brangwen generation of *The Rainbow* has the same simple connection with the external world. They lived on the Marsh Farm and "came and went without fear of necessity, working hard because of the life that was in them, not for want of the money".[26] The Brangwen men, like the ancient poet, enjoy simple farm life and prefer not to bother about what is happening beyond. Through their daily rituals they interchange with "the great sources of nourishment . . . in the universe".

American Buddhist scholar, ecologist and poet Gary Snyder put forward a different ecological vision, viewing nature as our community.[27] In this community, the single individual beings are a part of an ecological communion, while the whole communion is formed through the interrelation of all different individual entities.

In Snyder's community, the "ecological self is not indistinguishable from the whole. The self is *both* the individual *and* the whole", or simply "the one and the many".[28] In accordance with the Buddhist theory of global continuum, of which every individual is a part, the wholeness does not deny individuality at all. In Snyder's words, "All is one and at the same time all is many".[29]

One principal aspect of Snyder's theory of community is about the basic cycle of nature, particularly in the food web. For Snyder, the food web is a community that consists of "a gift exchange, a potluck banquet, and there is no death that is not somebody's food, no life that is not somebody's death . . . The shimmering food chain, food-web, is the scary, beautiful condition of the biosphere".[30] In this food-web community, all individuals participate in mutual gift exchange. Thinking of this "scary" yet "beautiful" food web, Snyder asks in his poem, "Just where am I in the food chain".[31] Lawrence expresses the same wonder in the "Reflections on the Death of a Porcupine": "Food, food, how strangely it relates man with the animal and vegetable world! How important it is! And how fierce is the fight that goes on around it". The skeletons of the porcupine, the inside of a rabbit, the never-stop-eating horses, his cow Susan, his chickens and his cat Timsy are all "*living* on other organisms". The crude devouring is a reality among all the creatures, "In nature, one creature devours another, and this is an essential part of all existence and of all being. It is not something to lament over, nor something to try to reform".[32] Seemingly contradictory to Lawrence's Darwinian notion, Snyder sees an intimate membership in all beings: "Looking closer at this world of oneness, we see all these beings as our flesh, as our children, our lovers. We see ourselves too as an offering to the continuation of life".[33] Different articulations speak the same thing: Lawrence is talking about the existing reality; Snyder is making our vision of food chain subtler by asserting a notion of love. Darwin's survival of the fittest, to Lawrence, only happens in the world of time-space dimension, in which "its existence impinges on other existence, and is itself impinged upon".[34] However, in the timeless and spaceless dimension, or the "fourth dimension" as Lawrence puts it in the essay "Reflections on the Death of A Porcupine", the individual beings are unrivalled, incomparable and unique. In this fourth dimension, every creature is a living unity in his own being, regardless of his condition of being higher or lower in human judgement, and is free in his interfusion with all other creatures of the universe.

* *

Francis H. Cook writes about the mutual identities of Buddhist totalism. In this "totalistic world" all are "simultaneously cause and result, or support and supported".[35] The existence of beings is not only interdependent, but also mutually conditioned; each one has his significance as an individual only when it plays a part within the whole. If one part fails to "support" the other, then the other individual has neither existence nor meaning, because they make and define each other. Viewing things in a sense of mutual definition is a fundamental belief in Mahayana Buddhism. This belief is further interpreted by Alan Watts that: "Nothing in the universe can stand by itself—no thing, no fact, no being, no event" and all things are intelligible only in terms of each other, since all things "exist only in relation to other things".[36] Cook and Watts' points of view draw our attention to Lawrence's perception of mutual identity, particularly in the aspect of human relations. In terms of human beings, real individuality exists only by certain relationships, without which he would become meaningless, "become trashy, conceited little modern egoists":

> Apart from our connexions with other people, we are barely individuals, we, amount, all of us, to next to nothing. It is in the living touch between us and other people, other lives, other phenomena that we move and have our being. Strip us of our human contacts and of our contact with the living earth and the sun, and we are almost bladders of emptiness. [37]

Man's existence and individuality is defined by his relationship with other individuals, other men, women, his family, and everything of the external world. On the other hand, the whole universe would mean nothing if there were no individual beings or creatures by which to define it. Lawrence talks at length about this mutual definition in the essay "We Need One Another". Any historical hero, he argues, no matter how clever he is, how great his philosophies are, would become nothing if he were isolated. Mary Queen of Scots, Napoleon, Immanuel Kant and so on, would become meaningless, and their philosophies useless, if he (or she) were cut off and isolated "in his own pure and wonderful individuality"—he remarks sarcastically. An individual's value or identity is dependent upon other individuals, and even Buddha is no exception:

> Take even Buddha himself, if he'd been whisked off to some lonely place and planted cross-legged under a bho-tree and nobody had ever seen him or heard any of his Nirvana talk, then I doubt he would have got much fun out of Nirvana, and he'd have been just a crank. [38]

This is in effect "a theory of human relativity" as he writes in "Fantasia of the Unconscious".[39] Even God's existence would be meaningless if there were no human beings. In order to maintain one's "real individuality", one has to keep a "living contact" with one's female partner or with other persons:

> It is in relation to one another that they have their true individuality and their distinct being: in contact, not out of contact. This is sex, if you like. But it is no more sex than sunshine on the grass is sex. It is a living contact, give and take: the great and subtle relationship of men and women, man and woman. In this and through this we become real individuals, without it, without the real contact, we remain more or less, nonentities.[40]

From interrelatedness we come to a point of relative identity. The fact that each influences the other and defines the other can be best understood when it is applied to relationships between two opposites. According to Zen Buddhism, each thing is defined by what it is not, "pleasure is defined by pain, life is defined by death..."[41] This mutual definition is seen in Buddhism as a genuine manner of existence, which is called "emptiness". It means that each thing has no self-nature or self-essence as it derives its existence purely through its dependence on everything else. Its lack of essence accounts for its lack of uniqueness. Each has no difference from the other; they are all identical in the sense that they "share in the universal interdependence, or intercausality, of all that exists".[42] This is a Buddhist way of understanding the nature of all things: all is empty, the whole universe is void. Lawrence, though he talks about "real individuality", in his later life holds the same view of "emptiness": individuals, everything in this world have no absolute identity or absolute existence. Being a part of the whole, the individual's existence is like an illusion only reflected by one's mind. "There is nothing that is alone and absolute except in my mind", he says in *Apocalypse*. Even mind itself "has no existence by itself, it is only the glitter of the sun on the surface of the waters". Mind, as well as every individual, is virtually "empty", or "illusion" in Lawrence's words, as it disappears in the whole: "So that my individualism is really an illusion, I am part of the great whole, and I can never escape".[43] In *The Plumed Serpent*, we find the same confusion of the loss of individuality in wholeness. In the chapter "Malintzi", when Kate is puzzling over Don Ramon's insistence that "Alone you are nothing . . . But together we are the wings of the Morning", she wonders if she must "admit that the individual (is) an illusion". She sees clearly her relation to Ramon is reciprocal: "Alone she was nothing. Only as the pure female corresponding to his pure male, did she signify". She feels "she was not real till she was reciprocal",[44] and only by then when the two are together "in strange reciprocity", the morning star would rise between them and grant each of them souls.

* * *

On the other hand, reciprocal human identification does not prevent Lawrence from thinking highly of the uniqueness of individuality and "the heroic soul in the greater man".[45] He respects the individual and his role in the shaping of history more than the individual's unison with society through mindless submission. He writes in "Study of Thomas Hardy": "The final aim of every living thing, creature, or being is the full achievement of itself". Each individual he stresses is new in its own degree, and like a flower can never have "its exact equivalent".[46] Therefore no comparison between individuals is necessary. In "Democracy" he states: "Each human self is single, incommutable, and unique. This is its *first* reality. Each self is unique, and therefore incomparable". Hence we understand his assertion that one man is neither equal nor unequal to another man, and neither inferior nor superior to anyone else, because "I am only aware of a Presence, and of the strange reality of Otherness . . .. Comparison enters only when one of us departs from his own integral being, and enters the material-mechanical world. Then equality and inequality start(s) at once".[47]

Lawrence is clearly aware of the negative influence of mechanical society upon the individual's integrity and spontaneous being. He writes in "Democracy" that a true individual should "fight for the soul's own freedom of spontaneous being, against (the) mechanism and materialism . . .", so that he can "*keep* whole" and "integral". However, it is no easy job for a man to keep whole and integral, for "man is unable to distinguish his own spontaneous integrity from his mechanical lusts and aspirations", as man is in "his present state of unspeakable barbarism". So laws and governments are needed in order to deal with the material-mechanical aspects of man and society. In Lawrence's opinion, any individual living in this material-worshiping world should consciously and purposely preserve his "spontaneous, single, pure being". He emphasizes:

> All our efforts in all our life must be to preserve the soul free and spontaneous. The whole soul of man must *never* be subjected to one motion or emotion, the life-activity must *never* be degraded into a fixed activity, there must be *no fixed direction*.

The "fixed direction" is to him a man-fixed "ideal goal", the goal to gain wealth, fame, and power, which, to him, "is a kind of illness of the spirit, and a hopeless burden upon the spontaneous self".[48] The "hopeless burden" of a "fixed direction" also harms the relationship between individuals. Lawrence believes a perfect relationship should be free of any mechanical restriction, or "ideal goal". From this point of view, he argues that the Christian commandment of "love thy neighbour as thyself" is in violation of spontaneous being. This is because love is a pure and spontaneous thing, which should not be looked upon as an ideal with its origin in the mind and commandment. Likewise, making a "model" housewife of a woman, or a "model" mother, are "fixed notions" that will kill "every possibility of true contact".[49] For Lawrence, "an ideal is superimposed from above, from the mind; it is a fixed, arbitrary thing, like a machine control", whereas, "A desire proceeds from within, from the unknown, spontaneous soul or self".[50] Lawrence's criticism of the imposed "love" and mechanical "model mother" bears a striking affinity with Taoist theory of "De" ("Virtue" in English). In Taoism, De is a kind of unaffected or spontaneous virtue which cannot be cultivated or imitated by any deliberate method. If a notion like "love your neighbour" is cultivated consciously and deliberately, it is then not a real virtue. As it becomes conventional, it will lose its genuine significance. Zhuangzi makes up an imaginary dialogue to criticise Confucius who prescribes a virtue which depends upon the artificial observance of rules and precepts. I quote the whole dialogue here as it serves to explain substantially what Lawrence is aiming to express:

> "Tell me," said Laozi, "in what consist charity and duty to one's neighbour?"
> "They consist," answered Confucius, "in a capacity for rejoicing in all things; in universal love, without the element of self. These are the characteristics of charity and duty to one's neighbour."
> "What stuff!" cried Laozi. "Does not universal love contradict itself? Is not your elimination of self a positive manifestation of self? Sir, if you would cause the empire not to lose its source of nourishment, there is the universe, its regularity is unceasing; there are the sun and moon, their brightness is unceasing; there are the stars, their groupings never change; there are the birds and beasts, they flock together without varying; there are trees and shrubs, they grow upwards without exception. Be like these: follow Tao, and you will be perfect. Why then these vain struggles after charity and duty to one's neighbour, as though beating a drum in search of a fugitive. Alas! Sir, you have brought much confusion into the mind of man." [51]

The ideals of modern society, for Lawrence, are all conventional virtues which are at odds with the achievement of true individuality. So an individual should fight his way out "from the fixed, arbitrary control of ideals, into free spontaneity", instead of being lumped into "the ideal of Oneness, the unification of mankind into the homogeneous whole".[52] From this point of view Lawrence expresses his hatred of artificial mankind: "Smash humanity, and make an end of it . . . Make an end of our holy oneness".[53] What disappoints Lawrence most is the lack of individuality caused by "the modern consciousness". He says, "In this individualistic age, there are no individuals left. People, men, women, and children, are *not* thinking their own thoughts, they are *not* feeling their own feelings, they are *not* living their own lives". [54] Thoroughly disappointed at the lack of individuality, Lawrence imagines that only "death" would possibly give us "our single being", and will "release me from the debased social body", as he writes in "The Reality of Peace".[55]

Lawrence finds mankind has done too much harm to individuals, which leads him to question his belief in the unison of purposive men. In a letter to Lady Cynthia Asquith in 1916, he expresses his hatred of war, and then writes:

> It comes to this, that the *oneness* of mankind is destroyed in me. I am I and you are you, and all heaven and hell lies in the chasm between. Believe me, I am infinitely hurt by being thus torn off from the body of mankind, but so it is, and it is right . . . there is a separation, a separate, isolated fate. [56]

Lawrence's life experience makes him feel that the individual is besmirched by the crowd. In a letter to Mark Gertler, there is a sense of bitterness in being rejected by society: "My heart shuts up against people—practically everybody—nowadays. One has been so much insulted and let down".[57] He has lost hope in man, and wants to keep his own individuality by turning away from his fellow men. Lawrence's nature and his plight are reflected in the story of Somers, the hero of *Kangaroo*, who is unwilling to make friends and always feels isolated. "He was the most forlorn and isolated creature in the world". A sense of detachment from society and mankind is illustrated everywhere in *Women in Love*, *Aaron's Rod* and *Kangaroo*. The main characters, Birkin, Aaron and Somers, trust no class, no collective social action. They are all "noble escapists", but at the same time dissatisfied by their solitariness and singleness. Their situation characteristically represents Lawrence's plight.

According to Lawrence, there are two ways of knowing things: "knowing in terms of apartness, which is mental, rational, scientific, and knowing in terms of togetherness, which is religious and poetic". Lawrence naturally favours the latter, which is his poetic vision of togetherness. From his overall sense of togetherness, he argues that "The Christian religion lost, in Protestantism finally, the togetherness with the universe, the togetherness of the body, the sex, the emotions, the passions, with the earth and sun and stars".[58] As Christian religion lost the pagan vision of the living universe, it not only "abstracted the universe into Matter and Force", but also abstracted men and women, men and men "into separate personalities—personalities being isolated units, incapable of togetherness . . ." If a person is isolated and "incapable of togetherness", he will turn out to be a menace to others and to society. Sir Clifford in *Lady Chatterley's Lover*, for example, "is purely a personality, having lost entirely all connexion with his fellowmen and women, except those of usage".[59] Without connections with his fellow men and women, he is isolated and has developed a sense of menace and fear. Any isolated individuals would turn out to be a menace to every other man's existence. Lawrence further analyses the harms of "apartness". Once "the old togetherness, the old blood-warmth has collapsed, and every man is really aware of himself in apartness", then there will arise "hostile groupings of men for the sake of opposition". This is "the tragedy of social life" and is "the ugly fact which underlies our civilization".[60] In this sense, Lawrence advocates the recovery of the "old togetherness", which is not in the sense of being lumped together by some man-made ideals; and the necessity of rejecting the "isolated individualism", which is in opposition to a living, spontaneous relationship between all the creatures.

* * * *

Lawrence's individualism and oneness tend to be criticised for lack of consistency. At times, he seems to waver between preserving identities and merging with the whole (as in the "Education of the People"); at other times, he puts forward a combined theory, claiming individual identities as a necessary condition for the achievement of wholeness (as in the "Reflection on The Death of Porcupine"). However, Lawrence in "Education of the People" explains explicitly his dualistic perception of individuality and wholeness: "Though man is first and foremost an individual being, yet the very accomplishing of his individuality rests upon his fulfilment in social life . . . Life consists in the interaction between a man and his fellows, from the individual, integral love in each".[61] Man's needs result in two paradoxical movements, as Lawrence puts it. On the one hand, we are single, isolated individuals, we have to achieve our own "wholeness" or "completeness"; on the other hand, we are in "a great concordant humanity". We have to establish, in an almost unconscious way, a true, living relationship with other human beings. He writes in "Love":

> There must be brotherly love, a wholeness of humanity. But there must also be pure, separate individuality . . . there must be both. In the duality lies fulfilment. Man must act in concert with man, creatively and happily. This is great happiness. But man must also act separately and distinctly, apart from every other man, single and self-responsible . . . moving for himself without reference to his neighbour.[62]

Danish artist Knud Merrild's book *With D H Lawrence in New Mexico* serves as the best illustration of the above passage through Lawrence's life in Taos and his close relationship with his male friends, the Danes.

Lawrence's seemingly contradictory concepts of individuality and oneness in every aspect strike close resemblance with the Buddhist theory of totalism and individuality. On the one hand, there is a continuum of life in the whole universe—Hua-yan's totalism in Buddhism—in which everything is interrelated with everything else; on the other hand, everything in this universe has its own individuality. Snyder interprets this issue as "the one and the many, the whole and parts". From this point of view, the big oneness does not violate against differentiation, neither should it deny nor devalue any individuality. Thus we come to another Buddhist principle. In Cook's opinion, within this "one organic body of interacting parts",[63] we shall accept all kinds of events and things willingly, viewing them equally in terms of their interrelationships. As all things in this totalistic universe are interrelated and everything functions as a causal condition for everything else, there is nothing which is not of value in the great harmony of nature, and there should be no differentiation imposed upon each one of them. Hence, death and birth, laughter and tears, and other opposites are thought to coexist equally with each other (this notion will be further examined in the next chapter). Their existence is a reality; we cannot ever have one without the other, the two always go together, and integrate into the total world. In the totalistic world of Lawrence's *White Peacock*, for example, Annable's death goes hand in hand with the beautiful spring sunshine; in *St. Mawr*'s world, the destructive force of nature and its extreme beauty are forever in coexistence, each has its own value in the great harmonious universe. The reality is a unity of multiple things and events, each mirrors the whole, and the whole penetrates each.

F. R. Leavis says that Lawrence's assertion of "The oneness of life; the separateness and irreducible otherness of lives; the supreme importance of 'fulfilment' in the individual" is "the peculiar Laurentian genius" that "manifests itself in the intensity, constancy and fullness of the intuition".[64] Thinking with intuition might be an important factor in explaining his acute awareness of the interrelatedness of all things in the universe, as well as the individual's balancing relationships with all of mankind. Moreover, his understanding of individuality and the continuum of nature represents an Eastern mind of ecological consciousness.

---

1 D. H. Lawrence, "Morality and Novel", in *D. H. Lawrence, A Selection from Phoenix*, p. 176.

2 D. H. Lawrence, "Aristocracy", in *Reflections on the Death of a Porcupine and Other Essays*, p. 367.

3 D. H. Lawrence, "We Need One Another", *Phoenix*, p. 190.

4 D. H. Lawrence, "Aristocracy", in *Reflections on the Death of a Porcupine and Other Essays*, p. 371.

5 D. H. Lawrence, *The Rainbow*, Ch. 1, pp. 10-11.

6 D. H. Lawrence, "Pan in America", *Phoenix*, p. 25.

7 D. H. Lawrence, *Kangaroo*, Ch. 8. p. 173.

8 Eddith Cobb, *The Ecology of Imagination in Childhood*, p. 24.

9 Frieda Lawrence, *Memories and Correspondence*, p. 273.

10 D. H. Lawrence, "Pan in America", *Phoenix*, P. 25.

11 D. H. Lawrence, *Apocalypse*, p. 200.

12 Alan Watts, *Nature, Man and Woman*, p. 4.

13 Gary Snyder, quoted in Mary E. Tucker, ed., *Buddhism and Ecology*, p. 189.

14 Francis H. Cook, "The Jewel Net of Indra", quoted in J. Baird Callicott, ed., *Nature in Asian Tradition of Thought: Essays in Environmental Philosophy*, pp. 213-4.

15 Ibid., p. 215.

16 Ibid., p. 213.

17 Ibid., p. 229.

18 D. H. Lawrence, *The Trespasser*, Ch. 3, pp. 20-1.

19 D. H. Lawrence, "Morality and Novel", *D. H. Lawrence, A Selection from Phoenix*, p. 176.

20 Paul O. Ingram, "The Jeweled Net of Nature", quoted in Mary E. Tucker, ed., *Buddhism and Ecology*, pp. 76-7.

21 Ibid., p. 77.

22 D. H. Lawrence, *A Propos of Lady Chatterley's Lover*, in *D. H. Lawrence, A Selection from Phoenix*, p. 355.

23 Ibid., p. 355.

[24] Yen Yuan (1635-1704), quoted in Dolores LaChapelle, *D. H. Lawrence, Future Primitive*, pp. 157-8.

[25] William Gerhardi, "Literary Vignettes II", in *The Saturday Review*, pp. 893-4, quoted in Dolores LaChapelle, *D. H. Lawrence, Future Primitive*, p. 158.

[26] D. H. Lawrence, *The Rainbow*, Ch. 1, p. 9.

[27] David Landis Barnhill, "Great Earth Sangha: Gray Snyder's View of Nature as Community", quoted in Mary E. Tucker, ed., *Buddhism and Ecology*, p. 187. Sangha means Buddhist community.

[28] Ibid., p. 190.

[29] Gray Snyder, "The Old Way: Six Essays", quoted in Mary E. Tucker, ed., *Buddhism and Ecology*, p. 190.

[30] Gray Snyder, "Grace", quoted in Mary E. Tucker, ed., *Buddhism and Ecology*, p. 188.

[31] Gray Snyder, *Earth House Hold: Technical Notes and Queries to Fellow Dharma Revolutionaries*, quoted in Mary E. Tucker, ed., *Buddhism and Ecology*, p. 188.

[32] D. H. Lawrence, "Reflections on the Death of a Porcupine", in *D. H. Lawrence, A Selection from Phoenix*, pp. 449, 451.

[33] Gray Snyder, "Grace", quoted in Mary E. Tucker, ed., *Buddhism and Ecology*, p. 188.

[34] D. H. Lawrence, "Reflections on the Death of A Porcupine", in *D. H. Lawrence, A Selection from Phoenix*, p. 453.

[35] Francis H. Cook, "The Jewel Net of Indra", quoted in J. Baird Callicott, ed., *Nature in Asian Tradition of Thought: Essays in Environmental Philosophy*, p. 223.

[36] Alan Watts, *The Way of Zen*, p. 63.

[37] D. H. Lawrence, "We Need One Another", *Phoenix*, p. 190.

[38] Ibid., p. 191.

[39] D. H. Lawrence, *Fantasia of the Unconscious and Psychoanalysis and the Unconscious*, p. 15.

[40] Ibid., p. 191.

[41] Alan Watts, *The Way of Zen*, p. 63.

[42] Francis H. Cook, "The Jewel Net of Indra", quoted in J. Baird Callicott, ed., *Nature in Asian Tradition of Thought: Essays in Environmental Philosophy*, p. 227.

[43] D. H. Lawrence, *Apocalypse*, p. 224.

[44] D. H. Lawrence, *The Plumed Serpent*, Ch. 24, pp. 403, 404.

[45] D. H. Lawrence, "Democracy", *Phoenix*, p. 716.

[46] *Lawrence on Hardy and Painting*, J. V. Davies, ed., pp. 15, 14.

[47] D. H. Lawrence, "Democracy", *Phoenix*, pp. 714, 716.

[48] Ibid., pp. 716, 715, 717.

[49] D. H. Lawrence, "We Need One Another", *Phoenix*, p. 191.

[50] D. H. Lawrence, "Democracy", *Phoenix*, p. 713.

[51] H. A. Giles, *Chuang-tzu*, quoted in Alan Watts, *The Way of Zen*, p. 26.

[52] D. H. Lawrence, "Democracy", *Phoenix*, p.713.

[53] D. H. Lawrence, "The Reality of Peace", *Phoenix*, p. 687.

[54] D. H. Lawrence, "The Individual Consciousness V. The Social Consciousness", *Phoenix*, p. 761.

[55] D. H. Lawrence, "The Reality of Peace", *Phoenix*, p. 687.

[56] *The Letters of D. H. Lawrence*, Aldous Huxley, ed., p. 379.

[57] *The Letters of D. H. Lawrence*, James T. Boulton, ed., Vol. III, p. 194.

[58] D. H. Lawrence, *A Propos of Lady Chatterley's Lover*, in *D. H. Lawrence, A Selection from Phonix*, p.357

[59] Ibid., pp. 357, 359

[60] Ibid., pp. 358-9.

[61] D. H. Lawrence, "Education of the People", *Phoenix*, pp. 613-4.

[62] D. H. Lawrence, "Love", *Phoenix*, p. 155-6.

[63] Francis H. Cook, "The Jewel Net of Indra", quoted in J. Baird Callicott, ed., *Nature in Asian Tradition of Thought: Essays in Environmental Philosophy*, p. 226.

[64] F. R. Leavis, *D. H. Lawrence: Novelist*, p. 102.

Chapter V

Duality and the Yin-Yang Principle

*

In the previous chapter we discussed the concepts of interrelationship, oneness and individuality, which reflect Lawrence's view of nature. Among his major worldviews, perhaps his theory of duality and polarity is one of the most striking central features of his philosophy of nature.

According to Lawrence, duality is an all-pervasive principle in the reality of this natural world, which exists in many kinds of relationships and is perceived as pairs of opposites: in nature, within the individual, in religion and in the movement of history itself. "Life itself is dual. And the duality is life and death".[1] "Everything that exists, even a stone, has two sides to its nature".[2] And so with the Christian religion: "The religion of the strong, renunciation and love. And the religion of the weak taught *down with the strong and the powerful, and let the poor be glorified*".[3] God, an eternal primary substance or force, is for him manifested in the division of opposites—the warm and the cold, the dry and the wet, light and dark, fire and water, male and female, and so on. "The true God is created every time a pure relationship, or a consummation out of twoness into oneness takes place".[4] In his expository writings, especially dealing with his dualistic outlook, Lawrence makes his point with a symbolic method and at a very high degree of generality. In this way, he proclaims his own duality: "I know I am compound of two waves . . . When I am timeless and absolute, all duality has vanished. But whilst I am temporal and mortal, I am framed in the struggle and embrace of the two opposite waves of darkness and of light".[5] Thinking in a much broader sense, the movement of history is to him forever undergoing a dualistic transformation:

> We must never forget that mankind lives by a twofold motive: the motive of peace and increase, and the motive of contest and martial triumph. As soon as the appetite for martial adventure and triumph in conflict is satisfied, the appetite for peace and increase manifests itself, and vice versa. It seems a law of life.[6]

The paintings of the Etruscan Tombs—the continual repetition of the images of lion against deer—strengthens his understanding of duality: "As soon as the world was created, according to the ancient idea, it took on duality. All things became dual, not only in the duality of sex, but in the polarity of action". This duality, he stresses, does not "contain the later pious duality of good and evil".[7] Because, taking the animal kingdom for instance, the lion and the deer and other pairs of animals are just "part of the great duality, or polarity of the animal kingdom. But they do not represent good action and evil action. On the contrary, they represent the polarized activity of the divine cosmos, in its animal creation".[8] "The divine cosmos" to him is a living unity that is constantly going through dual and "polarized activity":

> The universe, which was a single aliveness with a single soul, instantly changed, the moment you thought of it, and became a dual creature with two souls, fiery and watery, for ever mingling and rushing apart, and held by the great aliveness of the universe in an ultimate equilibrium.[9]

So, according to Lawrence, there is a universal law of polarity: "the law of all the universe is a law of dual attraction and repulsion, a law of polarity".[10] Being governed by this law, "She (the earth) rests for ever in perfect motion, consummated into absolution from a complete duality. Fulfilled from the two (the earth and the sun), she is transported into the perfection of her orbit." Therefore, a true peace is achieved "in that perfect consummation when duality and polarity is transcended into absorption". [11]

Lawrence's dualistic worldview, though first formulated in the works such as the "Study of Thomas Hardy" (1914) and *Twilight in Italy* (1916), can be traced back to his boyhood experience. His experience of the dual characters of the quarry caves, as well as his parents' deep contrast in their personalities and daily activities, probably contributed in a way to his future dualistic view of life. During the last visit to his hometown in 1927, Lawrence wrote an essay "Autobiographical Fragment", in which he recalls how he was fascinated by the caves in the quarry:

> I loved it because, in the open part, it seemed so sunny and dry and warm, the pale stone, the pale, slightly sandy bed, the dog-violets and the early daisies. And then the old part, the deep part, was such a fearsome place. It was always dark—you had to crawl under bushes. And you came upon honeysuckle and nightshade, that no one ever looked upon. And at the dark sides were little, awful rocky caves, in which I imagined the adders lived.[12]

The two parts of the caves with their noticeable "Yin-Yang" features "haunted" him. He says, " . . . and in this still, warm, secret place of the earth I felt my old childish longing to pass through a gate, into a deeper, sunny, more silent world".[13] This cave experience could be a prelude to his later developed concept of duality. The dark part is comparable to his father's mining life routine. He has to crawl down into the dark pit in the bright morning and return home in the evening to join the ordinary world, and he makes this journey from the dark pit every day, "Only a brief few hours—often no daylight at all during the winter weeks".[14] In this case, the father represents for Yin which means dark, cloudy, weak and feminine in Chinese, while the mother represents Yang: sunny, strong and masculine. Though the father is "deeply alive", his retreat from "the rational aspect of life"[15] and his drinking habit are naturally rejected by the family and have done much damage to the father-son relationship. His mother on the contrary represents all the qualities of Yang: brightness, vitality and intellect, and wins her children's love and admiration.

The basic elements of Lawrence's duality find similarities in the Yin-Yang philosophy of Taoism. Ben Willis in *The Tao of Art* discusses the meaning and function of the Yin-Yang principle.

As nature's most basic principle, it conceives every action and event as the effect of two primary elements or forces, the positive and the negative. It maintains a constant balance of conflicting elements in the physical reality of this world and is, as a matter of fact, an inherent law of compensatory harmony, or "the law of natural action and the action of natural law".[16] Both nature and man (as part of nature) are unavoidably governed by the same Yin-Yang principle of balanced opposition. Lawrence's dichotomy of duality has been illustrated in multiple instances under a great variety of names. Here are some major selected examples: [17]

Light	Dark
Sun	Moon
Male	Female
Intellect	Blood/Senses
Mind	Body/Senses/Intuition
Ideal	Desire
Rational	Intuitive/creative
Spirit /Will/Idea/Brain	Flesh/Body
Knowledge	Feeling/Nature
Love	Law
Consciousness	Feelings/Instinct/ unconsciousness
Motion	Inertia
Movement	Stability
Change	Immutability
Activity	Permanence
Time	Eternality
Multiplicity/ Diversity	Oneness/Wholeness
Duality/Polarity	Oneness/Harmony
God the Son	God the Father
Being	Non-being
Doing	Being
Utterance	Gratification in the Senses
Mental clarity	Sensation
Eagle	Dove
Tiger	Lamb
Lion	Unicorn
Movement towards Discovery	Movement towards the Origin

Though Lawrence is an amateur philosopher, his classification serves very well as a useful formula for the opposite elements with which he can illustrate his thoughts. They are used symbolically and express the same concept as Yin and Yang in Taoism. From this diagram we see that Lawrence identifies Yang (such as the masculine, active, conscious principle) with light and the spirit; Yin (such as the feminine, passive, unconscious principle) with darkness and body. But the sun and moon symbols sometimes change place. The sun presents the quality of the Yin of the moon, and the moon the quality of the Yang of the sun. Even male and female can sometimes play each other's parts, notably when we come to the example of Lawrence's parents. His father, as is discussed before, represents Yin because of his mining routine, and is on the same side as the female, while his mother, being intellectually superior, is regarded in the same light as the male. Hough in *The Dark Sun* points out that we should avoid two misunderstandings concerning Lawrence's duality. The first one is the conventional concept of spirit and matter, with matter usually representing the natural world, while spirit is seen as a supernatural reality set against it. In Lawrence's version, however, both of them are part of the natural world. The second "is to take the common view of Lawrence's belief and see the opposition as merely a sexual one". It is not like that. Lawrence's male-female opposition is just one instance among many of his dualistic views; and he does not inherit the Freudian psychology of sexuality by "constructing the world on the model of sexual duality". [18]

From his own experience, Lawrence may have learned the need and importance of the equilibrium of the positive and the negative. His relationship with Frieda, for example, is one of love and hate, attraction and repulsion, which is much the same as the relationships between his characters. He remarks in *Psychoanalysis and the Unconscious*: "The duality goes so far and is so profound. And the polarity!"[19] The equilibrium of positive and negative, dynamic and unconscious, is sometimes referred to by him as "love", or as the harmonious reality created by a third force called the Holy Ghost. This third force is similar to the creative power "Brahma" in Hinduism, a power that creates the natural balance. Alan Watts employs Hindu mythology to illustrate the reality of the existence of the opposing elements.

In Hindu mythology, there is a divine play that embraces the widest extremes of pleasure and pain, virtue and depravity. The opposites of light and darkness, good and evil, pleasure and pain suggest a reality that both the dark side and the bright side of life comprise an integral part of the whole.[20] For both Hindus and Taoists, the two opposing elements are not merely contrasted with each other; they are in a process of constant transformation through a continuous interaction. The polar forces of Yin and Yang, representing the balance of opposites in the universe, must work together in order to achieve a state of harmony. When they are equally present, and in a mutually compensate condition, all is calm, this is called "Great harmony", or "Da Tong" in Chinese, or in Lawrence's words "the reality of peace". When one outweighs the other, there is confusion and disorder.

Lawrence's early essay "The Crown" expounds the necessity of the existence of the two opposing elements. He employs imagery of lions, lambs and unicorns to discuss his notion of duality and polarity. According to Lawrence, the balance of opposites is achieved by attraction and repulsion in a new equilibrium of two in one, yet still one and one. Or in other words, the opposition between the two is seen as strife, as a combat; but the contrasting forces are not necessarily in a sense of hostility. Lawrence regards life as the combat for the crown between the two, which should never cease because this fighting itself "is their sole reason for existing":

> But think, if the lion really destroyed, killed the unicorn: not merely drove him out of town, but annihilated him! Would not the lion at once expire, as if he had created a vacuum around himself? Is not the unicorn necessary to the very existence of the lion, is not each opposite kept in stable equilibrium by the opposition of the other. . . . They would both cease to be, if either of them really won the fight which is their sole reason for existing.[21]

The lion and the unicorn are obviously symbols of the opposing forces. On the lion's side there is the mind, the active, the male principle, which is at strife with the unicorn—the senses, the passive, representing the female principle. And the crown is the symbol of victory that both sides fight for. Each side, the intellect and the senses, or Yin and Yang, wants to annihilate his opponent by winning the crown; yet if either of them succeeded, it would bring their life to an end, since the purpose of their existence has been completed. Lawrence further explains: "And there is no rest, no cessation from the conflict. For we are two opposites which exist by virtue of our inter-opposition. Remove the opposition and there is a collapse, a sudden crumbling into universal nothingness".[22] Just like light and darkness, none of the two opposites could be removed; they "want each other", they "consummate even in opposition", as their existence is the need for a greater cosmic peace. In this sense, the crown serves as a symbol of the eternal balance between the two forces, which is something indispensable in sustaining life. The same situation applies to human beings. "Flesh and spirit", "love and power, light and darkness, these are the temporary conquest of the one infinite by the other . . . But when the opposition is complete on either side, then there is perfection". If either side triumphs, it "shall perish". "The consummation comes from perfect relatedness . . . But he who triumphs, perishes",[23] as there is then no longer a third balancing force sustaining the life. Lawrence speaks of the same concept in the "Notes for *Birds, Beasts and Flowers*":

> Homer was wrong in saying, 'Would that strife might pass away from among gods and men!' He did not see that he was praying for the destruction of the universe; for if his prayer were heard, all things would pass away—for in the tension of opposites all things have their being. [24]

The tension of the opposites is for Lawrence a spiritual source for the being of all things, and between these contending forces something will be established, which is the new state of peace and tranquillity. Nevertheless, in terms of the man-woman relationship, too much tension between the opposites, or too much threat to one's individuality, can cause destruction to both sides. The struggle of Helena and Siegmund in *The Trespasser* is an example. The spiritual "dreaming woman" Helena needs Siegmund's love, but not a possessive one. She wants him to satisfy her desire for love without subjecting her to the degrading coarseness of animal sex. However, Siegmund's confidence and joy, born of his sexual fulfilment, seem to nullify her as an individual.

Later when Siegmund senses Helena's indifference, he feels that she is only *using* him. A sense of love and hate has arisen from a contest between them. Each needs the other, but each resents the other's threat to his or her individuality. Behind the battle of the opposing lovers, Lawrence projects a cosmic struggle. The male sun fights with the female moon; fire with water; spirit with flesh; day with night; light with darkness. The clash of opposites between men in the microcosm exemplifies the war of opposites in the macrocosm. As there is no balance, no conciliation between them, the battle ends up with Siegmund's suicide. Upon this ground, Lawrence puts forward a theory of two wills in human contradictory psychology: the will to union, and the will to separateness and self-responsibility. These are the two conflicting impulses working through all relationships between men and women. Schneider comments, "All of his late psychology would become a variation on the theme of this fundamental opposition in the human psyche, an opposition even more basic than that of spirit and 'the blood'".[25] The two-will concept contains the same elements as one's dualistic desire to keep one's individuality and to be consummated with the universe, which has been examined in the previous chapter.

The travel book *Twilight in Italy* records Lawrence's vision of the transcendental knowledge of the Yin and Yang polarities. Through his observation of local Italian places and people, he receives revelation from these dualistic phenomena, particularly those between sublimation and primitive sensuality. There in the Alpine mountains are crucifixes, which are seen as the centre of a dualistic scheme. Above the terrifying cold white mountains, every living thing is finally absorbed into "the radiance of changeless not-being". "The brightness of eternal, unthinkable not-being" embodies the absolute death of life. Power, heat, and life are all gone into that "radiant cold" hovering ahead, which "waits to receive back again all that which has passed for the moment into being". However in the hot valley of sensuality, there is "endless heat and rousedness of physical sensation which keeps the body full and potent, and flushes the mind with a blood heat, a blood sleep".[26] In another story, "The Spinner and the Monks", Lawrence writes about the duality of the churches in terms of their architectures and locations, which he conceives as "the churches of the Dove and the churches of the Eagle".[27] The churches of the Eagle represent the spirit of arrogance and self-assertion, and the churches of the Dove, the spirit of self-abnegation. The church of San Tommaso symbolizes dualistic characters of sunshine and darkness, abstraction and substance, openness and enclosure. Having escaped the heavy darkness inside the church—"the lair of some enormous creature", Lawrence enters into another pair of opposing images, that of an old woman and himself. The old woman is situated in bright blue clear surroundings, completely unselfconscious, and is untroubled by anything like Lawrence's concern about duality and polarity. She is like a sun in her innocent serenity, which forms a striking comparison with Lawrence's self-conscious night-creature image. Carefree and nonchalant, she is the whole universe to herself, while Lawrence is only aware of his "microcosm" in the "macrocosm". Leaving her, Lawrence again steps into his boyhood experience of dark depth and sunny height. He scrambles down into a little underground place, which is a "complete shadowless world of shadow" where the sunshine of normality seems far away. Afraid he will be benighted in the dark, "groping about like an otter in the damp and darkness", he struggles up to be immersed in the sun shining world again.[28] Through repeated metaphors and images of high and low, cold and hot, light and dark, sun and moon, Lawrence summarizes the significance of these existential realities. To him, man's transcendental knowledge will help to consummate the opposing extremes, and further man should be pleased to realize the greatness of the polarities in the universe, which brings "the supreme ecstasy in mankind":

> Where in the mankind is the ecstasy of light and dark together the supreme transcendence of the afterglow, day hovering in the embrace of the coming night like two angles embracing in the heavens? . . . Where is the transcendent knowledge in our hearts, uniting sun and darkness, day and night, spirit and senses? Why do we not know that the two in consummation are one; that each is only a part; partial and alone forever; but that the two in consummation are perfect, beyond the range of loneliness and solitude? [29]

Once we "pass beyond the scope of this duality into perfection", we are in a state of "actual living equipoise of blood and bone and spirit". [30]Lawrence writes in "The Reality of Peace": "When sense and spirit and mind are consummated into pure unison, then we are free in a world of the absolute. The lark sings in a heaven of pure understanding, she drops back into a world of duality and change".[31] According to Lawrence, we must acknowledge simultaneously both duality and the unity in duality. Unity in duality is a perfect state, which is a realization of the peace. "This is the state of heaven". "But there is getting there. And that, for ever, is the process of conquest".[32] The reality of duality and polarity is a matter of momentary revelations. Yet they must not be seen as short-lived or transient, but timeless, as they are "for ever" in the "process of conquest". Integration is therefore a durable condition. It is "extended in time, a continued recognition of unity in duality".[33] This integration, or he sometimes calls absorption or consummation, is equivalent to the great Tao, while the duality working toward the Tao represents the Yin-Yang principle in Taoism.

* *

Lawrence's position differs from most dualist philosophers in that, during the process of their conflicting interactions, the contending forces must retain their own identities. The new harmonious wholeness created from a relationship between opposites is not a complete fusing of the two into one but a complement of the one by the other. This understanding finds a perfect affinity in the Yin-Yang principle. In Taoism, Yin and Yang are not merely opposing elements of nature, they depend on one another; each complements the other, their "continuous interaction" provides a unified whole and a creative universe between the two.[34] Lao Zi explicitly summarizes this concept: "When opposites supplement each other, everything is harmonious".[35] The polarities of mind and body, consciousness and intuition, light and darkness, or tiger and lamb are, from a Taoist perspective, the consequences of the blind forces of nature. The two opposites must be allowed to exist with their own qualities, and at the same time undertake a complementary interaction in order to be transformed into a higher state of unity.

Ancient China serves as a remarkable example in the harmonious balance between the two extreme philosophies: Confucianism and Taoism. Confucianism represented the rational resources of the mind, maintaining a rational approach to solve all the problems of the society, and can be seen as the Yang of society; while Taoism represented the spiritual, insensible, intuitive aspects of nature and human society, maintaining a spontaneous way of living, the Yin of society. When these Yin and Yang work together, a perfect equilibrium between the positive and negative principles is achieved in a complicated society. A peaceful society is thus established without demanding that the two major opposing principles merge together or change their own characteristic features. In other words, this unity is not the result of a simple compromise, the harmony of society is not to the cost of the opposing philosophy. Further more, when Buddhism first entered China, the Chinese civilization was at least two thousand years old. It would be impossible for this new philosophy to enter into a solidly established culture without major adaptations to the Chinese mentality, that is to Confucianism; or without supplementing each other between Taoism and Buddhism, though there are some resemblances between the two. Undoubtedly the harmonious existence of the different philosophies is due to the extraordinary stability and maturity which the Chinese people have derived from both Confucianism and Taoism.[36]

In this chapter, I would like to further examine the significance of the mutual identity and mutual dependence of the opposing elements. Lawrence in "The Reality of Peace" emphasises the necessity of a co-existence between lion and lamb. The lion finds peace "when he carries the crushed lamb in his jaws", and the lamb finds "joyfulness" "when she quivers light and irresponsible within the strong, supporting apprehension of the lion".[37] In other words, without lambs, there would be no peace and no joy for lions, and vice-versa. This mutual dependence—each thing being defined by what it is not—is regarded as a classic Taoist view, which we discussed in terms of relative identity in the previous chapter. Watts in *The Way of Zen* explains that there is no separating the opposites—life and death, light and night, good and evil, strong and weak, gain and loss—they are two sides of the same coin. Each derives its existence purely through its dependence upon the opposing things.[38] This concept is called a doctrine of relativity in Indian Mahayana philosophy. It means that all things are without "self-nature" or independent reality since their existence is only in relation to other things. Nothing in the universe can stand by itself, no matter what it is, a thing, an event, a being, each exists only in relation to its own opposite, since what 'is' is defined by what 'is not', pleasure is defined by pain, light is defined by darkness, life by death, and motion by stillness. The two opposites are mutually defined and determined.[39] Lao Zi says in *Dao De Jing*:

> Beauty, for example, once distinguished, suggests its opposite, ugliness,
> And goodness, when we think of it, is naturally opposed to badness.
>
> In fact, all distinctions naturally appear as opposites. And opposites get their meaning from each other and find their completion only through each other. . . .
>
> Likewise, "difficult and easy," "long and short," "high and low," "loud and soft," "before and after,"—all derive their meanings from each other. [40]

It is because each thing that is distinct is only derived from it's opposite. All opposing things are mutually determined and interact continuously with each other. Laozi's philosophy finds a perfect interpretation in Lawrence's point in "the Reality of Peace": "It is not of love that we are fulfilled, but of love in such intimate equipoise with hate that the transcendence takes place. It is not in pride that we are free, but in pride, so perfectly matched by meekness that we are liberated as into blossom". [41]

Take the case of the lamb and the lion for example: since all opposites gain balance by their mutual existence, to destroy one side would lead to the destruction of the other, and they would vanish together. The two exist by virtue of juxtaposition in our polarity.[42] In another sense, whether it is good or bad, strong or weak, beautiful or ugly, each has its legitimacy in existence. Order is meaningless without disorder; pleasure is unrecognisable without pain. And evil things are no exception. For a traditional Buddhist or Taoist mind, there should be no problem in understanding the existence of "evil", as this conventional world is inevitably a world of opposites and it is unrealistic to live in a world without evil minds and evil actions. Hence there is no point in questioning the existence of plague or war (even the most evil crime like the German concentration camps), as it is an existential reality. Trying to get rid of them is a different issue.

* * *

From the principle of mutual identity between polar elements, Lawrence arrives at another aspect of this theory that is an identical quality shared by the two. He sees an absolute relation between the two opposites; each of them is virtually the same as the other:

> After all, eternal not-being and eternal being are the same. In the rosy snow that shone in heaven over a darkened earth was the ecstasy of consummation. Night and day are one, light and dark are one, both the same in the origin and in the issue, both the same in the moment of ecstasy, light fused in darkness and darkness fused in light, as in the rosy snow above the twilight. [43]

Similarly, departure is equivalent to coming together; and so is destruction to construction, corruption to creation:

> The spirit of destruction is divine, when it breaks the ego and opens the soul . . . In the soft and shiny voluptuous(ness) of decay, in the marshy chill heat of reptiles, there is the sign of the Godhead. It is the activity of departure. And departure is the opposite equivalent of coming together; decay, corruption, destruction is the opposite equivalent of creation. In infinite going-apart there is revealed again the pure absolute, the absolute relation. [44]

This passage speaks the same principle as Zhuang Zi's famous saying: "Construction is destruction. Destruction is construction", which is another aspect of the theory of mutual identity. Upon this ground, Alan Watts points out a very wrong notion from our "only alternative" mind, which is man's constant pursuance of the good. This is actually an illusion of the human mind. Watts writes of the absurdity of choosing "the good" with the hope to improve one's life. In his opinion, life is not a situation from which there is anything to be grasped or gained. Everything good or bad can only be seen in its relative sense. "To succeed is always to fail—in the sense that the more one succeeds in anything, the greater is the need to go on succeeding. To eat is to survive to be hungry".[45] The same identity principle is explicitly expressed in the following couplets compiled by a Zen master Toyo Eicho:

> To receive trouble is to receive good fortune;
> To receive agreement is to receive opposition.

It is more vividly expressed:

> At dusk the cock announces dawn;
> At midnight, the bright sun. [46]

The key point Watts and the Zen master make is this: do not pursue the good persistently, as it will lead to disillusionment. "Choose is absurd because there is no choice", for the human situation is like that of "fleas on a hot griddle". The flea that falls must jump, and the flea that jumps must fall, as Watts puts it, hence there is no alternative solution that could offer to solve this situation. So one had better behave naturally and not strain one's mind to reach any "better" solutions. However, the solution is there waiting for you, once you act in accord with the law of nature, and do not live exclusively on an ideal pursuance.[47] This is an attitude of life called Wu Wei in Taoism: choosing nothing but submitting to nature, a notion also being expounded by Lawrence in his *Twilight in Italy*, as well as in his Hardy essay.

The Yin-Yang balance can be applied to natural phenomena and human beings, as well as to art and psychology. If applied to art, it is the union of form and spirit; if applied to psychology, it is a complementary quality of the rational and intuitive faculties. It can be achieved between individuals and between psychic forces within the individual. When individuals arrive at a balanced state, the prolonged conflict is transcended. However, Yin and Yang, as Willis explains, are more like a flow with the rhythm of nature than a form of compromise. It is a natural blending of opposites, going with life happily, rather than always trying to compete with each other, or push against the natural currents of life.[48] When the Yin-Yang balance is applied to relationships between individuals, it means a state of mutual complementary balance, instead of a complete merging of opposites. Lawrence similarly compares man and woman to two flows of the river of life, each should maintain his or her own individuality. He criticizes the fixity of woman's role as "sweetheart, mistress, wife, mother", and wants us to,

> Break up this fixity, and realize the unseizable quality of real woman: that a woman is a flow, a river of life, quite different from a man's river of life: and that each river must flow in its own way, though without breaking its bounds: and that the relation of man to woman is the flowing of two rivers side by side, sometimes even mingling, then separating again, and traveling on.[49]

In the fields of love, marriage or sexual polarities, the most desirable status is obtained through a perfect consummation between man and woman—the "two complementary parts". Lawrence writes in the "Study of Thomas Hardy" about how the two arrive at a perfect consummation. It is a circle of "starting from connexion . . . of the genitals, and travelling towards the feelings and the mind, there becomes ever a greater difference and a finer distinction between the two", and finally the two parts complete "a perfect unity, the two as one, united by the Holy Spirit".[50] Graham Hough interprets Lawrence's vision of "circle" as "a perpetual travelling from one pole to the other and back again. Complete consummation in the flesh for the moment annihilates spirit and transcends all duality".[51] According to Lawrence's point of view, every living thing, every man and woman has a desire for consummation and completeness, and yearns for "the perfect union of the two". This is "the law of the Holy Spirit, the law of Consummate Marriage". But he stresses that a man shall first of all know "the natural law of his own individual being", and know the law of his female partner, and submit to it. "He must know that he is half, and the woman is the other half: that they are two, but that they are two-in-one".[52]

In *Women In Love*, Birkin realizes he and Ursula are the two halves. He is not quite sure what it is in Ursula that he wants, he only wants "two-in-one", which is something more than love: the "freedom together". Besides, he only wants to follow his "impulse", or "the primal desire" to love the other side. When Ursula accuses him of being "purely selfish" and demands his "love", Birkin replies:

> But it isn't selfish at all. Because I don't *know* what I want of you. I deliver *myself* over to the unknown, in coming to you, I am without reserves or defences, stripped entirely, into the unknown. Only there needs the pledge between us, that we will both cast off everything, cast off ourselves even, and cease to be, so that which is perfectly ourselves can take place in us . . .
> What I want is a strange conjunction with you— . . . not meeting and mingling;—you are quite right:—but an equilibrium, a pure balance of two single beings:—as the stars balance each other.[53]

Birkin, or Lawrence, believes that only in this "star- equilibrium" of love the two single beings will achieve a perfect balance without losing themselves. Each acknowledges the mystery and uniqueness of the other. If they mingle with each other, they should never finally "know" each other, as in the relationship between him and Hermione. Hermione wants to "know" Birkin by her one-sided demands, and finally their love breaks up owing to the lack of "pure balance". In the star-polarity of the Birkin-Ursula love, a peaceful balance is finally achieved when they surrender to the mystery of otherness, to the unknown "without reserves". It is the love gained from intuition that is in tune with the great law of nature, as Lawrence interprets: "They two together are one within the Great Law, reconciled within the Great Peace".[54] Hence in their relationship, they keep both individual self-sufficiency and wholeness, as well as their unforced spontaneous sensuality and sexual harmony.

In contrast to their love is the relationship between Gudrun and Gerald. The relationship Gerald seeks is the opposite of the star-polarity of love. Gerald's is either a desperate need or a complete dependence:

> He wanted to put his arm round her. If he could put his arm round her and draw her against him as they walked, he would equilibrate himself. For now he felt like a pair of scales, the half of which tips down and down and down into an indefinite void. He must recover some sort of balance.[55]

But he cannot achieve the balance. He and Gudrun, as Keith Sagar puts it, enclosed entirely in the old mechanical world of knowledge and sensationalism, "torture each other in a cage of nervous, furtive ecstasies". They "strain for knowledge of each other, and hence, power over each other". Their love implies "dependence, exploitation, violation", disintegration of self and soul, and even murder.[56] In Lawrence's words, Gerald's "tragedy" is "a stupendous assertion of not-being", because he has no trust, no confidence in life, his soul wants to die.[57] The two cannot be together without obeying or depending upon each other, which violates the Great Law of nature, and thus there is no hope of being "reconciled within the Great Peace". In *Kangaroo*, however, the relationship between Jack Callcott and his wife Victoria is perhaps of what Lawrence most approves. In their marriage bond, Jack does not "want to absorb her, or to occupy the whole field of her nature". He has confidence in their "permanent fidelity" without losing their respective integrities. He believes:

> But that part in each of them which did not belong to the other was free from all inquiry or even from knowledge. Each silently consented to leave the other in large part unknown, unknown in word and deed and very being. They didn't *want* to know—too much knowledge would be like shackles.[58]

This passage might in a way help us to understand Lawrence's own married life. Lawrence's wife Frieda is similarly very much loved by him "for her naïve sophisticated innocence", but she (Frieda) had several out of marriage encounters, about which Lawrence knew. Apparently, Lawrence chooses "not to know anything more about her than just so much as entered into the absolute relationship between them", as he writes in *Kangaroo*. Lawrence does not want to "make a cage" for his wife, so far as he believes "they were truly and intimately related".[59] Relatively speaking, he respects Frieda's individual integrity and thus enables the two flows of life to travel in their own way side by side harmoniously.

Lawrence in the "Study of Thomas Hardy" discusses at length the male-female "perfect frictionless interaction", and for the first time puts forward a concept of dual Will: "the Will-to-Motion and the Will-to-Inertia". According to this viewpoint, life consists in the interaction between the forces of change and the underlying forces of stability and inertia:

> The dual Will we call the Will-to-Motion and the Will—to-Inertia. These cause the whole of life, from the ebb and flow of a wave, to the stable equilibrium of the whole universe . . . And the Will—to-Motion we call the male will or spirit, the Will-to-Inertia the female. This Will to inertia is not negative, and the other positive. Rather, according to some conception, is Motion negative and Inertia, the static, geometric idea, positive.[60]

He then explains that Motion is absolute, while "rest is the lowest speed of motion", so the two Wills are actually the same—"The rapid motion of the rim of the wheel is the same as the perfect rest at the centre of the wheel". And "the interaction of the male and female spirit begot the wheel, the plough" of everything new in life.[61]

Lawrence's theory of Will-to-Motion and Will—to- Inertia, and the interaction of male and female spirits, bear close resemblance to the Yin-Yang transformations. In Taoism, the elementary units of reality are conceived primarily as changes from Yin to Yang or vice versa. A harmony is stable when all of its transformations repeat themselves. So stability can be seen as a type of harmonic change. And constant transformations of Yin and Yang bring forth a stable pattern of harmonious reality. In the case of the relationship between Lawrence's parents, there is also a changed Yin-Yang pattern. The male principle (Lawrence calls it "Love") implies spirit, intellect, transcendence and sublimation, which are all originally associated with his mother. While the female principle (the principle of "Law") represents the body, instinct, incarnation and immanence, which are the qualities associated with his father. This changing pattern or Yin-Yang transformation is in accord with the need of harmony and marriage stability. Unfortunately, there is no harmony and stability in his parent's marriage, because there are no constant transformations, neither is there any motional or inertial change, so the two rivers of life cannot flow along happily without hurting each other.

Graham Hough comments on the polar relationships of Lawrence's characters that his married men and women are all dependent on each other, "but they never merge; each recognizes at the core of the other's being an eternally separate spark. And the two poles are eternally opposed; the whole fruitfulness of the relationship depends on their opposition . . ."[62] In the course of mutual complementarity between the opposite sexes, opposition and conflict are seen as "emotional integrity" and "the springs of life", which "should be admitted, indulged, never shirked or avoided".[63] Once the male-female opposites allow themselves to develop in accord with their own spontaneous feelings and needs, they are on the same track of nature's "law of dual attraction and repulsion, a law of polarity", and they have actually built a sound foundation for a true marriage. Lawrence's personal life, especially his relationship with his wife Frieda, is a very good example of this. Had Lawrence always suppressed his unconventional insights and spontaneous inspiration in support of a preconceived social morality, he would never have had a married life with Frieda. Had he not allowed Frieda to develop her "spontaneous feelings" freely, their marriage would have been a disaster many times over. So long as the two opposing sides meet on equal terms without losing their own individuality, they will transcend their duality and attain a Yin-Yang balance:

> If it is to be life then it is fifty percent me, fifty per cent thee: and the third thing, the spark, which springs from out of the balance, is timeless. Jesus, who saw it a bit vaguely, called it the Holy Ghost. "Between man and woman, fifty per cent man and fifty per cent woman: then the pure spark. Either this, or less than nothing." [64]

"The Holy Ghost" or "the spark" is like the other balancing elements in Lawrence's perception: the crown, the rainbow, the rose, the plumed serpent, and the phoenix. It is not only an

Dr. Tianying Zang

important balancing agent in transcending the conflicting duality into a balanced harmony, but also "a true being" that signifies no distinction between any opposing elements, be it positive or negative, life or death.

[1] D. H. Lawrence, *Fantasia of the Unconscious and Psychoanalysis and the Unconscious*, p. 147.
[2] D. H. Lawrence, ". . .Love was Once a Little Boy", *Phoenix II*, p. 455.
[3] D. H. Lawrence, *Apocalypse*, p. 17.
[4] D. H. Lawrence, "The Crown", in *Reflection on the Death of a Porcupine and Other Essays*, p. 303.
[5] Ibid., p. 265.
[6] D. H. Lawrence, *Movements in European History*, p. 306.
[7] D. H. Lawrence, "The Painted Tombs of Tarquinia", in *Mornings in Mexico and Etruscan Places*, p. 154.
[8] Ibid., p. 154.
[9] Ibid., p. 147.
[10] D. H. Lawrence, "The Reality of Peace", *Phoenix*, p. 692.
[11] Ibid., p. 693.
[12] D. H. Lawrence, "Autobiographical Fragment", *Phoenix*, pp. 823-4.
[13] Ibid., p. 824.
[14] D. H. Lawrence, "Nottingham and Mining Countryside", *Phoenix*, p. 136.
[15] Ibid., p. 136.
[16] Ben Willis, *The Tao of Art*, p. 63.
[17] References from Graham Hough, *The Dark Sun*, p. 224, and Lawrence, "Study of Thomas Hardy".
[18] Graham Hough, *The Dark Sun*, p. 225.
[19] D. H. Lawrence, *Fantasia of the Unconscious and Psychoanalysis and the Unconscious*, p. 234.
[20] Alan Watts, *The Way of Zen*, p. 35.

[21] D. H. Lawrence, "The Crown", in *Reflections on the Death of a Porcupine and Other Essays*, pp. 253-4.

[22] Ibid., p. 256.

[23] Ibid., pp. 264-258-261-2.

[24] D. H. Lawrence, "Notes for *Birds, Beasts and Flowers*", *Phoenix*, p. 67.

[25] Daniel J. Schneider, *The Consciousness of D. H. Lawrence: An Intellectual Biography*, p. 64.

[26] D. H. Lawrence, "The Crucifix Across the Mountains", in *Twilight in Italy*, p. 12.

[27] D. H. Lawrence, "The Spinner and the Monks", in *Twilight in Italy*, p. 25.

[28] Ibid., p. 34.

[29] Ibid., pp. 37-8.

[30] D. H. Lawrence, "The Reality of Peace", *Phoenix*, p. 681.

[31] Ibid., p. 680.

[32] D. H. Lawrence, "Reflections on the Death of a Porcupine", in *Reflections on the Death of a Porcupine and Other Essays*, p. 457-8.

[33] Graham Hough, *The Dark Sun*. p. 229.

[34] Ben Willis, *The Tao of Art*, p. 64.

[35] Laozi, *Dao De Jing*, Archie J. Bahm, ed., Ch. 32, p. 35.

[36] Ben Willis, *The Tao of Art*, p. 141.

[37] D. H. Lawrence, "The Reality of Peace", *Phoenix*, p. 692.

[38] Alan Watts, *The Way of Zen*, p. 63.

[39] Ibid., p. 63.

[40] Laozi, *Dao De Jing*, Archie J. Bahm, ed., Ch. 2, p. 12.

[41] D. H. Lawrence, "The Reality of Peace", *Phoenix*, p. 693.

[42] Ibid., p. 692.

[43] D. H. Lawrence, "The Spinner and the Monks", in *Twilight in Italy*, p. 36.

[44] D. H. Lawrence, "The Crown", in *Reflections on the Death of a Porcupine and Other Essays*, p. 292.

[45] Alan Watts, *The Way of Zen*, p. 116.

[46] Quoted in Alan Watts , *The Way of Zen*, p. 117.

[47] Alan Watts, *The Way of Zen*, pp. 116-7.

[48] Ben Willis, *Tao of Art*, p. 65.

[49] D. H. Lawrence, "We Need One Another", *Phoenix*, p. 194.

[50] D. H. Lawrence, "Study of Thomas Hardy", *Phoenix*, pp. 514—5.

[51] Graham Hough, *The Dark Sun*, p. 229.

[52] D. H. Lawrence, "Study of Thomas Hardy", *Phoenix*, p. 515.

[53] D. H. Lawrence, *Women in Love*, Ch. 13, pp. 146-7.

[54] D. H. Lawrence, "Study of Thomas Hardy", *Phoenix*, p. 515.

[55] D. H. Lawrence, *Women in Love*, Ch. 24, p. 328.

[56] Keith Sagar, *The Art of D. H. Lawrence*, pp. 94., 93.

[57] *The Collected Letters of D. H. Lawrence*, Harry T Moore, ed., Vol. I, p. 446.

[58] D. H. Lawrence, *Kangaroo*, Ch. 2, p. 40.

[59] Ibid., p. 40.

[60] D. H. Lawrence, "Study of Thomas Hardy", *Phoenix*, p. 448.

[61] Ibid., p. 448.

[62] Graham Hough, *The Dark Sun*, p. 228.

[63] Ibid., p. 233.

[64] D. H. Lawrence, "Him with his Tail in his Mouth", in *Reflections on the Death of a Porcupine and Other Essays*, p. 141.

Chapter VI

Life and Death

*

A discussion of Lawrence's duality and polarity is by no means complete without the examination of his interest in life and death. Lawrence's work constantly shows his fascination with the continuum of nature and its special way of transforming life and death. He is delighted at the truth that man is born out of an unknown creative force, and is equally delighted at the knowledge that life is a long ever-changing river carrying us to its opposite equivalent—death. Frederick Carter, Lawrence's friend, comments: "Beyond all, what he desired most to know was the history—the real true myth—of the descent of man into this life's bondage of the spirit. Why did he come from heaven? What had he left? Towards what did he purpose journeying?"[1] In Lawrence, a religious seeker, there is always a deep reverence for life for its beauty, mystery and wonder. His work registers his "thought adventures", among which is his preoccupation with issues concerning life and death.

Lawrence, who denies evolution and a personal god, of course refuses to acknowledge that man's life has evolved gradually out of certain chemical elements. "At no moment can man create himself", he writes in the essay "Life", "He can but submit to the creator, to the primal unknown out of which issues the all". [2] The creator he is talking about is not a Christian god, but a creative unknown. His life concept is a reversal of Western cosmogonies.

Both modern scientists and ancient materialists assume that life has developed from matter and is evolved through the combination of atoms or by ever more complicated chemical processes. For Lawrence, however, life precedes matter, it has sprung from the unknown force of the cosmos. We shall never know the origin of our creation, except the unknown from which we come:

> Midway between the beginning and the end is man, midway between that which creates and that which is created, midway in an otherworld, partaking of both, yet transcending . . . At every moment we issue like a balanced flame from the primal unknown. We are not self-contained or self-accomplished. At every moment we derive from the unknown.[3]

This unknown origin, as he summarizes, "is the first and greatest truth of our being". Lawrence imagines that man's whole life is "like a flame between the two darknesses, the darkness of the beginning and the darkness of the end":

> It is our business to burn, pure flame, between the two unknowns. We are to be fulfilled in the world of perfection, which is the world of pure creation. We must come into being in the transcendent otherworld of perfection, consummated in life and death both, two in one.[4]

According to Lawrence's metaphorical vision, the burning of a flame is a transitional process of life and death. It is "a flame conducting unknown to unknown, through the bright transition of creation".[5] His notion of burning is close to the idea of "burning" in Buddhism. In a book entitled *Science and Buddhism*, P. Dahlke makes a metaphorical summary that in theology everything stands, in science everything falls, and in Buddhism everything burns. "The notion of burning is a metaphysical expression of transience and impermanence", which is "a very early statement of energy flow point of view".[6] This flowing energy is in constant "burning" or "flaming", in Lawrence's terms, towards a finally consummation of life and death. Scientifically speaking, this ever-flowing universal energy sustains everything, including individual human lives. At the same time it also indicates a burning process of a life in its transient existence. Once an individual's burning completes, he is transferred into Lawrence's "transcendent otherworld of perfection", and has fulfilled his final consummation.

Lawrence compares life—the transient existence—to "wind", to "wave". We are blown away by the wind or the wave of flood, he says. "It is the wind of time" that carries us away "in the seethe of morality", and "So we shall be swept away as long as time lasts".[7] Life is sometimes compared by him to "a travelling to the edge of knowledge". People live and die, towards the "edge of knowledge", which is a timeless process. He argues, "We know that in the process of life we are purely relative. But timelessness is our fate, and time is subordinate to our fate. But time is eternal".[8] "Timelessness" is only in the sense of the bigger unknown life that contains both earthly life and after life. His essay "On Human Destiny" carries his vision that a human being is like a tree. "A tree slowly rises to a great height, and quickly falls to dust. There is a long life-day for the individual. Then a very quick, spacious death-room". He is glad of the fact that "I live and I die. I ask no other. Whatever proceeds from me lives and dies". Human life is just like the life circle of the tree in that "at the very last, the great tree will go hollow . . . and it will disappear like a ghost back into the humus". He is glad because he knows that a tree, and man the same, will finally enter into eternity, and that eternity is a result of the countless cycles of life: "It is the cycle of all things created, thank God. Because, given courage, it saves even eternity from staleness". [9] In terms of an individual's earthly life, it is brief and transitory, eternally fixed between the two poles of being and non-being. Lawrence's view of the life-process between "the two unknowns" reflects a Buddhist thought: everything is process— "from being to non-being"—a process only persisting by virtue of some universal kind of energy flowing through the universe. Though the individual's "process of life" comprises of only one wave within successive waves, it is a life among numerous lives sustaining the whole life flood of the universe. So in a broader sense, life is "timeless", like the wind or flood forever rushing and ebbing towards an unknown eternity.

In Lawrence's point of view, the physical cosmos is established upon the living individual's death:

> The cosmos is nothing but the aggregate of the dead bodies and dead energies of bygone individuals. The dead bodies decompose as we know into earth, air, and water, heat, and radiant energy and free electricity and innumerable other scientific facts.[10]

The dead souls for him play a magic role in the creation of the psychic life of living individuals. "The dead souls likewise decompose . . . into some psychic reality, and into some potential will". Lawrence seems to mix soul with individuality, believing that "the dead soul . . . always retains its individual quality". The dead soul will never "disappear", but "re-enter into the living psyche of living individuals".[11] So living individuals sustain a constant interchange of energy with the cosmic realities through the surviving life soul. Thus, life and death are both part of the sustaining force of the cosmos. Life contains death, and death predicts life. They are both "timeless" and, in Lawrence's interpretation, this "is our fate". Likewise, in Buddhist Zen, death and life are identical. In actual life, as Hokuseido puts it, life and death are inseparable: "From the moment we are born to the moment we die, we have life-death, a stream of mental and physical changes, which at no point can be called life and at no point death, but which at every point is both".[12] Lawrence voices the same view in different language. He writes in "The Crown":

> The actual physical fact of death is part of the life-stream. It is an incidental point when the flux of light and dark has flowed sufficiently apart for the conjunction, which we call life, to disappear. We live with the pure flux of death, it is part of us all the time. But our blossoming is transcendent, beyond death and life.[13]

He describes life as "a travelling to the edge of knowledge, and then a leap taken". But "the leap taken" is "into the beyond", just like "a lark leaps into the sky". He says, "But it is not death. Death is neither here nor there. Death is a temporal, relative fact. In the absolute, it means nothing".[14] Just as Jesus Christ's death brings the world life and hope, Buddha's anguished search for enlightenment finally enables him to reach nirvana. For them, death is truly the gateway of life, not the dissolution of the body, but the consummation and integration of death with life.

Lawrence acknowledges that though he is "fully aware of" the "relation between life and death, the living and the dead", he does not know it: "The universe of life and death, of which we, whose business it is to live and to die, know nothing".[15] However, he tries to avoid any scientific explanation. He strongly disapproves of the mechanic explanation of this physical universe: "concerning the universe of Force and Matter we pile up theories and make staggering and disastrous discoveries of machinery and poison-gas, all of which we were much better without". The enigma of life and death to him has nothing to do with any scientific theories. Anyway, "It is life we have to live by", he says, "not machines and ideals. And life means nothing else, even, but the spontaneous living soul which is our central reality".[16]

Maintaining a "spontaneous living soul" is, in Lawrence's vision, "the only clue" to being truly alive. The interchange between an individual's "living soul" and the dynamic cosmos sustains the eternal life of the universe, which stimulates Lawrence's imagination. He writes in the *Fantasia of the Unconscious*:

> How it is contrived that the individual soul in the living sways the very sun in its centrality, I do not know. But it is so. It is the peculiar dynamic polarity of the living soul in every weed or bug or beast, each one separately and individually polarized with the great returning pole of the sun, that maintains the sun alive. For I take it that the sun is the great sympathetic centre of our inanimate universe.[17]

The living souls in his belief provide an eternally circulated energy which interpenetrates among the living creatures and planetary bodies, and makes the world live, move and forever change. Upon this ground, Lawrence repeatedly emphasises the purpose of our life: "our life *consists* in this achieving of a pure relationship between ourselves and the living universe about us".[18]

For Lawrence, man truly alive is living through all his senses and desires, living with a vital connection to his people and everything in the natural world. It is genuine life of which Lawrence most approves, which must be achieved through an individual's spontaneous openness to receive "the source of joy and strength" from the creative unknown. He particularly admires the Indian's "deep streams of life", and writes with great enthusiasm about their life in "New Mexico": "the whole life-effort of man was to get his life into direct contact with the elemental life of the cosmos, mountain-life, cloud-life, thunder-life, air-life, earth-life, sun-life. To come into immediate felt contact, and so derive energy, power, and a dark sort of joy".[19] He also admires the pagan Greeks and Romans for their simple yet powerful religions with no prescribed and conventional mode of worship and belief, as he mentioned in the *Movements in European History*. He is particularly impressed by their spontaneous, intuitive attempts to secure a "living relationship" with the dynamic universe. The living relationship is not difficult to achieve for those who are living a spontaneous life, it "was all part of the active, actual everyday, normal life—not something apart". [20]

Again we return to the simple mode of living an "everyday, normal life". By contributing their life-flow in doing simple jobs, people are building a vital connection with the external world. Lawrence's own life serves as a good example. In his youth he enjoys doing different kinds of manual work. Later when he lives with Frieda, he is very enthusiastic in doing odd jobs, such as planting, mending, cooking, digging ditches and painting walls. Being engaged in these moments of activity with all his attention, he experiences a unity with the external world and is happy and satisfied. In a letter in 1916, he tells Catherine Carswell that they were "doing our cottage, and helping the Murrys", and "made a dresser", then he says, "I feel fundamentally happy and free, beyond".[21] A man who is involved in the living moment is in Lawrence's words "a man in his wholeness wholly attending", and he will derive great joy and freedom from it.[22] Being absorbed in the moments of everyday activity, one preserves one's true individuality and spontaneous self. Ordinary life contains "creative spirit" and it is "life itself", Lawrence remarks in "Reviews of Books", that is "in touch with the heart of all things . . . It is a state of absorption into the creative spirit, which is God".[23] Lawrence writes to Brewster about life flow, about Gandhi's *ashram* (thatched cottage) and his enthusiasm for hand spinning and weaving:

> All we possess is life—weaving, carving, building—this is the flow of life, life flows into the object—and life flows out again to the beholder. So that whoever makes anything with real interest, puts life into it, and makes it a little fountain of life for the next comer. Therefore a Gandhi weaver is transmitting life to others—and that is the great charity.[24]

Brewster recollects that Lawrence often says to him, "I would rather work with you, each doing something with our hands, than to talk together". Brewster admires his ability in finding happiness while doing any small manual work. "He was able to find in the humblest occupation a rhythm and a flow of life which gives him satisfaction".[25] Being completely absorbed in the living moment, whether physical or spiritual, the individual transcends the barriers of time and space, and enters with freedom into a heaven of peace. Every individual achieving this state is at once living in the spatial universe of three dimensions and yet above it, in the fourth dimension of existence. Or as Lawrence sometimes puts it, he is living in the creative unknown, in that other mode of existence. In oriental traditions, being completely involved in the present moment is regarded as a virtue, which is encouraged and admired. The moment suggests a moment of true life and is regarded as a moment of eternity. It is called natural Tao in Taoism, "Shantih" in Hinduism, and "every-minute Zen" in Buddhist Zen. It is an initial awakening experience and is described in Zen as the "embodiment of enlightenment in one's daily life" and is a process that takes a whole life.[26] Living in the moment of daily activities implies living with the rhythm of the universe. One who concentrates his efforts on a simple daily activity will live in ever deeper awareness of the mystery of each present moment, and will enjoy the beauty of life and recognize the power of the unknown.

Unfortunately, our modern life, in Lawrence's opinion, is in an increasing state of dissolution and deterioration. The balance and harmony of life are often destroyed by growing technicalization and materialization of modern society, such as the situation in

Women in Love. Civilization and religion are to him the two major factors that prevent man from building a connection with the wondrous mystery of life. Lawrence's works very often aim to depict the tragedies of human life, and at the same time, he tries to inject hope and renewal to modern life. He hopes that modern people can possess an awareness of the life-flow of the cosmos and live in it, so that they can be renewed by the unknown:

> Turn back to the life that flows invisibly in the cosmos, and will flow for ever, sustaining and renewing all living things . . . it is a question of renewal, of being renewed, vivified, made new and vividly alive and aware, instead of being exhausted and stale, as men are today. How to be renewed, reborn, and revivified? [27]

In the essay "the Real Thing" Lawrence points out that "There are millions of ways of living, and it's all life. But what is the real thing in life? What is it that makes you feel right, makes life really feel good?" He then goes on,

> What makes life good to me is the sense that, even if I am sick and ill, I am alive, alive to the depths of my soul, and in touch somewhere (in touch) with the vivid life of the cosmos. Somehow my life draws strength from the depths of the universe, from the depths among the stars, from the great 'world'. Out of the great world comes my strength and my reassurance . . . But there *is* a flame or a Life Everlasting wreathing through the cosmos forever and giving us our renewal, once we can get in touch with it.[28]

Lawrence himself seems to have had this good sense of life, a sick man most of his life, yet he is vitally alive. His lifelong illness makes him more aware of the preciousness of being alive, and more conscious of the importance of living to his true self or, in his words, being truly "alive to the depths of my soul". A fragile body with a strong mind, Lawrence's life is like "a flame" renewed and strengthened by the elements of the universe. "Nothing is important but life", he says in "Why the Novel Matters", "And for myself, I can absolutely see life nowhere but in the living". [29] He concludes: "To be alive, to be man alive, to be whole man alive: that is the point". [30]

Leavis expresses his admiration for Lawrence's insight on life, commenting that Lawrence has the "power to charge 'life' with the special Lawrentian value". The words "alive", "living" and "lives" in Lawrence are "intimately associated with 'wonder', the 'unknown', 'imagination', 'religious' and 'responsible'", Leavis remarks in *Thought, Words and Creativity*. [31] After interpreting Lawrence's imaginings of how new life comes forth from the unknown and enters us, he says: "In any case his thought (and that is his art) was in general—I include myself in the generalization—uncomprehended, it was basically too new and important".[32]

* *

Lawrence's understanding of life and death not only gives us further insight into the polar relationship between life and death, construction and destruction, but also invites us to read what is the "thought adventure" in a dying man's mind. On his deathbed, the more urgent question Lawrence asks is not whether we shall be able to live, but if we shall ever be able to die. "Let us prepare now for the death of our present 'little' life, and the re-emergence in a bigger life, in touch with the moving cosmos".[33] The "bigger life" in Taoism is an afterlife that is bound to the moving cosmos forever, which is the same as Lawrence's similar perspective of final consummation. Having realized the utter futility and frustration of life, Lawrence sometimes yearns for a final consummation with the living universe. His consummation does not mean final death. In his view, life is not simply in opposition to death; it might in a way suggest a state of "not being", a "negation" of death. Thinking in a macrocosmic way, he views life as "never finished". Death "can but abruptly close the individual life. But life itself, and even the forms men have given it, will persist and persist and persist".[34] He argues in "The Crown", "The actual physical fact of death is part of the life-stream. It is an incidental point when the flux of light and dark has flowed sufficiently apart for the conjunction, which we call life, to disappear".[35] Being and not being are interdependent with each other and can be "transfused into oneness". Just as destruction is the opposite equivalent of creation, life is the opposite equivalent of "not-being". Birkin in *Women in Love* compares people to "flowers of dissolution", saying to Ursula: "Dissolution rolls on, just as production does . . . It is a progressive process—and it ends in universal nothing—the end of world . . . But why isn't the end of the world as good as the beginning?" [36] Death and corruption are therefore natural conditions for life and creation, and vice versa, which is a thought characteristic of both Buddhist and Taoist philosophies.

For a Taoist, life and death are correlated with each other. "To be or not to be" is *not* the question, for pure being and pure non-being alike are conceptual ghosts. In Taoism this is called "inner identity". As soon as one feels the "inner identity" of the correlatives, death seems simply to be a return to that unknown inwardness out of which we were born. Life is ever related to death, as is creation to destruction. The co-existence of life and death is seen by Lawrence as two equivalents: "There is in me the great desire of creation and the great desire of dissolution. Perhaps these two are pure equivalents. Perhaps the decay of autumn purely balances the putting forth of spring".[37] As corruption and creation are mutually dependent, he believes, "Death will take its place in me . . . I shall be fulfilled of corruption within the strength of creation".[38] Jack in *The Boy in the Bush* claims that life and death have the same Lord: "The two are never separate, life and death. And in the vast dark kingdom of afterwards, the Lord of Death is Lord of Life, and the God of Life and creation is Lord of Death".[39] Lawrence is always concerned with the dark stillness beneath the bright activity of life, the oneness underlying duality. He claims in "The Reality of Peace" that we should be able to submit to the fundamental nature of our real self by achieving the balance between corruption and creation:

> We are not only creatures of light and virtue. We are also alive in corruption and death. It is necessary to balance the dark against the light if we are ever going to be free. We must know that we, ourselves, are the living stream of seething corruption, this also, all the while, as well as the bright river of life. We must recover our balance to be free. From our bodies comes the issue of corruption as well as the issue of creation. We must have our being in both, our knowledge must consist in both. [40]

In line with this fundamental nature of man's existence, Lawrence further points out that destruction and corruption are the two things that are "necessary", "inevitable" and interdependent. They should not be something of which we feel ashamed or feel like to deny: "How shall it be a shame that from my blood exudes the bitter sweat of corruption on the journey back to dissolution . . .?" It is human nature to be "dissolved from my old being". To attempt to deny one's nature is to prevent self-fulfilment: "There is in me the desire of creation and the desire of dissolution. Shall I deny either? Then neither is fulfilled. If there is no autumn and winter of corruption, there is no spring and summer. All the time I must be dissolved from my old being". However, in Christian tradition, death and life are not viewed as an original part of the divine plan of nature. God is associated with being and life to the exclusion of non-being and death, so Christians celebrate the triumph over death by the miracle of resurrection. Those who are of this point of view associate death and decay with evil, and shudder at the thought of corruption and death. It is because they separate the two desires—the desire of life and desire of death. They do not realize that, though the two desires are "forever contrary and complementary", they are of the same nature and can be transcended. If they understand it, they will be prepared for anything non-being or death, and expect to enter a new world—Lawrence's fourth dimension, and "there we are immune and perfect, there the two are one".[41]

With regard to this view, we can never conquer death, because "only by death do we live". "Death and the great dark flux of undoing, this is the inevitable half. Life feeds death, death feeds life". We have Lawrence's dialectical view on the common "mistaken interpretation" of life and death:

> We wish to conquer death. But it is absurd, since only by death do we live, like the leopard. We wish not to die; we wish for life everlasting. But this is mistaken interpretation. What we mean by immortality is this fulfilment of death with life and life with death in us where we are consummated and absolved into heaven, the heaven on earth.[42]

So death can never be destroyed, it can only be transcended "in pure understanding", which is a transcendence of sense and spirit. Taoism subscribes to the same thought that death, like life, is part of an endless process of transformation of being from form to form. The problem of death is not an issue to be solved by the abolition of death, which is almost like chopping off the head to cure the headache. The problem lies in man's revulsion and unwillingness to "encompass death" in one's living mind, to borrow Lawrence's words. Death in Taoism is regarded as a fulfilment, a stage being transformed. With regard to people's fear of death, Zhuangzi makes a metaphoric interpretation of the relation between life and death: "Who am I to say that rejoicing in life is not an illusion? Who am I to say that in despising death we do not resemble children who are lost and have no idea how to get home?" [43] He comments on his wife's death as merely a transformation of the same sort that gives her birth, and he even beats drums and strikes gongs to celebrate her death.

Lawrence's interpretation of life and death suggests the same understanding as that in Zhuangzi's sayings. Physical death is regarded by Lawrence as "a transcendent state of existence". Once death is understood by us, he believes, it can be transcended:

> That is how we know death, having suffered it and lived. It is now no mystery, finally. Death is understood in us, and thus we transcend it. Henceforward actual death is a fulfilling of our own knowledge.

> Nevertheless, we transcend death by understanding down to the last ebb the great process of death in us. We can never destroy death. We can only transcend it in pure understanding. We can envelop it and contain it. And then we are free.
> By standing in the light we see in terms of shadow. We cannot see the light we stand in. So our understanding of death in life is an act of living.
> If we live in the mind, we must die in the mind, and in the mind we must understand death. Understanding is not necessary mental. It is of the senses and the spirit.
> . . .

> Therefore the first great activity of the living mind is to understand death in the mind. Without this there is no freedom of the mind, there is no life of the mind, since creative life is the attaining (of) a perfect consummation with death. When in my mind there rises the idea of life, then this idea must encompass the idea of death, and this encompassing is the germination of a new epoch of the mind.[44]

For Lawrence, the transcendence of an actual death is a kind of fulfilment "of our own knowledge". This knowledge is also recognized in Taoism, that not only life and death but also other pairs of opposites will eventually be transformed into oneness. Andre Breton has made a similar point: "Everything leads us to believe that there exists a certain point of the intelligence at which life and death, the real and imaginary, the past and the future . . . cease to be perceived as opposites". [45]

Without a positive understanding of death, people would live in the past with the deceased, like Paul with his mother in *Sons and Lovers*. It is not her death that really matters; it is his mind holding on to her memory:

> And his soul could not leave her, wherever she was. Now she was gone abroad into the night, and he was with her still. They were together. But yet there was his body, his chest, that leaned against the stile . . . where was he?—one tiny upright speck of flesh, less than an ear of wheat lost in the field. He could not bear it. On every side the immense dark silence seemed pressing him, so tiny a spark, into extinction, and yet, almost nothing, he could not be extinct. Night, in which everything was lost, went reaching out, beyond stars and sun.[46]

Paul is confronted with such a situation that he feels it hard to get away from the bitter memories his mother's death brought to him. But there is no rebirth for him if he cannot get over it. Lawrence finally helps him to turn away from the dead. "He would not take that direction, to the darkness, to follow her"; instead, "He walked towards the faintly humming, glowing town, quickly".[47] Thus, darkness is to be transformed into light, so is death into life. In *Women in Love*, after Diana is drowned,

Birkin expresses the same worry about the difficulty of tearing away from the dead. He tells Ursula: "I don't mind about the dead . . . once they are dead. The worst of it is, they cling on to the living, and won't let go". [48] In Lawrence's novels, there is never a situation like, for example, Heathcliff's crazy pining for Catherine Emily in *Wuthering Heights*. In the episode of Tom Brangwen's drowning, Lawrence describes how by next morning the spell of death was already waning. When the mother Lydia Brangwen sees his body, "her heart cold, knowing her own singleness", she simply says: "I shared life with you, I belong in my own way to eternity". She realizes, "He was beyond change or knowledge, absolute, laid in line with the infinite . . . who was revealed in the stripped moment of transit from life and death". [49] Lawrence is conveying a message that it is no good pining for the dead, for death is the opposite equivalent of life. One should in one's living mind learn how to die in the past and live in the present. Thus we understand George's misery in his unwillingness to let his past die. When Gerald in *Women in Love* in the end dies tragically, Birkin, though being torn with grief at the sight of the frozen corpse, "turned away" from his friend. Looking at "the beautiful face of one whom he had loved, and who had died still having the faith to yield to the mystery", Birkin expects a new life is gestating in the dead body: "No one could remember it without gaining faith in the mystery, without the souls warming with new, deep life-trust". [50] His attitude towards death is romantic, as he believes that both life and death belong to "non-human mystery", only transcendental knowledge could help one to get over the fear of death.

Unsatisfied with love or with societal life, Lawrence's characters tend to yearn for death, through which one hopes to gain rebirth or to be consummated with the unknown. Birkin in the "Death by Water" episode secretly yearns for death, which would enable him to escape from society and the obligations of humanity. Ursula, after the exciting yet ultimately frustrating passion, is happy to slip into a pure oblivion. Here we read of her weariness of life and her yearning for "a great consummation"—death:

> She was fulfilled in a kind of bitter ripeness, there
> remained only to fall from the tree into death . . . After

all, when one was fulfilled, one was happiest in falling into death, as a bitter fruit plunges in its ripeness downwards. Death is a great consummation, a consummating experience. It is a development from life . . . better die than live mechanically a life that is a repetition of repetitions. To die is to move on with the invisible. To die is also a joy, a joy of submitting to that which is greater than the unknown; namely the pure unknown . . . death is never a shame. Death itself, like the illimitable space, is beyond our sullying . . . To know is human, and in death we do not know, we are not human . . . The promise of this is our heritage, we look forward like heirs to their majority.[51]

This text epitomises Lawrence's life-death philosophy. Death, as Ursula realizes, is not a thing to be frightened of; it is a part of the rhythm of the bigger universe. "To die is also a joy". It is not only an escape from the never satisfying earthly life, but also a chance to experience a non-human life in the greater unknown. Birkin says to Ursula that death "is our real reality . . . that dark river of dissolution . . . the black river of corruption".[52] Like Birkin and Ursula, Lawrence, in "The Reality of Peace", cries for death, as death can be the means to end one's sufferings and can "save us from humanity":

> Sweet death, save us from humanity. Death, noble, unstainable death . . . smash humanity, and make an end of it. Let there emerge a few pure and single men—men who give themselves to the unknown of life and death and are fulfilled . . . Release me from the debased social body . . . Let me derive direct from life or from death, according to the impulse that is in me.[53]

From this monologue, we can imagine that the dying Lawrence does not flinch when facing the oncoming longer journey; instead, he might feel a sense of fulfilment and expect secretly a thorough relief. Here is his "Song of Death":

> Sing the song of death, oh sing it!
> For without the song of death, the song of life
> becomes pointless and silly.

> Sing then the song of death, and the longest journey
> and what the soul carries with him, and what he leaves
> behind
> and how he finds the darkness that enfolds him into utter
> peace
> at last, at last, beyond innumerable seas.[54]

So he asks people to be prepared for the journey to oblivion:

> So build your ship of death,
> and let the soul drift to dark oblivion.
> may be life is still our portion
> after the bitter passage to oblivion.[55]

There are mainly two kinds of death for Lawrence. One is a day-to-day death in the life of an individual, death in the mind instead of a physical death, which is a living death. It is the death of Lady Chatterley's marriage to Clifford, or George's self-abandoning life. It is the death of the lives of Rico and the vicar Lawrence portrays and attacks in *St. Mawr*. The other is physical death, death of the body, which is the "hereafter", the long journey to oblivion. In the last section of his "Last Poems", death is described as a great "journey" from "the entanglements of life" to a "dark oblivion": "My soul has had a long, hard day/ she is tired,/ she is seeing her oblivion." "Bavarian Gentians" reflects the same romantic thought :

> Reach me a gentian, give me a torch!
> let me guide myself with the blue, forked torch of this
> flower
> down the darker and darker stairs, where blue is darkened
> on blueness.[56]

The repeated words associated with darkness and blueness suggest symbolically that the journey of death is part of an unknown mystery. However, for Lawrence, to die is not easy: "Be careful, then, and be gentle about death. / For it is hard to die, it is difficult to go through the door, even when it opens", he writes in "All Souls' Day".[57] Lawrence is probably speaking of his own experience here, as he goes through those dying days with acute anguish and with anticipation for the otherness of oblivion. His poem "The difficult Death" reflects his thoughts on his deathbed:

> It is not easy to die, O it is not easy
> to die the death.
>
> For death comes when he will
> not when we will him.
> And we can be dying, dying, dying
> and longing utterly to die
> yet death will not come.[58]

Lawrence in his death poems clearly differentiates the dead who depart for the new journey with a feeling of contentment from those "unhappy dead" who in actual life failed to confirm the creative meaning of life. For the former, death is a hopeful adventure to the new beauty as he describes in "So Let Me Live":

> So let me live that I may die
> eagerly passing over from the entanglement of life
> to the adventure of death, in eagerness
> turning to death, as I turn to beauty
> to the breath, that is, of new beauty
> unfolding in death.[59]

For the latter, the poem "Death" tells us:

> They dare not die, because they know
> in death they cannot anymore escape
> the retribution for their obstinacy.
>
> Old men, old obstinate men and women
> dare not die, because in death
> their hardened souls are washed with fire, and washed
> and seared
> till they are softened back to life-stuff again, against which
> they hardened themselves.[60]

Those who have denied the creative life are to Lawrence the greatest of evils. They were dead when they were living, and when they are dead they cannot die a good death. His sympathy for them is shown in "The Houseless Dead":

> Oh pity the dead that are dead, but cannot take
> the journey, still they moan and beat
> against the silvery adamant walls of life's exclusive city.
>
> Oh pity the dead that were ousted out of life
> all unequipped to take the long, long voyage
> . . .
> The poor gaunt dead that cannot die
> into the distance with receding oars,
> but must roam like outcast dogs on
> the margins of life! [61]

The imaginative metaphor of the houseless dead matches exactly the vision of the "hungry ghost" in Buddhism. Those Eastern hungry ghosts either did something seriously wrong or were wrongly put to death in their earthly lives. As a result of abnormal death, they are living like "outcast dogs", roaming in the dark underworld without shelter or food. They are uneasy spirits, angry and malignant and threatening. Lawrence's vision of these "angry unappeased dead" in his poem "Beware the Unhappy Dead!" precisely depicts a classic Buddhist belief:

> Beware the unhappy dead thrust out of life
> unready, unprepared, unwilling, unable
> to continue on the longest journey.
> . . .
> Oh, now they moan and throng in anger . . .
> seeking their old haunts with cold, ghostly rage
> . . .
> Oh, but beware, beware the angry dead.
> Who knows, who knows how much our modern woe is due
> to the angry, unappeased dead
> that were thrust out of life, and now come back at us
> malignant, malignant, for we will not succour them.[62]

In order to "succour" these "lost souls, the uneasy dead", Lawrence invites the living to alleviate their anger and pain by serving them the best food and wine, to give them peace so that they will not disturb our life:

> Oh, on this day of the dead, now November is here
> set a place for the dead, with a cushion and soft seat
> and put a plate, and put a wine-glass out
> and serve the best of food, the fondest wine
> for your dead, your unseen dead, and with your hearts
> speak with them and give them peace and do them honour.[63]

Lawrence's imagination echoes a Buddhist tradition where in annual sacrificial practice all the angry or misleading souls, together with the ancestors, shall receive good treatment from the living. Lawrence, like all religious thinkers, is able to visualize the self after death, in some form or other, in the dark unknown world. What he is curious about is whether and how the soul of the angry dead can be united with the unknown and hence have its peace. Maybe he is suggesting the souls of war criminals, or those unfortunates who miss the fullness and happiness of the living moment. Whatever the angry souls could be, Lawrence reasserts that only when they have done with the known will they be ready for the unknown.

It may have been his illness and approaching death that stimulated his thinking and endowed him with images of the afterlife. His studies of the myths of Odysseus and Osiris, and the legends of the Etruscan tombs might have triggered a hope that something continues after death. In many of his death-poems and prose, Lawrence not only describes an afterlife world, but also projects a positive attitude towards man's departure from this time-space life. In the story "The Flying Fish", for example, when the malaria-ridden Gethin Day is preparing to return to his own womb and tomb, he recalls an Elizabethan metaphysical chronicle of his family, "The Book of Days", through which we are given an imaginative vision of the lesser day of ordinary life and the greater day of life in death. In his illness, Gethin Day had glimpsed the greater day when the lesser day,

> had cracked like some great bubble, and to his uneasiness
> and terror, he had seemed to see through the fissures the

deeper blue of the other Greater Day where moved the other sun shaking its dark blue wings . . . He was ill, and he felt as if at the very middle of him, beneath his navel, some membrane were torn, some membrane which had connected him with the world and its day.[64]

Day's death is interpreted as returning back to home, or to one's womb. It is a Taoist insight into death: returning to where the dead were born. The "Elizabethan book" presents a jolly attitude towards the mysterious long journey of death. Death is to Day a joyful reunion with the womb prior to man's life. The "sheer joy of life", the "purest achievement of joy" of the flying fish—the image of man—is beyond description, and man can never accomplish such joy. [65] "Beautiful it is to be dead!" Day says, "It is the refrain which hums at the centre of every Indian heart, where the greater day is hemmed in by the lesser".[66]

Lawrence compares death to a "silence", a "sheer oblivion", "a silent sheer cessation of all awareness". Death, to him, is also a form of sleep in which there is "a hint of lovely oblivion", or the "sleep of god" in which "the world is created afresh". Chaman Nahal in his *D. H. Lawrence: An Eastern View* points out the striking closeness between Lawrence's metaphor of "deep sleep", "dreamless sleep" and the same description in Hindu Vedantic thought (Hindu philosophy). In the two short poems, "Sleep" and "Sleep and Waking", Lawrence explains what sleep after life means to him:

Sleep is the shadow of the death, but not only that.
Sleep is a hint of lovely oblivion.
When I am gone, completely lapsed and gone

and healed from all this aching of being.
In sleep I am not, I am gone
I am given up.
And nothing in the world is lovelier than sleep,
Dark, dreamless sleep, in deep oblivion!
Nothing in life is quite so good as this.

Yet there is waking from the soundest sleep,
Waking, and waking new.

Did you sleep well?
Ah yes, the sleep of God!
The world is created afresh.[67]

In the state of dreamless sleep, his mind is completely dead to the known, to worldly knowledge. Only in this "deep oblivion" is he capable of being in total contact with the unknown without the interference of the known. Though Lawrence never read the Upanishads (a series of philosophical compositions concluding the exposition of the Vedas), his own intelligent reasoning gives exactly the same metaphor of "deep sleep" as that of the Upanishads. For ancient Hindus, one's mind is completely silent when one is in a dreamless sleep, "So the Upanishads say that the state of perfect stillness of the mind is reached by man in Deep Sleep alone".[68] In a sleep with dreams, the visualized images are the result of the known. Only in the dreamless sleep, in a state of oblivion, there the mind is altogether free of the known, and will then allow the self to be united with the god, with the unknown. It is a paradoxical situation as Nahal suggests: How can one have an "image" when one is in a deep sleep absent of any image? In Upanishads theory, briefly speaking, the deep sleep (the *samadhi*, or the *mukati*, or salvation) "does not mean total extinction; it means only extinction of the known. The unknown is implicitly accepted".[69] Therefore, in his "Dark, dreamless sleep, in deep oblivion", Lawrence gives in to both the known and the unknown, flowing towards a final "waking": it is a rebirth into god's new world and a return to the very same oblivion.

Lawrence imagines how the eternal world is built: "When the living individual dies, then is the realm of death established. Then you get Matter and Elements and atoms and forces and sun and moon and earth and stars and so forth. In short, the outer universe, the cosmos".[70] The cosmos is eternal, but it is established upon the numerous dead individuals who have lived their "little" earthly life. According to Lawrence, "Everything human" will finally "perish" and he shows no sorrow, but gladness:

> I live and I die. I ask no other. Whatever proceeds from me lives and dies. I am glad, too. God is eternal, but my idea of Him is my own, and perishable. Everything human, human knowledge, human faith, human

emotions, all perishes. And that is very good; if it were not so, everything would turn to cast-iron.[71]

Lawrence's understanding of life and his life-long illness strengthened his religious vision of the long journey to oblivion, and also endowed him with a Taoist carefree attitude towards life and death.

Lawrence, though clearly realizing the mutual identity between life and death, always grants more significance to a physical life than a physical death. He says in *Fantasia of the Unconscious* that it is life that contributes to the formation of the universe: "At length, for *my* part, I know that life, and life only, is the clue to the universe. And that the living individual is the clue to life". [72] Through the man in *The Man Who Died*, Lawrence speaks his own mind: "And the destiny of life seemed more fierce and compulsive to him even than the destiny of death. The doom of a death was a shadow compared to the raging destiny of life, the determined surge of life". [73] Leavis points out that the affirmation of life never wavers in Lawrence, "the life in him was something like unshaken invincible faith".[74] In the end of the same book, Leavis again eulogizes Lawrence's "indestructible life-courage", commenting, "His religious intuition of the primacy of life was such that he was capable of saying that even if human life extinguished itself, or was eliminated from the world, new life would be generated in the universe." This life-courage is clearly "in the product of his creativity", which, Leavis predicts, "makes it inevitable for us to carry on the creative effort with all our intelligence, courage and resource".[75]

[1] Frederick Carter, *D. H. Lawrence and the Body Mystical*, p. 28.

[2] D. H. Lawrence, "Life", *Phoenix*, p. 695.

[3] Ibid., p. 695.

[4] Ibid., pp. 695, 696.

[5] Ibid., p. 697.

[6] Quoted in J. Baird Callicott, ed., *Nature in Asian Traditions of Thought: Essays in Environmental Philosophy*, p. 47.

[7] D. H. Lawrence, "Life", *Phoenix*, p. 263.

[8] Ibid., pp. 263-4.

[9] D. H. Lawrence, "On Human Destiny", *Phoenix II*, p. 629.

[10] D. H. Lawrence, *Fantasia of the Unconscious and Psychoanalysis and the Unconsciousness*, pp. 148-9.

[11] Ibid., p. 149.

[12] Hokuseido, *Zen in English Literature and Oriental Classics*, p. 338.

[13] D. H. Lawrence, "The Crown", in *Reflection on the Death of a Porcupine and Other Essays*, p. 282.

[14] Ibid., p. 262.

[15] D. H. Lawrence, *Fantasia of the Unconscious and Psychoanalysis and the Unconscious*, p. 149.

[16] Ibid., p. 149.

[17] Ibid., p. 150.

[18] D. H. Lawrence, "Morality and the Novel", *Phoenix*, p. 528.

[19] D. H. Lawrence, "New Mexico", *Phoenix*, p. 146.

[20] D. H. Lawrence, *Movements in European History*, p. 21.

[21] *The Letters of D. H. Lawrence*, Aldous Huxley, ed., p. 346.

[22] *The Complete Poems of D. H. Lawrence*, Vivian de Sola Pinto, ed., p. 673.

[23] D. H. Lawrence, "Reviews of Books", *Phoenix*, p. 395.

[24] Earl Brewster, *D. H. Lawrence: Reminiscences and Correspondence*, p. 174.

[25] Ibid., p. 49.

[26] Ruben L. F. Habito, quoted in Mary E. Tucker, ed., *Buddhism and Ecology*, p. 169.

[27] D. H. Lawrence, "The Real Thing", *D. H. Lawrence, A Selection from Phoenix*, p. 380.

[28] Ibid., p. 379.

[29] D. H. Lawrence, "Why the Novel Matters", *Phoenix*, p. 534.

[30] Ibid., p. 537.

[31] F. R. Leavis, *Thought, Words and Creativity*, p. 28.

[32] Ibid., p. 136.

[33] D. H. Lawrence, "Autobiographical Fragment", *Phoenix*, p. 817.

34 D. H. Lawrence, "The Crown", in *Reflection on the Death of a Porcupine and Other Essays*, p. 292.

35 Ibid., p. 282.

36 D. H. Lawrence, *Women in Love*, p. 173.

37 D. H. Lawrence, "The Reality of Peace", *Phoenix*, p. 679.

38 Ibid., p. 676.

39 D. H. Lawrence, *The Boy in the Bush*, p. 331.

40 D. H. Lawrence, "The Reality of Peace", *Phoenix*, p. 676.

41 Ibid., pp. 678-9, 681.

42 Ibid., p. 680.

43 Brandon Toropov, ed., *The Complete Idiot's Guide to Taoism*, p. 161.

44 D. H. Lawrence, "The Reality of Peace", *Phoenix*, p. 682.

45 Brandon Toropov, ed., *The Complete Idiot's Guide to Taoism*, p. 162.

46 D. H. Lawrence, *Sons and Lovers*, Ch. 15, p. 510.

47 Ibid., p. 511.

48 D. H. Lawrence, *Women in Love*, Ch. 14. p. 185.

49 D. H. Lawrence, *The Rainbow*, Ch. 9, p. 233.

50 D. H. Lawrence, *Women in Love*, Ch. 31, p. 480.

51 Ibid., Ch. 15, pp. 191-3.

52 Ibid., Ch. 14, p. 172.

53 D. H. Lawrence, "The Reality of Peace", *Phoenix*, pp. 686-7.

54 *The Complete Poems of D. H. Lawrence*, Vivian de Sola Pinto, ed., p. 965.

55 Ibid., p. 721.

56 Ibid., pp. 725, 960.

57 Ibid., p. 721

58 Ibid., p. 720.

59 Ibid., p. 676.

60 Ibid., p. 663.

61 Ibid., p. 722.

62 Ibid., p. 722.

63 Ibid., p. 723.

64 D. H. Lawrence, "The Flying Fish", *Phoenix*, p. 782.

65 Ibid., pp. 794-5.

66 Ibid., p. 784.

67 *The Complete Poems of D. H. Lawrence*, Vivian de Sola Pinto, ed., pp. 724-5.

68 Chaman Nahal, *D. H. Lawrence: An Eastern View*, p. 248.

69 Ibid. 249.

70 D. H. Lawrence, *Fantasia of the Unconscious and Psychoanalysis and the Unconscious*, p. 148.

71 D. H. Lawrence, "On Human Destiny", *Phoenix II*, p. 629.

72 D. H. Lawrence, *Fantasia of the Unconscious and Psychoanalysis and the Unconscious*, p. 148.

73 *The Tales of D. H. Lawrence*, p. 1106.

74 F. R. Leavis, *Thought, Words and Creativity*, p. 137.

75 Ibid., p. 156.

Chapter VII

Mind and Body

*

Ever since attending university, Lawrence was fascinated by the power of the unconscious. Influenced by nineteenth-century scientific readings, he began to accept their insights into issues concerning mind and body, mental consciousness and blood consciousness, rationality and intuition. He later devoted several essays to expounding his belief in the "creative unconscious". To him, "there is a whole science of the unconscious in its law-abiding activities". It is as incomprehensible as nature's law, but once we admit its presence we are liberated and will "live from the spontaneous initial prompting". He writes in *Psychoanalysis and the Unconscious*:

> What we are suffering from now is the restriction of the unconscious within certain ideal limits. The more we force the ideal the more we rupture the true movement. Once we can admit the unknown, but incomprehensible, presence of the integral unconscious; once we can trace it home in ourselves and follow its first revealed movements; once we know how it habitually unfolds itself; once we can scientifically determine its laws and processes in ourselves: then at last we can begin to live from the spontaneous initial prompting, instead of from the dead machine-principles of ideas and ideals.[1]

Daniel J. Schneider in *The Consciousness of D. H. Lawrence* examines the influences upon Lawrence's conception of mind and body. During his early twenties, Lawrence began to read Schopenhauer and to connect part of his philosophy with the ideas of other Rationalist writers such as Darwin, Huxley, Spencer and Haeckel. Their scientific perceptions contribute a great deal to Lawrence's "Psychoanalysis" of "the Unconscious". According to Schopenhauer, feeling or desire comes prior to reason. In Spencer's theory, mental activity is the effect of bodily activity instead of the cause of it, as consciousness is in the service of the organism, and seeks to adjust its internal needs to the environment. From this concept comes William James' theory that physiological activity precedes emotional or conscious response. "I do not strike because I am angry, I am angry because I strike; I do not weep because I am unhappy, I am unhappy because I weep".[2] Emotions, or love and hate, do not come from the conscious mind, and their existence suggests the very physical foundation of life. Mind or consciousness on the other hand is in the service of body or impulse. James' theory confirms Lawrence's understanding in Schopenhauer and Nietzsche: the mind does not represent the "true self"; ideas are falsification of the intellect, which can never know the reality but only its own representations of reality; the visible world of time and space is only an illusion-maya; the reality can be found only through instinct or intuition instead of one's mind.[3]

Throughout his intellectual development, as Schneider observes, Lawrence was deeply influenced by Edward Carpenter's thought. Perhaps the most significant idea, for the young Lawrence, was that the project of building a new heaven and a new earth could not be confined to political and economic changes. A healthy humanity should be based upon a cosmic unity, "a new consciousness, a new naturalism joined to the religious sense of the unity of all things: *tat tvam asi*. The basis of this cosmic unity was *feeling*, the impulse that attracted one body to another and ultimately to identification with the All".[4] This conception was bound to be ignored or ridiculed by intellectuals, such as Russell and the Bloomsbury-Cambridge group, who believed that mind or consciousness plays the role of an autonomous instrument, capable of conducting human behaviour. Carpenter's argument about the "great sympathetic"—the system of nerves as the seat of emotion—may have provided Lawrence with the physiological centre that he later used in his theory of the unconscious and the solar plexus. Carpenter advocates that emotion and desire are only associated with the nervous system of the body and not with the mind. Lawrence accepts Carpenter's idea and develops it further into his own theory that through desire one is united with others and ultimately with the whole cosmos.

Nietzsche is probably one of the most influential writers who followed this mind-body pattern that Lawrence read or was acquainted with during and after his formative period.[5] For Nietzsche, reality is not recognized through science or mind, but is known through great impulses—the immediate body and the deepest desire. Nietzsche concludes, "There are no mental causes". Man is motivated by deep instinctive will (both "will to live" and "will to power"), not by spirit or mind. To him, "Everything good is instinct"; every error is "a degeneration of instinct".[6] He justifies the pride of "the noble man", whose mission it is "to create a new, vital world in which the instincts are not condemned but rather are joyfully affirmed". Lawrence also "joyfully affirmed" the instinctive life of Nietzsche's "noble man":

> When it comes to living, we live through our instincts and our intuitions. Instinct makes me run from little over-earnest ladies; instinct makes me sniff the lime blossom and reach for the darkest cherry. But it is intuition which makes me feel the uncanny glassiness of the lake this afternoon, the sulkiness of the mountains, the vividness of near green in thunder-sun, the young man in bright blue trousers lightly tossing the grass from the scythe, the elderly man in a boater stiffly shoving his scythe-strokes, both of them sweating in the silence of the intense light.[7]

Nietzsche argues that in Western civilization, the emphasis on mind and science dominates our life and has destroyed innocent passions and instincts. Christianity is the cause of man's abhorrence of the body and flesh, its ethics poison man's spontaneous wholeness. Following Nietzsche, Lawrence also attacks Christianity for its preaching of demanding love and "love of neighbour", for its slave assertion of selflessness and self-sacrifice for the common good, and for its "vicious" intention to subdue man's pure sexuality and all instinctive desires. The mental consciousness according to Nietzsche's interpretation is "the last and latest development of the organic and consequently also the most finished and weakest part of it". "Thinking which has become conscious is only the smallest part of (thought)" and "the worst part". "Man, like every living creature, thinks continually but does not know it", so man's deepest and most accurate thought is unconscious, and the conscious thought is for him "an illness".[8] Lawrence in a letter explicitly voices the same belief: "My great religion is a belief in the blood, the flesh, as being wiser than the intellect. We can go wrong in our minds. But what our blood feels and believes and says is always true. The intellect is only a bit and a bridle".[9]

Lawrence's belief in blood consciousness is most strengthened by the air of Bloomsbury. In 1915, with a strong hope of finding an intellectual group to help him establish a new foundation for English life, Lawrence entered into the Bloomsbury-Cambridge group. But he was thoroughly disappointed at what Bertrand Russell and the other Cambridge elite could provide. The synopsis of the lectures that Russell sent to him was thought of by Lawrence as "pernicious". What Lawrence wanted was a radical change, a new utopian world based upon organic life and a cosmic unity. But on the contrary what he saw was the corrupting atmosphere of Cambridge with its homoeroticism, rationalism and cynicism. He particularly objected to the Cambridge-Bloomsburians' new ideas of "modern morality": "The primacy of reason; the available truths of science; the superiority of exquisite states of mind developed through the contemplation of beauty, art, and cultured conversation".[10] Reason, science and mind are at odds with Lawrence's dream of building an organic life. The organic life, according to Lawrence, is not based upon mechanisms such as reason, science, mind or mental consciousness, but upon instinct, intuition, and impulse, which belong to the unconscious body, or are categorized by him as "blood consciousness". In a letter to Russell, Lawrence accuses him of being the "enemy of all mankind". He says, "it is *not* the hatred of falsehood which inspires you. It is the hatred of people, of flesh and blood".[11] Later in December of the same year, Lawrence wrote to Russell again, expressing his conviction after reading Frazer's *The Golden Bough* and *Totemism and Exogamy*:

> Now I am convinced of what I believed when I was about twenty—that there is another seat of consciousness than the brain and the nerve system: there is a blood-consciousness which exists in us independently of the ordinary mental consciousness . . . One lives, knows, and has one's being in the blood, without any reference to nerves and brain . . . And the tragedy of our life, and of your life, is that the mental and nervous consciousness exerts a tyranny over the blood consciousness and that your will has gone completely over to the mental consciousness, and is engaged in the destruction of your blood being or blood -consciousness, the final liberating of the one, which is only death in result. Plato was the same.[12]

With regards to Lawrence's blood-consciousness, Russell wrote in return that he felt Lawrence was a "positive force for evil". He condemned his "mystic philosophy of 'blood'", saying it "seemed frankly rubbish" to him, and "I rejected it vehemently".[13] Lawrence later parodies and satirizes Russell in *Women in Love* as Sir Joshua Matheson, "a learned, dry Baronet of fifty" who was always talking endlessly "with a strong mentality working", and "yet always known, everything he said known beforehand". Maynard Keynes, one of the main members of the Cambridge group, whom Lawrence met through Russell's introduction, and whom Lawrence disliked vehemently, however admits later in his memoirs:

> As cause and consequence of our general state of mind we completely misunderstood human nature, including our own. The rationality which we attributed to it led to a superficiality, not only of judgement, but also of feeling . . . The attribution of rationality to human nature, instead of enriching it, now seems to me to have impoverished it . . . What a combination of qualities we offered to arouse his passionate disaster; this thin rationalism skipping on the crust of the lava, ignoring both the reality and the value of the vulgar passions . . . That is why I say that there may have been just a grain of truth when Lawrence said in 1914 that we were "done for".[14]

Lawrence, by that time, saw England as an entirely critical society, founded on books and the mind. He talks at length in *A Propos of Lady Chatterley's Lover* about how a society worshipping rationality and mental knowledge exclusively could only produce "false feelings" or "mental feelings" instead of "real feelings": "Today, many people live and die without having any real feelings—though they have had a 'rich emotional life' apparently, having showed strong mental feeling. But it is all counterfeit". He comments, "Never was an age more sentimental, more devoid of real feeling, more exaggerated in false feeling, than our own". The false feeling he blames is a result of a rational mind, which is the product of society and education.[15] Lawrence, using extreme and radical terms in a letter, criticises the depressing mind-worshiping society, a society which is creating an "almost overwhelming incubus of falsity and ugliness on top of us, so that we are almost crushed to death".[16] The Bloomsbury and Cambridge group is composed of the leading intelligentsia of England, to which Lawrence is no match in educational credentials, so whatever he said was either ignored or regarded as something "rubbish" or "evil".

During Lawrence's time, the imagists and surrealists were enthusiastic rebels against intellect, and Freud and the symbolists showed them the way to the unconscious, instinct and intuition. In this general tendency, Lawrence becomes its epitome in his distrust of intellect and mind, and his maintaining of the intuitive power of body and soul. In *Lady Chatterley's Lover*, Clifford's friends are intelligent, in a superficial way, but their mental life cannot satisfy Connie's needs and cannot alleviate a sense of utter nothingness in her life. Her dark, dull life is finally lit up by the sensuous gamekeeper Mellors, as he is living in both his mind and body. Through Tommy Dukes, one of Clifford's friends, Lawrence depicts the danger of solely living in a mental life:

> I was not talking about knowledge . . . I was talking about the mental life. Real knowledge comes out of the whole corpus of the consciousness; out of your belly and your penis as much as out of your brain and mind. The mind can only analyse and rationalise . . . And if you've got nothing in your life but the mental life then you yourself

> are a plucked apple . . . you've fallen off the tree. And then
> it is a logical necessity to be spiteful, just as it's a natural
> necessity for a plucked apple to go bad.

Tommy Dukes and his friends then talk about Bolshevism, accusing it of being "superlative hatred of the things they call the bourgeois" which indicates "feelings and emotions", and the blood consciousness.[17]

The mind and body conflict inevitably leads us to explore the problems of love and marriage. Lawrence once said to his engaged friend Louie Burrows, trying to undo her prudery, "I say only that is wicked which is a violation of one's feeling and instinct".[18] There are many "wicked" elements in love and marriage, such as the arranged marriage in the East, and the marriage seeking security in the West. According to Lawrence, there is no genuine love generated from "feeling and instinct" in modern love. Love and emotion today are all to him "counterfeit". He writes in *A Propos of Lady Chatterley's Lover* that it becomes a stereotyped thing that all the young know how they ought to feel and how they ought to behave according to the anticipation of society. Lawrence realizes that he himself is contradictory, embodying at once counterfeit and true feelings of love. However, what he emphasizes is that one should be able to know one's true feeling and real wants, and act accordingly. Unfortunately, as he points out, the "true flame of real loving communion" is likely to be extinguished by a "peculiar", calculated society. This is the tragedy of marriage because the initial desire and initial impulse to marry is not based on intuition, on the voice of the soul; instead it is based on the will of the ego, calculating advantages and disadvantages according to egoistic ideals and societal requirements. He asserts that genuine love should have a different kind of goal: "There is a goal, but the goal is neither love nor death. It is a goal neither infinite nor eternal. It is the realm of calm delight, it is the other-kingdom of bliss".[19] The realm of bliss only comes from the unknown, and the unknown can be united with man through the power of intuition and spontaneity. In order to be in tune with the unknown, the mind must be free of the known, and thus be ready for urges from the unknown. Because the reasoning mind is unable to receive the unknown, only "pure spontaneous morality" has the power to do it. Lawrence explains this in the lines at the end of the essay "Love": "It is our business to go as we are impelled, with faith and pure spontaneous morality, knowing that the rose blossoms, and taking that knowledge for sufficient".[20] This is the key to a real marriage: the coming together of a man and woman, completely absent of mind and egoistic goals.

Chaman Nahal illustrates this point of view through Lawrence's characters. In the cases of Tom Brangwen and Lydia in *The Rainbow*, and Rupert and Ursula in *Women in Love*, we find their love and union are most successful. Both men are looking for a lifetime woman according to their instinctive regards. Their relationships are not built upon any pre-conceived rules except "the urge of the soul". So far as the urge is spontaneous, it must be from the unknown, and then it is creative and healthy and will bring the couple a "kingdom of bliss". When Tom sees Lydia on the road for the first time, his involuntary response is "That's her".[21] This short exclamation is highly valued by Leavis: "we have a very specific sense, even so early in the book, of the forces registered in the exclamation—the complexity speaking".[22] Leavis is talking about the instinctive motive behind the intense attraction. At the time when Ursula in *The Rainbow* and Gudrun in *Women in Love* meet the men, they both have formed a certain pre-conceived notion of the type of man they would like to be wooed by. And the two men Skrebensky and Gerald fill the ideal image of the lover these two women have in mind. Ursula's love for Anton is actually for her own long designed dream, which is "a mere reaction, reaction as the result of a desired end in the mind".[23] And Gerald is in Gudrun's eyes a social success, and has a taste for the arts. Their intense love is thus the result of their ego, it is therefore deceptive and unreliable. As the story proceeds, their relationships come to a sad end. But the intensity of Tom's desire for Lydia falls into different category. Tom's love for Lydia is just a state of readiness, without knowing exactly what he wants of that woman, except feeling that the woman has stirred his soul. On Lydia's side, it is also an instinctive love: "Her instinct fixed on him—just on him. Her impulse was strong against him, because he was not of her own sort. But one blind instinct led her, to take him, to have him, and then to relinquish herself to him. It would be safety".[24] Their love is what Nahal describes as "a symbol of the unprepared for, unforeseen urge of the soul".[25]

In *Aaron's Rod*, Lilly gives Aaron some significant advice: "You've never got to deny the Holy Ghost which is inside you, your own soul's self". He then explains that, "If your soul's urge urges you to love, then love. But always know that what you are doing is the fulfilling of your own soul's impulse".[26] This line was heavily attacked by Eliseo Vivas in his *D. H. Lawrence, The Failure and the Triumph of Art*: "it is an expression of Lawrence's unmitigated, immature, foot-stamping, table-pounding, fretting, pouting, cry-baby, petulant selfishness—a sheer, uncomplicated, unrestrained, colossally arrogant, self-centred selfish- ness".[27] Vivas' impetuous criticism suggests a grave misunderstanding shared with some other critics, such as Russell. Lawrence's advice of "following your own soul's impulse" is a key issue concerning his belief in "blood consciousness", and is exactly what he would like to see in our everyday life. To Lawrence, "soul's impulse" is more reliable than mental consciousness. Blood-consciousness can never misguide you; only the conscious mind or the will of ego can go wrong. It is true that Aaron has left his wife, and ends up in what would conventionally be termed "unethical" situations. However Lawrence's talk about the soul's impulses is by no means intended to justify Aaron's behaviour. Lawrence's interest is not in making any impartial justification of his behaviour. His purpose is to raise the importance of accepting the reality in a particular situation and at a particular time, and to encourage people to make their own judgment in answering one's soul's urge. "This is the greatest secret of behavior" Lawrence writes in *Kangaroo*, all one has to do is "to stand alone, and judge oneself from the deeps of one's own soul. And then, to know, to hear what the others say and think: to refer their judgment to the touchstone of one's own soul-judgment".[28] Love and marriage will come initially from the soul as an unavoidable fate: this is a true love and above reasoning. The motivating power behind Aaron's dramatic action is undoubtedly in line with Lawrence's doctrine that things should happen with a natural ease and natural inevitability. Aaron's action is in accordance with his intuition and impulse, coming naturally without being interrupted by any ethics. On the other hand, Lawrence believes that instinct and fidelity are not opposed to each other, or in other words, true love is the foundation of fidelity. He argues:

> All the literature of the world shows how profound is the instinct of fidelity in both man and woman, how men and women both hanker restlessly after the satisfaction of this instinct . . . The instinct of fidelity is perhaps the deepest instinct in the great complex we call sex. Where there is real sex there is the underlying passion for fidelity.[29]

Buddhist belief maintains that in a man's life, as in love and marriage, there is an element of fatalism. This "fatalism" can be best explained by *The Book of Changes* ("Yi Jing" in Chinese, which is not to be elaborated here). Achsah Brewster once recalled Lawrence's words in one of their conversations: "the Hindus were right to believe that the hand of Fate deals out three events—birth, marriage and death—and that no man can escape his fate".[30] Aaron's desertion of his wife is in the hands of fate, and his action, in a natural inevitability, falls justifiably within the range of Lawrence's "urge of the soul".

* *

In Lawrence's perception, the modern world is characterized by a division between will and feeling, mind and body, consciousness and unconsciousness, rationality and intuition. There is always a war between the two or between the "two different living principles" as Lawrence puts it. Accordingly, as mentioned before, there are "two ways of knowing": "knowing in ways of apartness, which is mental, rational and scientific, and knowing in terms of togetherness, which is religious and poetic". The two ways of knowing reflect the noticeable division in the spheres of consciousness between Eastern intuitionism and Western rationalism. Here is Ben Willis' interpretation of the two ways of knowing:

> The Western intellectual tradition has accused the Eastern attitude of not dealing in empirical evidence and fact, of illogic, inexactitude, and especially of impracticality, typically rational objections which could

apply as well to Western religion, the Western creative arts, and the Western right brain . . . It is heartening, however, that the Western intellectual community seems to be at last becoming dimly aware that the most creative advances in science and scholarly research are brought about precisely through inexplicable intuitional leaps.[31]

The war between the two consciousnesses is a characteristic theme of Lawrence's *Studies in Classic American Literature.* There will always exist the mutually destroying forces of blood consciousness and mind-consciousness:

> Blood-consciousness overwhelms, obliterates, and annuls mind-consciousness. Mind-conscious- ness extinguishes blood-consciousness, and consumes the blood. We are all of us conscious in both ways. And the two ways are antagonistic in us. They will always remain so. That is our cross.[32]

Lawrence further analyses the problems in our modern culture: "There is a basic hostility in all of us between the physical and the mental, the blood and the spirit. The mind is 'ashamed' of the blood. And the blood is destroyed by the mind, actually".[33] In the essay, "Herman Melville's *Moby Dick*", he remarks on Moby Dick as "the deepest blood-being of the white race; he is our deepest blood-nature". But he is hunted "by the maniacal fanaticism of our white mental consciousness". "This last phallic being of the white man" is "hunted into the death of upper consciousness and the ideal will: Our blood- consciousness sapped by a parasitic mental or ideal consciousness". This is to Lawrence the "great horror" of "our civilization". Lawrence believes that Melville knew that "his race", "his white soul", "his great white epoch", the "idealist", himself and the spirit were all "doomed".[34] In James Fenimore Cooper's major novels, Lawrence detects and enjoys his most unconscious element. Cooper's blood consciousness and his reliance on the unconscious creative imagination are, as Lawrence puts it, central to his position as an artist and a moral being.

The novelette *St. Mawr* provides the richest understanding of Lawrence's message of the conflict between mental consciousness and blood consciousness. Lou Witt's husband Rico and the vicar are living exclusively within their mental consciousness, while the stallion St. Mawr together with the two grooms, Lewis and Phoenix, represents an altogether different world, a world absent of human ideology.

Lou feels instinctively that the stallion's world, full of "mysterious fire" and "splendid demon", is beyond her. [35] She "seemed to hear the echoes of another, darker, more spacious, more dangerous, more splendid world than ours . . . And there she wanted to go". In contrast with "the triviality and superficiality of her human relationships", the stallion presents Lou with "an older, heavily potent world". It arouses a vision in her "as if the walls of her own world had suddenly melted away, leaving her in a great darkness", and even "forbade her to be her ordinary, common-place self". Lawrence with his own sensitivity of animal consciousness depicts two different realities. The contact between animal and man is described as "a battle between two worlds". Lou's handsome husband Rico is a representation of those who are obsessed with all the ideas and ideals of social conventions. Rico is all about "attitude" and "so self-controlled" to the point that he is not "real"; everything about him is "perfectly prepared for social purposes". He lives entirely in the world of the "personal" and is unable to imagine another world in which the horse is "undominated and unsurpassed". For the two grooms, reality is beyond "the personal" and the purely human. They think and feel with their blood consciousness. Like St. Mawr, though under the control of their employers, they remain intact and "unyielding", their "impersonal", "intuitive mind(s)" know things "without thinking them". Their thinking is "straight from the source". They feel in their bones that the reality of London is like "a mirage" or a "prison", and know that the trap of civilization blocks the natural life flow. They are intimate with the otherness of the animal kingdom. The story registers an overall sense that natural man thinking with his "immediate intuition" is more powerful than the rational intellect in knowing the reality.[36]

In the "Introduction to These Paintings", Lawrence criticises the English attitude to the arts and life, for its lack of intuition and its suppression of "instinctive-intuitive consciousness". He argues that "the English failure in the visual arts" is a result of an ignorance of the significance of intuitive knowledge, from "a terror, almost a horror of sexual life", and of a horror of man's own body.[37] With a preoccupied "'spiritual-mental' consciousness", man intends to "suppress with all his might his instinctive-intuitive consciousness, which is so radical, so physical, so sexual". This suppression of man's physical emotions and reactions will lead to "the crippling of the consciousness of man", because the "very elementary in man is his sexual and procreative being", on which "depend many of his deepest instincts and the flow of his intuition". He argues:

> A deep instinct of kinship joins men together, and the kinship of flesh-and-blood keeps the warm flow of intuitional awareness streaming between human beings. Our true awareness of one another is intuitional, not mental. Attraction between people is really instinctive and intuitional, not an affair of judgement.

But unfortunately,

> We have become ideal beings, creatures that exist in idea, to one another, rather than flesh-and-blood kin. And with the collapse of the feeling of physical, flesh-and-blood kinship, and the substitution of our ideal, social or political oneness, came the failing of our intuitive awareness, and the great unease, the *nervousness* of mankind.[38]

This creates, particularly in Western society, a false relationship based on the intellectual, on "ideal or social or political entities", which is "fleshless, bloodless, and cold". All arts, painting and novel, to Lawrence, should "depend entirely on the intuitional perception of the *reality* of substantial bodies" and "the reality of substantial bodies can only be perceived by the imagination, and the imagination is a kindled state of consciousness in which intuitive awareness predominates".[39]

According to Lawrence's perception, painting and writing involve both "mind consciousness" and "blood consciousness", they "are made by the whole consciousness of man working together in unison and oneness: instinct, intuition, mind, intellect all fused into one complete consciousness". These "two modes must act complementary to one another". However, he is aware of the prejudice most intellectuals hold towards intuitions and instincts. There are too many scientists who "work with the mind alone, and force the intuitions and instincts into a prostituted acquiescence", he says. Lawrence admires the French artist Cézanne for his struggle against clichés and his objectivity in paintings. Throughout his painting life, Cézanne is true to his body and intuition. He wants to paint people and landscapes "intuitively and instinctively", always trying hard to get rid of the interference of "his mental consciousness". Lawrence thought highly of his life principle, especially the instincts and intuition embodied in him as an artist: "He wanted to live, really live in the body, to know the world through his instincts and his intuitions, and to be himself in his procreative blood, not in his mere mind and spirit".[40]

For Lawrence, an instinctive consciousness of body is an important aspect of complete consciousness. His paintings manifest his worship of the vitality of body and flesh, as well as his strong phallic consciousness, which is stimulated furthermore by the strong sinuous lines of Etruscan paintings. He believes that man's hatred and fear of the body have led to the lack of sensual qualities in English paintings. It seems to him that William Blake is the only exception to this: "Blake paints with real intuitional awareness and solid instinctive feeling. He dares handle human body, even if he sometimes makes it a mere ideograph". According to Lawrence, "an artist *can* only create what he religiously *feels* is truth, religious truth really felt, in the blood and the bones". Feeling of what is true is not from any "ready-made mental concept", it is an intuitive understanding in the body. In Lawrence's interpretation, "By intuition alone can man *really* be aware of man, or of the living, substantial world", and "By intuition alone can man live and know either woman or world, and by intuition alone can he bring forth again images of magic awareness which we call art".[41]

For Taoists, reality is above thought, and cannot be reached by rational analysis, but only by "immediate intuition". Lawrence gives this "immediate intuition" other names such as "spontaneous centres", "soul", "the unconscious", or "the blood consciousness". The conscious mind, from a Taoist point of view, can only accumulate experiences and biases in analytical and critical tendencies; it cannot arrive at spiritual awareness, by the nature of its own limitations. A conventionally bounded mind is incapable of understanding or achieving a "full knowledge" of reality, for that is above and beyond the boundaries of rational thought. "There is nothing either good or bad, but thinking makes it so". In other words, the idea coming from thinking is not necessarily always right. Thus it is of no use depending solely upon the ever-searching rational mind and letting it be the "director or controller of the spontaneous centres".[42] Lawrence does not trust the rational mind either. "We can go wrong in our minds", he says, as the rational mind is largely an artificial, acquired intelligence, the warehouse of all the education and experience accumulated in the physical world. In his view, the "whole mental consciousness and the whole sum of the mental content of mankind" has great limitations. It is merely a "tithe of all the vast surging primal consciousness, the affective consciousness of mankind". If we depend too much on our mental centre, "We have limited our consciousness, tethered it to a few great ideas, like a goat to a post". He then comments on a prevailing phenomenon: "We insist over and over again on what we know from one mere centre of ourselves, the mental centre".[43]

Lawrence therefore asserts, "It is the impulse we have to live by, not the ideals or the idea".[44] Many of his characters, like Aaron and Tom, are living by impulse and are submissive to its power, and in defiance of conventional ideas and ideals. In the story "The Woman Who Rode Away", Lawrence, through the white woman's sacrifice to the Chilchui Indians, exhibits an intuitive understanding that primal realities are inaccessible to the ideal and rational consciousness. The woman is sick of her meaningless, stale life, and is drawn intuitively to the mysterious Indian community. She realizes that the consciousness prevailing within the Indian community is different from her own white consciousness. The Indians do not act from the egoistic will, but rather live voluntarily with the mystery of the great tides of creation and destruction, attraction and repulsion. Their passions and powers, seen as the deepest promptings of nature, are dynamically associated with the circumambient universe. As the white woman observed, in the eyes of the Indian there is an intense power which goes deep to the heart of the earth, and the heart of the sun. Their love and hatred are voluntary impulses of their blood consciousness. Being with these "impersonal" Indians, the woman's white consciousness has gradually succumbed to the Indians' cosmic consciousness:

> More and more her ordinary personal consciousness had left her, she had gone into that other state of passional cosmic consciousness, like one who is drugged. The Indians, with their heavily religious natures, had made her succumb to their vision.[45]

Despite being praised for his excellence in science and being a great examination passer, Lawrence sees falsity and uselessness in one's complete dependence upon mind and science. With the belief in blood and unconsciousness, he enjoys the company of mindless animals, birds and plants, with which he feels he is intimately connected. "There is a sort of relation" between Susan and Lawrence, "And this relation is part of the mystery of love".[46] The animals do not know the white consciousness, they are congenial to the quality of nature, and are thus the symbol of good and truth. "Religion was right and science is wrong",[47] Lawrence proclaims. With his "great religion", Lawrence rejects the idea of fixed, mechanical law, the science of biology and even Darwin's evolution. He hates to think that water is nothing but the elements of Hydrogen and Oxygen; neither does he feel comfortable imagining that the sun is but a ball of blazing gas, or that the living earth is seen by the man of science as merely a turning wheel. He regards all scientific explanations of natural elements as "thought-forms", which he says are "derived from experiments with water" or fire. But these "thought-forms . . . do not make our life".[48] To him, the truth or living mystery of the elements of the universe is beyond civilized man's comprehension, and possibly known only by primitive people, since they have the capacity to view the world with blood and intuition instead of by scientific analysis. He prefers the living mystery to the cause and effect of man's logical mind. But unfortunately, living in modern society, we simply cannot get rid of the habitual conscious mentality. Since it is this world that produces all scientific and mechanical things, as well as all the imposed ideas and ideals, it is even more urgent to raise our consciousness in the need to protect man's organic spontaneous growth. In *Aaron's Rod*, Lilly tells Levison that "The idea and the ideal has for me gone dead—dead as carrion—". To Levison's request for an explanation, Lilly's answer provides us with a glimpse of what ideas and ideals Lawrence is "precisely" up against:

> The ideal of love, the ideal that it is better to give than to receive, the ideal of liberty, the ideal of the brotherhood of man, the ideal of the sanctity of human life, the ideal of what we call goodness, charity, benevolence, public spiritedness, the ideal of sacrifice for a cause, the ideal of unity and unanimity—all the lot—all the whole beehive of ideals—has all got the modern bee-disease, and gone putrid, stinking.[49]

In his *Fantasia of the Unconscious* and *Psychoanalysis and the Unconscious*, Lawrence expounds his point of view about mind and body, mental consciousness and intuition. He has observed a danger in over-rationalizing human lives, hoping no ideas or ideals should interfere with or suppress the individual's impulses of their spontaneous life. The ideas and ideals to him only play the role of the "dry, unloving, insentient plumage which intervene between us and the circumambient universe, forming at once an insulator and an instrument for . . . subduing the universe".[50] It is wrong for our society and our education to put too much importance upon the acquisition of ideas, and "to force each individual to a maximum of mental control, and mental consciousness". The corruption of ideology is the enemy of man's spontaneous creative life. He criticizes idealism: "pure idealism is identical with pure materialism, and the most ideal peoples are the most completely material . . . The ideal is but the god in the machine—the little, fixed, machine- principle which works the human psyche automatically". Though "Mental consciousness is a purely individual affair . . . for the vast majority, much mental consciousness is simply a catastrophe, a blight. It just stops their living". Thus Lawrence wants us to eliminate the dangerous influence of "stale ideas": "The ideal mind, the brain, has become the vampire of modern life, sucking up the blood and the life.

There is hardly an original thought or original utterance possible to us. All is sickly repetition of stale, stale ideas".[51]

One of the crucial elements of Lawrence's disbelief in "mental consciousness" is its falsity and incapability in knowing true reality. By transferring man's vivid experience into a set of fixed precepts, concepts and ideas, the mind can become the terminal instrument of the dynamic consciousness. He writes in *Fantasia of the Unconscious*: "The primal consciousness in man is pre-mental, and has nothing to do with cognition. It is the same as in the animals . . . The mind is but the last flower, the *cul de sac*". The rational mind is for Lawrence the "dead end" of man's experience of the world, for it can only acquire a priori knowledge, which he thinks is "dead". He explains:

> To know is to lose. When I have a finished mental concept of a beloved, or a friend, then the love and the friendship is dead. It falls to the level of an acquaintance. As soon as I have a finished mental conception, a full idea even of myself, then dynamically I am dead. To know is to die.[52]

The rational mind mechanically imposes an unjustified image upon man's understanding of the external world and upon his moral judgment. What we know about nature is the "finished" and immutable knowledge our mind derived from the senses. "Let us not have mental knowledge before us as the goal of the leading", he pleads, as "Understanding is a fallacy and a vice in most people". According to his analyses, "everything vital and dynamic", such as our active desire, love and hope, all generate mysteriously from the body; the mind only plays the function of registering "that which results from the emanation of the dynamic impulse and the collision or communion of this impulse with its object". The mind does not know things by itself, and "we can never know ourselves".[53] Once we know, we come to a dead end.

We find in Taoism the same text: "Not-knowing is a beginning but knowing is an ending. Not-knowing is the uncertainty that permits movement". Along with knowledge, we come to "certainty" and thus come to the end of our quest. Facing the unknown we would move in questions and answers, which brings us freedom. Thus a Taoist believes, "If there was only known, no one could move in the certainty. Proceed from unknown to unknown. Certainty binds, uncertainty frees".54

Lawrence points out that the fact we cannot know ourselves does not mean we should not know anything. The purpose of knowing your self is to be able to "be yourself", "not just for the sake of knowing". "The aim is *not* mental consciousness. We want effectual human beings, not conscious ones. The final aim is not *to know*, but *to be*". Here is his conclusion about "to know" and "to be":

> Yet we *must* know, if only in order to learn not to know. The supreme lesson of human consciousness is to learn how *not to know*. That is how not to *interfere*. That is, how to live dynamically, from the great Source, and not statically, like machines driven by ideas and principles from the head, or automatically, from one fixed desire. At last knowledge must be put into its true place in the living activity of man.55

Yutang Lin, the famous modern Chinese philosopher, when talking about mental pleasures, argues, "All human knowledge comes from sensuous experience. We can no more attain knowledge of any kind without the sense of vision and touch and smell than camera can take pictures without a lens and a sensitive plate".56 He holds that mere thinking is not enough in obtaining the knowledge of life; "one has to feel one's way about—to sense things as they are and to get a correct impression of the myriad things in human life and human nature not as unrelated parts but as a whole".57 Only through this co-operation of the senses, can we gain an intuitive understanding of the world.

Lawrence's interpretation of senses, flesh and mind speaks of the same vision as Yutang Lin's. He writes in the essay "The Lemon Gardens" that the flesh and the senses are "self-conscious. They know their aim. Their aim is in supreme sensation. They seek the maximum of sensation". The mind "subserves the senses" all the time, as it "is submerged, overcome" by the senses. He argues further:

> The senses are the absolute, the god-like. For I can never have another man's senses. These are me, my

senses absolutely me. And all that is can only come to me through my senses. So that all is me, and is administered unto me. The rest, that is not me, is nothing.[58]

It is through all the senses and intuition, or through "feeling", "touching" or the "impulse" of the body that we know the world. He condemns it "wrong" to understand nature by means of pure thought or by the "brain system", which he says is "the tragedy of our life". His perception of this knowledge is clearly indicated in one of his early letters:

Somehow, I think we come into knowledge (unconscious) of the most vital parts of the cosmos through touching things . . . there must be some great purposeful impulses impelling through everything to move it and work it to an end. The world says you feel the press of these impulses, you recognize them, in knowledge—science; but I joining hands with the artists, declare that also and supremely the sympathy with and submission to the great impulses comes through *feeling*—indescribable—and, I think unknowable.[59]

In Lawrence's perspective, the body is the headquarters through which true knowledge from nature is received, while the mind only has a temporary reflection. Moreover, the body has more intense feelings and emotions than the mind:

The body's life is the life of sensations and emotions. The body feels real hunger, real thirst, real joy in the sun or the snow, real pleasure in the smell of roses or the look of a lilac bush; real anger, real sorrow, real love . . . All the emotions belong to the body, and are only recognized by the mind. We may hear the most sorrowful piece of news, and only feel a mental excitement. The hours after, perhaps in sleep, the awareness may reach the bodily centres, and true grief wrings the heart. [60]

In *The Rainbow*, Lawrence describes the body's intense emotional life when one is in love. Tom, realizing his love with the foreign woman Lydia, feels there is "some invisible connection" with her in his body:

A daze had come over his mind, he had another centre of consciousness. In his breast, or in his bowels, somewhere in his body, there had started another activity. It was as if a strong light were burning there, and he was blind within it, unable to know anything, except that this transfiguration burned between him and her, connecting them, like a secret power.[61]

* * *

Lawrence, however, does not ask for a radical elimination of the whole mental consciousness. In *Psychoanalysis and the Unconscious*, Lawrence interprets what the mental consciousness can do for us. Apart from its limitations and drawbacks, it provides us with the means to balance the external universe and ourselves:

> True, we must all develop into mental consciousness. But mental consciousness is not a goal; it is a cul-de-sac. It provides us only with endless appliances which we can use for the all-too-difficult business of coming to our spontaneous-creative fullness of being. It provides us with means to adjust ourselves to the external universe. It gives us further means for subduing the external, material-mechanical universe to our great end of creative life. And it gives us plain indication of how to avoid falling into automatism, hints for the *applying* of the will, the loosening of false, automatic fixations, the brave adherence to a profound soul-impulse. This is the use of the mind—a great indicator and instrument. The mind as author and director of life is anathema.[62]

In *Fantasia of the Unconscious* Lawrence mentions the positive aspects of the mind:

> The business of the mind is first and foremost the pure joy of knowing and comprehending, the pure joy of consciousness. The second business is to act as medium, as interpreter, as agent between the individual and his object. The mind should *not* act as a director or controller of the spontaneous centres. This soul alone must control:

the soul being that forever unknowable reality which causes us to rise into being.[63]

Therefore "any creative act occupies the whole consciousness of a man", not only the 'spiritual-mental' consciousness", but also the instinctive consciousness of the body. Only with "one complete consciousness" can we finally arrive at "a complete truth":

> The truly great discoveries of science and real works of art are made by the whole consciousness of man working together in unison and oneness: instinct, intuition, mind, intellect all fused into one complete consciousness; and grasping what we may call a complete truth.[64]

The complete truth comes from both mind and body, so there should be a balance between the two: "But I stick to my book and my position: Life is only bearable when the mind and body are in harmony, and there is a natural balance between them, and each has a natural respect for the other".[65] Lawrence sometimes talks about the significance of following tradition in one's life, and suggests that we should live by mind and body, as well as tradition: "We *know* we cannot live purely by impulse. Neither can we live solely by tradition. We must live by all three, each in its hour. But the real guide is the pure conscience, the voice of the self in its wholeness, the Holy Ghost".[66]

However, when Lawrence talks about wholeness, he always gives emphasis to the unconscious mind or to one's blood consciousness. On the one hand he is fully aware of the fact that modern culture stresses too much rationality and ideology in the individual's life, so that, for a civilized man, "his head and his spirit have led him wrong", and he is "sadly off the track".[67] On the other hand, he believes that a "full knowledge" mainly comes from the unconscious:

> Knowledge is always a matter of whole experience, what St Paul calls knowing in full, and never a matter of mental conception merely. This is indeed the point of all full knowledge: that it is contained mainly within the unconscious, its mental or conscious reference being only a sort of extract or shadow.[68]

Bergson—one of the greatest Western philosophers, and whose theory Lawrence was familiar with during his formative years—has summarized the functions of the conscious and the unconscious, and the necessity of the development of them both:

> Consciousness, in man, is pre-eminently intellect. It might have been, it ought, so it seems, to have been also intuition. Intuition and intellect represent two opposite directions of the work of consciousness: intuition goes in the very direction of life, intellect goes in the reverse direction, and thus finds itself naturally in accordance with the movement of matter. A complete and perfect humanity would be that in which these two forms of conscious activity should attain their full development.[69]

Bergson's "full development" of the "two forms of conscious activity" speaks of an impartial solution, which should be in no conflict with Lawrence's notion of balance between mind and body, intuition and intellect.

Gregory Bateson, one of the greatest thinkers of our time in the related fields of anthropology, biology and psychiatry, explains the source of one's full knowledge from a different angle. In his *Mind and Nature: A Necessary Unity*, a lifetime's work of more than seventy years, Bateson studied the issue of mind and nature. He found an overall organic "pattern" in receiving a full knowledge. In his theory, as man is part of a living world, all knowledge of the external world he receives is from his immediate environment, including all aspects of nature. LaChapelle in *D. H. Lawrence, Future Primitive* summarizes:

> Bateson's basic premise is that the mental world—the mind—is not limited to our skin. The information coming to us includes all the external pathways along which information travels, such as other minds, light, sound, temperatures, and all aspects of earth and sky. The basic unit of mind is not the rational individual but the relationships between all these aspects.[70]

LaChapelle uses Bateson's theory to justify the effect Lawrence's writing has brought to us. She says the overall picture of his descriptive narrations suggests a powerful vision generated from such comprehensive relationships. The natural elements of the immediate environment surrounding his characters, the smell and texture of the air, the colour and taste of the vegetation, which are generally overlooked or dismissed by some critics as mere scenery, present a strange and haunting power in his descriptive narrations, particularly in *The White Peacock* and his New Mexico stories.[71] This is due to his awareness of the organic oneness of mind, body and nature. The achievement of true knowledge requires a total human being with both his mind and body merging completely with the whole external world. During this process, human consciousness is replaced by a primary, organic, non-moral body.

Alan Watts in his *Man, Woman and Nature* examines the separate functions of the conscious mind and intuitional body. His study shows that human beings' thought is analytic, divisive, and selective. When they become preoccupied with concentrated attentiveness, they cease to notice the mutuality of contrasting "things" and the "identity" of differences. However the fundamental realities of nature are not separate things as we may think. Nature cannot be studied piecemeal; nature is through and through relational. The interrelationship can only be understood by other means than analysis and step-by-step thinking. The right way of knowing is through intuition. As the steps of knowing nature are unconscious, the intuitive body could grasp all fields of related details simultaneously. [72]

Both Bateson and Watts' perceptions justify Lawrence's viewpoint of the organic relationship between mind, body and nature. Lawrence is right in his assertion of the limitations of mind. Decades after his death, medical experiments on the mind suggest that the left and right hemispheres of one's brain process information separately and in a different manner. Ben Willis in his *The Tao of Art*, when studying the oriental way of thinking, points out that the left mind is conceived as the rational. It operates in a verbal manner, and is responsible for reasoning, abstraction, speech, logic and scientific analysis, in which things and events must be handled one at a time and in order. The right hemisphere is intuitional, and many different events can occur all at once. The right mind deals with intuition, imagination, feeling, symbolism, the artistic, the musical, and is spontaneous, non-verbal and synthesis-oriented. The problem is that modern culture stresses too much the rational activity of the left mind. People, having long since admired logic, reason and scientific technology, only trust the rational mind; they dismiss the intuitive mind for its "vaguely unattainable intangibility".[73] It is tragic that, in the history of mankind, intuition has almost completely given way to intellect. Most modern men are living in their intellectual consciousness, which "inhibits the creative process by its own habit and superficiality".[74] So paradoxically, more intellectual consciousness, less genuine creative art can be achieved, as there is no intuitive mediator to transcend intuitive knowledge into genuine creative art.

Lawrence strongly opposes the way children receive their education, which he deems harmful to their "natural intelligence":

> We talk about education—leading forth the natural intelligence of a child. But ours is just the opposite of leading forth. It is a ramming in of brain facts through the head, and a consequent distortion, suffocation, and starvation of the primary centres of consciousness.[75]

The primary centre of consciousness is to Lawrence the unconscious of the body that knows the outer world. He writes in *Fantasia of the Unconscious*, "The child is *not* a little camera. He is a small vital organism which has direct dynamic rapport with the objects of the outer universe".[76] Child development is basically non-mental, and therefore the best and the only way is to "leave him alone"; let them know the world through their own connection with the different elements of nature. He criticises the falsity of pure "verbal and logical abilities" in education, and warns adults not to irrigate "mental knowledge" into a child's innocent mind. "It is a crime to teach a child anything at all, school-wise. It is just evil to collect children together and teach them through the head".[77] Instead, the children should be left alone. "Leave his sensibilities, his emotion, his spirit, and his mind severely alone". [78]

For Edith Cobb, the child's body is a means of knowing when it interacts with the external world. Having traced the roots of genius to a child's relationship with the natural world, Cobb states:

> Body and universe are engaged in some harmoniously integrated ongoing process . . . evoking a passionate response . . .. The exaltation that the child feels is a passionate response to an awareness of his own psychophysical growth potential as a continuity of nature's behaviour.[79]

Joseph Chilton Pearce in his book "Magical Child" foresees that if the early child is forced "to deal prematurely with adult abstract thought", his "ability to think abstractly later on" can be crippled.[80] Likewise Lawrence sees the danger in forcing mental knowledge into a child's head. He argues,

> Education means leading out the individual nature in each man and woman to its true fullness. You can't do that by stimulating the mind . . . Every extraneous idea, which has no intrinsic root in the dynamic consciousness, is as dangerous as a nail driven into a young tree.[81]

The acquisition of "true fullness" needs both conscious and unconscious minds.

* * * *

Instinct or intuition does not mean something in opposition to reason and knowledge. The opposite of reason is unreason; and Lawrence, like any sensible person, is strongly against it. The reason Lawrence emphasises instinct or intuition is because he believes that they are freer, more powerful and more reliable in knowing the unknown reality. Living intuitively means, in Lawrence's words, following one's deepest whole self. "IT being the deepest whole self of man, the self in its wholeness, not idealistic halfness", he writes in his introductory essay "The Spirit of Place", "The deepest self is way down, and the conscious self is an obstinate monkey".[82] Living in this deepest whole self is to him a state of genuine freedom, during which one enjoys integrity and freedom of soul. One is then independent of praise or blame, and of any other worries and conflicts.

Acting in accordance with "the deepest self" is the highest state of freedom in Taoism. "The deepest self" is termed in Laozi's book as "the inner self", which means soul or spirit, the original substance, and hence it has the same nature as Tao. "The inner self is our true self; so in order to realize our true self, we must be willing to live without being dependent upon the opinions of others".[83] Laozi defines the true self as "simplicity" or "Uncarved Block"; it exists in an original, primal state, untouched by the preoccupations of personal life and the limitations of the physical world. Zhuangzi calls this highly spiritual state of man the "Real Self" (elsewhere it is referred to as Zi Ran, literally, the "self-so", or "self suchness", which means natural or spontaneous.) The Way, the Taoist path to fulfilment, is directed to find one's real self and to live in it. This Taoist way of life is simple, detached and impartial, living according to one's intuitive and spontaneous self instead of depending upon the others. This characteristic way of living in Taoism is identical with Lawrence's notion of living in one's deepest whole self and enjoying one's "true, deeper, spontaneous self ". [84]

In Laozi's opinion, "He who wisely devotes himself to being self-sufficient, and therefore does not depend for his happiness upon external ratings by others, is the one best able to set an example for, and to teach and govern, others".[85] Lawrence is surely an example of one who "does not depend for his happiness upon external ratings". He consciously takes responsibility for his own life. He puts the questions to himself: "Am I, like all the others, condemned to submission to the marriage trap and to respectability? Or am I unique? Do I have the courage to break free—to rise above the sad entanglements of a life that has no other purpose than survival?"[86] It is this independent and unconventional point of view that accounts for his courage to answer his "deepest desire" to marry Frieda, a German aristocrat, a woman who in every aspect is so different from himself. In the story "Daughters of the Vicar", Lawrence is actually hailing his father's spontaneous selfhood, which seems "blind stupidity" at his time: "He saw some collier lurching straight forward without misgiving, pursuing his own satisfactions, and he envied him. Anything, he would have given for this spontaneity and this blind stupidity which went to its own satisfaction direct".[87] For this "way of living"—to be truly living "through our instincts and our intuitions"—Lawrence meets much misinterpretation and even hostility.

In accordance with his unconventional preference for the spontaneous way of living, Lawrence claims "all I want is to answer to my blood, direct, without fribbling intervention of mind". His desire arouses from his deepest belief that creative originality only springs from imagination, from blood knowledge, instead of from mental knowledge. So he admires the unconscious quality in artists and novelists.

His proposition of unconscious creativity contains the spirit of Wu Wei. In Taoist Wu Wei, it is highly recommended to reach the state of "suspending the will, reducing egoist extremes of unrest and possession, and the stilling of the interfering rational process".[88] Only from this mental stillness, from the non-action of the mind, can Taoist sages achieve intuitional enlightenment. The total stillness of the rational mind generates spontaneously intuitive creation in one's artwork. When one's rational mind does not interfere, the self is liberated and develops a very high level of integrity in creative art. The artist achieves this high level often in an unconscious way and with little effort. Lawrence's experience is a very good example in revealing the advantages of following one's intuition while producing imaginative art. In *Fantasia of the Unconscious* Lawrence describes his way of writing:

> It's *no good* looking at a tree to know it. The only thing is to sit among the roots and nestle against its strong trunk, and *not bother*. That's how I write all about these planes and plexuses—between the toes of a tree, forgetting myself against the great ankle of the trunk. And then as a rule, as a squirrel is stroked into its wickedness by the faceless magic of a tree, so am I usually stroked into *forgetfulness*, and into scribbling this book. My tree-book, really.[89]

In this text, we find a striking resemblance between his way of writing and the way of traditional Chinese artists. Simply "sit between the toes . . . forgetting myself" is his spontaneous way of writing. His description is seemingly paradoxical: how could he be at once "stroked into forgetfulness" and "into scribbling this book". The forgetfulness here means the very lack of self-consciousness, eliminating various external interferences and concentrating on writing. Lawrence writes, "I lose myself among the trees. I am so glad to be with them in their silent, intent passion, and their great lust. They feel my soul".[90] The spiritual unity he is experiencing gives his writings intuitional enlightenment. Forgetting or ignoring the complicated ideas coming forth to his rational mind while writing in his unconsciousness, he actually reaches a state of inner peace and complete freedom. In art and creativity, this freedom is possible when the self is undergoing the same "forgetfulness" of the rational mind.

Lawrence's "not bother" attitude echoes Taoist non-attachment. In Zen Buddhism, we also find a similar freedom in the practice of Zen's "silent contemplation". While writing his book without strenuous thinking, Lawrence is actually following Zen's teaching of "feeling without thinking", or looking at nature, staring subject, without thinking in the sense of narrowed attention. A Zen Buddhist believes, when writing or painting, the sensation of the ego or the effort of consciousness is unnecessary, it could only result in a state of confusion. According to Alan Watts' analysis, the practices of seeking, staring, and straining one's mind use more energy than is necessary to think, see, hear, or make decisions. These efforts are as futile as trying to leap into the air and fly. Lawrence does not stare hard at the tree in order to know it, to write it. Instead, he resorts to his feelings, and the spontaneous flow of feeling enables him to scribble his book in a manner of "forgetfulness". Lawrence's "not bother" (when one is writing) also matches the Taoist "Wu Nian" or "Wu Xin" meaning "no-thought" or better "no second thought". It is a psychological practice of free association, a kind of technique to get rid of obstacles preventing the free flow of thought from the unconscious. No thought or no strained contemplation should be employed to "block" the individual's natural organism that performs the most complex activities. One should "not bother" to make conscious efforts in writing books, because conscious efforts are not necessarily helpful. Being natural and spontaneous is the prerequisite of creativity, which, as understood by the Taoists, reflects the most fundamental laws of nature. This "nonthinking mode of awareness" is, as Watts argues, the only way that guarantees achievement of an "effortless, spontaneous, and sudden dawning of a realization".

Watts finds the same mode of thinking—a Taoist principle of "using no-knowledge to attain knowledge" -- employed in the most important scientific insights, or intuitions, and also recognized and practiced in the West. Watts' further elaborates: "For the most creative research, men of science must be trusted and encouraged to let their minds wander unsystematically without any pressure for results".[91] So the most creative advances in science and scholarly research are brought forth precisely through inexplicable intuitional leaps. Einstein's enlightenment leading to his theory of relativity and Newton's discovery of gravity are undoubtedly to a great extend due to their unconscious, unsystematic mode of thinking, as is Lawrence's own experience in writing his "tree-book". This spontaneous way of thinking is productive and imaginative in Lawrence's "thought adventure". Here is a poem written by Seng-ts'an about his interview with Hui-k'o.[92] It illustrates Taoist principles of Wu Wei and spontaneity, letting one's mind alone and trusting it to follow its own nature:

> Follow your nature and accord with the Tao;
> Saunter along and stop worrying,
> If your thoughts are tied you spoil what is genuine . . .
> Don't be antagonistic to the world of the senses,
> For when you are not antagonistic to it,
> It turns out to be the same as complete awakening.
> The wise person does not strive (Wu Wei);
> The ignorant man ties himself up . . .
> If you work on your mind with your mind,
> How can you avoid an immense confusion? [93]

Lawrence is always criticised for a lack of form in his imaginative works. His friend J. M. Murry writes in *Sons of Women* that Lawrence's greatness is attributed to the fact that "at bottom he was not concerned with art":

> He gave up, deliberately, the pretence of being an artist. The novel became for him simply a means by which he could make explicit his own 'thought-adventures' . . . To charge him with a lack of form, or of other of the qualities

which are supposed to be necessary to art, is to be guilty of irrelevance. Art was not Lawrence's aim. [94]

Murry is obviously wrong in saying Lawrence "was not a great artist".[95] Though he is wrong in his judgement, which has been under attack by some other authoritative critics such as Keith Sagar and F. R. Leavis, one point he is certainly right is that Lawrence does not particularly care about forms, and the novel is "simply a means by which he could make explicit his own 'thought-adventures'". It is true, there are no consistent forms for his novels. Some are superbly constructed such as *Women in Love*; some are rambling and almost formless such as *Kangaroo*, a full-length novel written within six weeks during his visit to Australia. So long as the form is appropriate and convenient for him to launch his "thought-adventures", it is employed regardless of any literary conventions of the time. So Murry's view that "at bottom he was not concerned with art" or form, is not groundless. Lawrence himself, believing in a spontaneous way of writing, is happy to "get rid of the stereotyped" artificial forms:

> We can get rid of the stereotyped movements and the old hackneyed association of sound or sense. We can break down those artificial conduits and canals through which we do so love to force our utterance. We can break the stiff neck of habit. We can be in ourselves spontaneous and flexible as flame, we can see that utterance rushes out without artificial form or artificial smoothness.[96]

His writing is characteristically quick, spontaneously reflective and fluid like running water murmuring with his own emphatic voices. Graham Hough's comment is revealing: "It is true that most of Lawrence's consummate successes are in immediate intuition, and that the shifting kaleidoscopic pattern of his intuitions must always be a richer thing than any fixed doctrine that could be deduced from it".[97] Lawrence's principle of writing undoubtedly rejects the arbitrary rules of a sophisticated world. His way of writing the tree-book is exactly the same as the "method of no-method" in the characteristic Tao-painting:

The spontaneous reflection from one's inner reality, unbound by arbitrary rules from without and undistorted by confusion and limitation from within. In this spontaneous reflection one's potentialities are set free and great creativity is achieved without artificial effort. This method of no-method in painting is the application of Taoist philosophy.[98]

Lawrence considers forms and rhythms of poetry to be "arbitrary rules from without". His desire to create as little distance as possible between the reader and the felt experience leads him eventually to abandon rhyming quatrains altogether. In early 1914, Lawrence had an argument with Edward Marsh (editor of the collected Georgian poems, and later war time secretary of Winston Churchill) over poetic form and technique which lasted for five months. He disliked Marsh's suggestion regarding improvement in the forms and rhythms he constantly used in his poems. When writing poetry, he shows little regard for the rules, preferring to see the rhythm as natural images: "when I think of meter, I think more of a bird with broad wings flying and lapsing through the air, than anything". He further explains, "It all depends on the pause—the natural pause, the natural lingering of the voice according to the feeling—it is the hidden emotional pattern that makes poetry, not the obvious form".[99] In an earlier letter, he wrote to Marsh: "I don't think, don't you know, that my rhythms fit my mood very well, in the verse . . . I have always tried to get an emotion out in its own course, without altering it. It needs the finest instinct imaginable, much finer than the skill of craftsmen".[100] Lawrence's writing philosophy is in fact the application of Taoist philosophy of Wu Wei and spontaneity.

What Lawrence believes in is the necessity of a commitment to pure expression and a rejection of restraint. He wrote many letters and articles in defense of his own art of writing. He argues that, while writing, if we are "thinking and feeling at the same time, we do not think rationally". So he insists that,

The free verse . . . is or should be the direct utterance from the instant, whole man. It is the soul and the mind and body surging at once, nothing left out. They speak all together. There is some confusion, some discord. But the confusion and discord only belong to the reality, as noise belongs to the plunge of water.[101]

Lawrence's overall approach in writing poetry naturally allows "more looseness", and even "formlessness". He says, "We need an apparent formlessness, definite form is mechanical".[102] The usual form, being just the medium to carry art, is not that important and even "wants smashing". Lawrence's wife Frieda is the first to understand Lawrence's "revolutionary" experiment of new form for his art, as she explains to Garnett in 1912:

> I have heard so much about 'form' with Ernest; why are you English so keen on it? Their own form wants smashing in almost any direction, but they can't come out of their snail-house. I know it's so much safer. That's what I love Lawrence for, that he is so plucky and honest in his work, he dares to come out into the open and plants his stuff down bald and naked; really he is the only revolutionary worthy of the name, that I know; any new thing must find a new shape, then afterwards one can call it 'art'.[103]

Here is a free-soul Lawrence who lives and writes with his intuition. He refuses to be kept inside the "snail-house" of preconceived form, and is free of limitations and all literary rules. Without this attitude to writing, it would be unlikely that Lawrence could have produced such an amount of literary works in so many forms and genres over such a short life.

* * * * *

Lawrence's belief in intuition or blood-consciousness does not mean his achievements spring purely from his own creation, or have nothing to do with the influence of tradition. On the contrary, he is to a great degree assimilative of the ideas, techniques and styles from the books of his Romantic predecessors as well as his contemporaries. Jessie said of him that he "seemed to consider all his philosophical reading from the angle of his own personal need".[104] Harold Bloom's *The Anxiety of Influence* places Lawrence among the "great deniers of influence", which is effectively refuted by the overwhelming evidence in J. Meyers' *D. H. Lawrence and*

Tradition. The literary influence of the major writers during and before his time could not only be traced in his style, structure, theme and technique, but also in the aesthetics, psychology and philosophy of his work. Lawrence himself admits that he has taken suggestions from "all kinds of scholarly books, from the Yoga and Plato and St. John the Evangelist and the early Greek philosophers like Herakleitos down to Fraser and his *Golden Bough,* and even Freud and Frobenius".[105] But his way of absorbing knowledge is free of sole mental consciousness, as he tells us that he remembers only hints, and proceeds by intuition. And the reader is told that he is free to put aside this "whole wordy mass of revolting nonsense, without a qualm".[106]

In answering the question of "what the unconscious actually is", Lawrence writes in his *Psychoanalysis and the Unconscious*:

> It is that active spontaneity which rouses in each individual organism at the moment of fusion of the parent nuclei, and which, in polarized connection with the external universe, gradually evolves or elaborates its own individual psyche and corpus, bringing both mind and body forth from itself. Thus it would seem that the term *unconscious* is only another word for life . . . Thus it is that the unconscious brings forth not only consciousness, but tissue and organs also . . . And consciousness is like a web woven finally in the mind from the various silken strands spun forth from the primal centre of the unconscious.[107]

He emphasises, "the unconscious is never an abstraction, *never to be abstracted*". It can be dealt with "quite tangibly" through tracing "its source and centres in the great ganglia and nodes of the nervous system".[108] This knowledge of the unconscious and its centres comes from James M. Pryse, who is a theosophist, and whose work *The Apocalypse Unsealed* inspired Lawrence in his understanding of Yoga.[109] In Yoga the body is divided into seven chakras, each of them is homologous with various aspects of the cosmos. In other words, aspects of human beings' bodies are polarized with fixed aspects of the universe. The veins of the heels are polarized to the centre of the earth. The blood itself is polarized to the moon and at the same time akin to the sea. Man's chest is polarized with the sun, the constant luminary. Thus, suspended between sun and moon, man lives in constant vital touch with the two heavenly bodies, and is meanwhile polarized to the stability of the earth centre. The practice of Yoga is to maintain a suitable circulation of energies within the individual through correspondent nerve centres (chakras) in order to communicate with the various aspects of the cosmos. Lawrence writes in *Psychoanalysis and the Unconscious*, "Having begun to explore the unconscious, we find we must go from centre to centre, chakra to chakra, to use an old esoteric word".[110] Lawrence here borrows Pryse's description of seven chakras, but only adopts four of them.

Lawrence's version of the nervous system is based upon a fourfold polarity that occurs below the neck in the unconscious. The unconscious has four principle centres and is divided by the diaphragm into two levels: a lower dark-dynamic with the centres of the solar plexus and the lumbar ganglion, and an upper objective dynamic level with the cardiac plexus and the thoracic ganglion in the breast.[111] The lower set of centres located in the solar plexus is to him the "subjective" set, and is identified with the sensual will. The "objective", "higher" set located in and around the chest is made up of a complex of nerves that serve the love-function. Among all the centres, Lawrence stresses, the solar plexus is "the greatest and most important centre of our dynamic consciousness". It is "The first seat of our primal consciousness" or "the deepest seat of awareness", in which "the root of all knowledge and being is established".[112]

Though his theory does sound nonsensical, Lawrence is trying to use these mystical or theosophical terms to clarify his own thinking of psychic realities, such as in the field of love and sexuality. His Hindu friend Earl Brewster, upon receiving the copy of his *Psychoanalysis and the Unconscious*, immediately knew it is an interpretation, "by a genius", of the ancient Hindu idea of the chakras. Frederick Carter—of whose book *The Dragon of Revelation* Lawrence wrote a review, which led to his last book *Apocalypse*—points out that Lawrence has found his seven centres in some American book on the Vedanta.[113] Lawrence's theory of the great nerve-system implies his embrace of Eastern philosophy, not only Hindu Yoga, but also Chinese Tai Qi and Japanese Aikedo (boxing). The solar plexus, which "lies in the middle front of the abdomen, beneath the navel", is to him the most important nerve centre, an unconscious media linking his body to the external universe. He mentioned the solar plexus on many occasions, and greatly surprised his friends. Rhys Davies in his essay "D. H. Lawrence in Bandol" writes about a dialogue between himself and Lawrence. Lawrence tells him, "When you have come to a decision, whatever your mental calculations tell you, go by what you feel here", then "with his quick intent gesture he placed his hands over and around his belly—'go by that, what you feel deep in you, not by what your head tells you'". [114]When he first meets Brewster, Lawrence advises him not to be governed by the centre between the eyebrows but rather by the centre of the solar plexus.[115] Lawrence regards this lower body centre as one's deepest life, a source for issuing power and achieving equilibrium. He says to Brewster:

> We should not pass beyond suffering: but you can find the power to endure, and equilibrium and a kind of bliss, if you will return to the deepest life within yourself. Can't you rest in the actuality of your own being? Look deep into the centre—to your solar plexus.[116]

Lawrence believes there is in one's lower centre "a true dynamic psychic activity" which "means a dynamic polarity ... between him and his immediate surroundings, human, physical, geographical".[117] He repeatedly emphasizes in his writing that in this polar plexus "you are triumphantly aware of your own individual existence in the universe", as there is "the keep and central stronghold of your triumphantly-conscious self". He remarks playfully in *Fantasia of the Unconscious,* "Let us pronounce the mystic Om, from the pit of the stomach, and proceed . . ."[118] Lady Asquith has a feeling that it seems to her as if Lawrence's "body thought". She recalls that he thought "with his solar plexus rather than with his brain", and he seemed to have a "strange perceptive sense of his own, which made it possible for him to probe into elements in a hidden world lying beyond the range of others".[119] The "strange perceptive sense" obviously comes from his solar plexus, instead of from his brain. Richard Aldington, when analyzing Lawrence's "Last Poems", writes playfully about his nerve consciousness, "It seems to me that nearly all these Pansies and Nettles came out of Lawrence's nerves, and not out of his real self".[120]

Lawrence's interest and belief in the solar plexus invited more ridicules from Western critics than any of his other views. However, Lawrence's stress on the solar plexus is not incomprehensible at all for an Eastern mind if we turn our attention towards Eastern traditional belief. This "other brain" is called "Hara" in Japanese, "Dian Tian" in Chinese, and is located in that particular plexus, a little below the navel inside one's belly. Through exercises and practices, this spot can open to the external world and receive energy from the universe. This is a particular centre of awareness, which is so precise that it can register the emotions of those nearby, as well as sense danger from behind, or even from beyond. It has the function of balancing the energy flow between mind and body, between the self and the external world. The study of man's physical functions has proved that "there was considerable reflexive automatic spinal control of movement from the lower spinal area, in that the reflexes for some tasks went only between the spine and the lower extremities and not through the central brain process at all", as explained by Dolores LaChapelle.[121] The power of this lower area also accounts for the incredible ability of the Japanese Aikido (boxing) in anticipating attacks from every side at the same time.

This solar plexus has some vivid expressions in Chinese traditional language and culture. It is the very spot through which we not only breathe or exhale (in Tai Qi exercise for instance), but also feel and think. The Chinese seem to think always with emotion and rarely with their analytic reason of the mind. It is no mere accident that the Chinese traditionally regard the belly (or solar plexus) as the seat of all their scholarship and learning, as in the expressions of "a bellyful of essays" or "a bellyful of scholarship". Since no one thinks completely without emotion and the belly is the seat of our emotions, the more emotional the type of thinking, the more responsible the intestines are for one's thoughts. While in English we say a man "ransacks his brain" for ideas in writing a composition, we say in Chinese he "ransacks his dry intestines" for a good line of poetry or prose. The belly plays the function of "warm heartedness", so we have the old saying as "warm intestines" denoting warm-heartedness. In the Chinese way of thinking, the broad minded and the narrow minded are also associated with one's belly, as the saying goes, "Big (or small) belly tolerance". When one is full of pent-up anger, the anger should fill one's belly instead of one's heart. To put it plainly "How could I know what is going on in his mind?" is obviously less affective than the Chinese saying, "Am I a tapeworm in his belly?" Hence the belly (Lawrence's solar plexus) is regarded in Chinese as a representative of the body, and is equivalent to the central nerve of consciousness that is able to think, to know and to feel.

In *Aaron's Rod*, Lawrence mentions the power at the base of the spine. In the essay "The Lemon Gardens", he talks about the spirit and will of the soldier and Italian, who "walks with his consciousness concentrated at the base of the spine, his mind subjugated, submerged".[122] His hero Birkin in *Women in Love* realizes what it is to have this magical, mystical force along his backbone. The spiritual exercise Don Ramon performs in *The Plumed Serpent* suggests the inspiration he receives is from the "mindless" Yoga. Ramon's sermon mentions the nerves' connection with the sky and the earth, claiming the "earth has kissed my knees, and put strength in my belly".[123] When he is filling his mind with the darkness of the room, and concentrating with the unconscious fashion of Yoga, Ramon feels "the dark fecundity of the inner tide washing over his heart, over his belly, his mind dissolved away in the greater, dark mind, which is undisturbed by thoughts". Ramon's belly can feel and has emotion. He feels that his wife Carlota is to him a torture: "She seemed to have the power still to lacerate him, inside his bowels. Not in his mind or spirit, but in his old emotional, passional self: right in the middle of his belly, to tear him and make him feel he bled inwardly".[124] As a serpent is coiling at the base of the spine, the initiated man like Cipriano has the strange power in his spine, and is able to control the sleeping or walking serpent in the bellies of men. Pryse's esoteric vision lends inspiration to Lawrence's *Apocalypse* and his *Fantasia of the Unconscious*. Lawrence emphasises time and again that "the sun itself is the soul of the inanimate universe". What really sustains the sun is not just the dead, but also "the dynamic relation between the solar plexus of individuals and the sun's core, a perfect circuit". Lawrence visualizes a dynamic relationship between the sun, the moon and our human body. "We live between the polarized circuit of sun and moon", he imagines, the sun is polarized with "the solar plexus of individuals", while "the moon is polarized with the lumbar ganglion, primarily, in man. Sun and moon are dynamically polarized to our actual tissue, they affect this tissue all the time".[125] From the oriental knowledge, we come to comprehend Lawrence's assertion that it is the lower, dark centres of the human body—the solar plexus and the lumbar ganglion—that are polarized with the whole universe. When the lower centres combine with our mental consciousness, we have our individual life and gain an overall understanding and feeling of reality.

Lawrence's reverence for body and intuitive life, his rejection of reason, materialism, science, and other mechanical things of our civilization are of the same core as that of primitivism, which will be dealt with in my next chapter, "Primitivism and Theosophy".

[1] D. H. Lawrence, *Fantasia of the Unconscious and Psychoanalysis and the Unconscious*, p. 212.

[2] Daniel J. Schneider, *The Consciousness of D. H. Lawrence*, p. 50.

[3] Ibid., p. 51

[4] Ibid., p. 57.

[5] According to Jessie Chambers, Lawrence read his books and began to talk about Nietzsche's ideas after going to Croydon. Among the books he read are *The Will to Power, The Gay Science*, and *Thus Spoke Zarathustra*, to which Lawrence's thought corresponds closely and on many counts.

[6] F. Nietzsche, *A Nietzsche Reader*, p. 163, quoted in Daniel J. Schneider, *The Consciousness of D. H. Lawrence*, p. 58.

[7] D. H. Lawrence, "Insouciance", in *Selected Essays*, p. 106.

[8] F. Nietzsche, *A Nietzsche Reader*, p. 66, quoted in Daniel J. Schneider, *The Consciousness of D. H. Lawrence*, p. 58.

[9] *The Collected Letters of D. H. Lawrence*, Harry T. Moore, ed., Vol. I, p. 180.

[10] Kim A. Herzinger, *D. H. Lawrence in His Time: 1908—1915*, p. 177.

[11] *The Collected Letters of D. H. Lawrence*, Harry T. Moore, ed., Vol. I, p. 367.

[12] Ibid., p. 393.

[13] Bertrand Russell, "Portraits from Memory—III: D. H. Lawrence", quoted in Dolores LaChappelle, *D. H. Lawrence, Future Primitive*, p. 83.

[14] John Maynard Keynes, *Two Memoirs*, pp. 101, 103, quoted in Dolores LaChappelle, *D. H. Lawrence, Future Primitive*, pp. 84-5.

[15] D. H. Lawrence, *A Propos of Lady Chatterley's Lover*, in *D. H. Lawrence, A Selection from Phoenix*, pp. 334-5.

[16] *The Collected Letters of D. H. Lawrence*, Harry T. Moore, ed., Vol. I, p. 362.

[17] D. H. Lawrence, *Lady Chatterley's Lover*, Ch. 4, p. 40.

[18] Quoted in Daniel J. Schneider, *The Consciousness of D. H. Lawrence*, p. 59.

[19] D. H. Lawrence, "Love", *Phoenix*, p. 153.

[22] F. R. Leavis, *D. H. Lawrence: Novelist*, p. 111.

[23] Chaman Nahal, *D. H. Lawrence: An Eastern View*, p. 145.

[24] D. H. Lawrence, *The Rainbow*, Ch. 2, p. 54.

[25] Chaman Nahal, *D. H. Lawrence : An Eastern View*, p. 148.

[26] D. H. Lawrence, *Aaron's Rod*, p. 344.

[27] Eliseo Vivas, *D. H. Lawrence, The Failure and the Triumph of Art*, p. 44.

[28] D. H. Lawrence, *Kangaroo*, p. 278.

[29] D. H. Lawrence, *A Propos of Lady Chatterley's Lover*, in *D. H. Lawrence, A Selection from Phoenix*, p. 343.

[30] Earl and Achsah Brewster, *D. H. Lawrence: Reminiscences and Correspondence*, p. 276.

[31] Ben Willis, *The Tao of Art*, p. 35.

[32] D. H. Lawrence, *Studies in Classic American Literature*, p. 91.

[33] Ibid., p. 92.

[34] Ibid., p. 169.

[35] D. H. Lawrence, *St. Mawr* in *St. Mawr and Other Stories*, p. 36.

[36] Ibid., pp. 50, 36, 42, 40, 42, 36.

[37] *Lawrence on Hardy and Painting*, J. V. Davies, ed., p. 129.

[38] Ibid., pp. 130, 134.

[39] Ibid., pp. 134, 137.

[40] Ibid., pp. 152, 147, 146.

[41] Ibid., pp. 138, 140, 160, 134.

[42] Hokuseido, *Zen in English Literature and Oriental Classics*, p. 117.

[43] D. H. Lawrence, "Education of the People", *Phoenix*, p. 629.

[44] Ibid., p. 64.

[45] D. H. Lawrence, *The Woman Who Rode Away*, in *The Woman Who Rode Away and Other Stories*, p. 76.

[46] D. H. Lawrence, " . . .Love Was Once a Little Boy", in *Reflections on the Death of a Porcupine and Other Essays*, p. 334.

47 D. H. Lawrence, *Fantasia of the Unconscious and Psychoanalysis and the Unconscious*, p. 210.

48 D. H. Lawrence, *Apocalypse*, p. 168.

49 D. H. Lawrence, *Aaron's Rod*, p. 326.

50 D. H. Lawrence, *Fantasia of the Unconscious* and *Psychoanalysis and the Unconscious*, p. 246.

51 Ibid., pp. 64, 207, 65.

52 Ibid., pp. 29, 68.

53 Ibid., pp. 89, 72.

54 Ray Grigg, *The Tao of Being*, p. 21.

55 D. H. Lawrence, *Fantasia of the Unconscious and Psychoanalysis and the Unconscious*, p. 64.

56 Yutang Lin, *The Importance of Living*, p. 135.

57 Ibid, p. 135.

58 D. H. Lawrence, "The Lemon Gardens", in *Twilight in Italy*, pp. 42-3.

59 *The Letters of D. H. Lawrence*, James T. Boulton, ed., Vol. I, p. 99.

60 D. H. Lawrence, *A Propos of Lady Chatterley's Love, in D. H. Lawrence, A Selection from Phoenix*, p. 334.

61 D. H. Lawrence, *The Rainbow*, Ch. 1, p. 38.

62 Ibid., p. 248.

63 Ibid., p. 130.

64 *Lawrence on Hardy and Painting*, J. V. Davies, ed., pp.151-2.

65 D. H. Lawrence, *A Propos of Lady Chatterley's Lover*, in *D. H. Lawrence, A Selection from Phoenix*, p. 333.

66 D. H. Lawrence, *Fantasia of the Unconscious and Psychoanalysis and the Unconscious*, p. 131.

67 Ibid., p. 732.

68 Ibid., p. 211.

69 Henri Bergson, *Creative Evolution*, p. 291.

70 Dolores LaChapelle, *D. H. Lawrence, Future Primitive*, p. 93.

71 Ibid., pp. 93-4.

72 Alan Watts, *Nature, Man and Woman*, pp. 51-69.

73 Ben Willis, *The Tao of Art*, p. 33.

74 Ibid., p. 143.

75 D. H. Lawrence, *Fantasia of the Unconscious and Psychoanalysis and the Unconscious*, p. 89.

76 Ibid., p. 87.

77 Ibid., p. 88.

78 D. H. Lawrence, "Education of the People", *Phoenix*, p. 620.

79 Edith Cobb, *The Ecology of Imagination in Childhood*, pp. 32-3.

80 Joseph Chilton Pearce, *Magical Child*, p. 27.

81 D. H. Lawrence, *Fantasia of the Unconscious and Psychoanalysis and the Unconscious*, pp. 72-3.

82 D. H. Lawrence, *Studies in Classic American Literature*, p. 13.

83 Laozi, *Dao De Jing*, Archie J. Bahm, ed., Ch. 13, p. 20.

[84] D. H. Lawrence, "Democracy", *Phoenix,* p. 710.

[85] Laozi, *Dao De Jing,* Archie J. Bahm, ed., Ch. 13, p. 20.

[86] Daniel J. Schneider, *The Consciousness of D. H. Lawrence: An Intellectual Biography,* pp. 52-3.

[87] D. H. Lawrence, "Daughters of the Vicar", in *The Collected Short Stories of D. H. Lawrence,* p. 154.

[88] Ben Willis, *The Tao of Art,* p. 69.

[89] D. H. Lawrence, *Fantasia of the Unconscious and Psychoanalysis and the Unconscious,* p. 38.

[90] Ibid., pp. 38-9.

[91] Ibid., p. 67.

[92] Hui-k'o (about 486-593), Chinese Zen master , disciple of Indian monk Bodhidharma (about d. 520.), the second Patriarch of Zen in China. Seng-ts'an (d. 606), the successor to Hui-k'o.

[93] Quoted in Alan Watts, *The Way of Zen,* p. 89.

[94] J. M. Murry, *D. H. Lawrence: Son of Woman,* p. 173.

[95] Ibid., p.174.

[96] D. H. Lawrence, "Prefaces and Introductions to Books", *Phoenix,* p. 221.

[97] Graham Hough, *The Dark Sun,* p. 218.

[98] Ben Willis, *The Tao of Art,* p. 55.

[99] *The Letters of D. H. Lawrence,* Aldous Huxley, ed., pp. 154-5.

[100] Ibid., p. 135.

[101] D. H. Lawrence, "Prefaces and Introductions to Books", *Phoenix,* pp. 220-1.

[102] D. H. Lawrence, "Translator's Preface to Cavalleria Rusticana", in *D. H. Lawrence, A Selection from Phoenix,* p. 264.

[103] Frieda's letter to Ernest Garnett in Sept. 1912, quoted in Keith Sagar, *The Art of D. H. Lawrence,* p. 43.

[104] Chambers Jessie, *D. H. Lawrence: A Personal Record,* p. 113.

[105] *The Collected Letters of D. H. Lawrence,* Harry T. Moore, ed., Vol. I, p. 184.

[106] Ibid., p. 184.

[107] D. H. Lawrence, *Fantasia of the Unconscious and Psychoanalysis and the Unconscious,* p. 241.

[108] Ibid., pp. 241-2.

[109] William Y. Tindall, *D. H. Lawrence & Susan His Cow,* pp. 150-1.

[110] D. H. Lawrence, *Fantasia of the Unconscious and Psychoanalysis and the Unconscious,* p. 90.

[111] Lawrence writes at length about the nerve system in both his psychological writings: "Fantasia of the Unconscious", and "Psychoanalysis and the Unconscious". It is the lower solar plexus, contrary to the upper cardiac plexus, that I intend to draw the similarities to the oriental belief.

[112] D. H. Lawrence, *Fantasia of the Unconscious and Psychoanalysis and the Unconscious,* pp. 22, 29.

[113] Frederick Carter, *D. H. Lawrence and the Body Mystical,* p. 25.

[114] Rhys Davies, "D. H. Lawrence in Bandol", quoted in Dolores Chapelle, *D. H. Lawrence, Future Primitive,* p. 98.

[115] Earl Brewster and Achsah Brewster, *D. H. Lawrence: Reminiscences and Correspondence*, p. 18. Here Lawrence refers to the traditional "Third Eye" between the eyebrows in Hinduism and Buddhism. But he ignores it.

[116] Edward Nehls, *D. H. Lawrence: A Composite Biography*, Vol. II. p. 60.

[117] D. H. Lawrence, *Fantasia of the Unconscious and Psychoanalysis and the Unconscious*, p. 55.

[118] Ibid., pp. 22, 14.

[119] Cynthia Asquith, *Remember and Be Glad*, pp. 144, 189.

[120] Richard. Aldington, "Introduction to Last Poems", *The Complete Poems of D. H. Lawrence*, Vivian de Sola Pinto, ed., p. 595.

[121] Dolores LaChapelle, *D. H. Lawrence, Future Primitive*, p. 99.

[122] D. H. Lawrence, "The Lemon Gardens", in *Twilight in Italy*, p. 43.

[123] D. H. Lawrence, *The Plumed Serpent*, p. 211.

[124] Ibid., pp. 205, 219.

[125] D. H. Lawrence, *Fantasia of the Unconscious and Psychoanalysis and the Unconscious*, pp. 150-1.

Chapter VIII

Primitivism and Theosophy

*

Lawrence's novels are filled with contempt for modern industrial civilization, which in his view has poisoned all phases of human life, from politics and arts to personal relationships. The ugly industrial surroundings he describes in *Sons and Lovers*, *The Rainbow*, and *Lady Chatterley's Lover* not only spoil the landscape, but also degrade human beings by destroying man's spontaneous, organic value. He writes in a letter, expressing his dislike of the modern world, saying, "I am feeling absolutely at an end with the civilized world. It makes me sick at the stomach". [1] He has a strong desire to change that filthy, unclean world. Men must gather "with one accord in purity of spirit", must pull down London and "build up a beautiful thing". [2] There must be "a new heaven and a new earth, a clear, eternal moon above, and a clean world below. So it will be". [3] In a letter to Lady Cynthia Asquith in November 1915, he cursed the corruption of the existing society that must be cleansed away:

> It is a great thing to realize that the original world is still there—perfectly clean and pure. . . .
> It is this mass of unclean world that we have super-imposed on the clean world that we cannot bear. When I looked back, out of the clearness of the open evening, at this Littlehampton dark and amorphous like a bad eruption on the edge of the land, I was so sick I felt I

could not come back: all these little, amorphous houses like an eruption, a disease on the clean earth: and of them full of such a diseased spirit, every landlady harping on her money, her furniture, every visitor harping on his latitude of escape from money and furniture: The whole thing like an active disease, fighting out the health . . . It is a dragon that has devoured us all: these obscene, scaly houses, this insatiable struggle and desire to possess, to possess always and in spite of everything, this need to be an owner, lest one be owned. It is too horrible . . . One feels a sort of madness come over one, as if the world had become hell . . . It can be cleaned away.[4]

Since industrial civilization and modern man are unbearable, one of the positive alternatives Lawrence believes is to restore the long since banished primitive cultures. Criticism of industrial civilization did not, of course, originate with Lawrence; there are numerous precedents in nineteenth-century literature. However, as Raymond Williams points out, "This observation has to be made again and again" in order to "shift the ugliness and evil of industrialism out of the present, back into the 'bad old days'".[5]

The modern hopeless world can be reborn, Lawrence holds, only by a fusion with the primitive past, by a return to the living worshipful universe of early man. Through his descriptions of bucolic countryside life and primitive cultures against the civilized industrial world, Lawrence expresses his esteem for the virtue, wisdom and innocence of natural man, the peasant and gamekeeper for instance. William Y. Tindall points out in *D. H. Lawrence & Susan His Cow* that the recovery of the natural world of those savage men becomes a thematic thread running through the most of Lawrence's later essays and novels. He calls Lawrence "the most conspicuous primitivist of our times", for he "turned to the savage as the embodiment of instinct, feeling, spirit, intuition, all that nature had given mankind, all that civilization had destroyed".[6]For Lawrence, primitive people in many aspects have set examples to modern people in their living style and life philosophy, such as their instinctive way of thinking and living. Though, naturally, their primitive philosophy is due to their absence of ideology, the machine and science, in their religion Lawrence sees sanity and reverence for nature and life, which correspond to his own belief in the health and wholeness of human existence.

Going back to the primitive consciousness means back to that religious closeness to nature, to that communion with the sun, the earth and the flowers enjoyed by ancient man; it also means leading forward, picking up again the natural power and glory from the old societies of the Egyptians, Etruscans, Hindus and Mexican Indians. In a letter to J. M. Murry, Lawrence points out:

> Anyhow, though England may lead the world again, as you say, she's got to find a way first. She's got to pick up a lost trail. And the end of the lost trail is here in Mexico. The Englishman, per se, is not enough. He has to modify himself to a distant end. He has to balance with something that is not himself.[7]

Lawrence's assertions about the balance between mind and body, consciousness and unconsciousness, are his way of reviving the qualities of ancient man. The recovery of those qualities "destroyed" by the modern white men, he believes, can save them from their decadent civilization. It becomes his prolonged effort to furnish modern men's minds with primitive modes of thought and feeling. In an article written in 1922 for the *New York Times* Lawrence tries to arouse interest in Indian aboriginal spirit and culture as a creative influence that could shape the future of a new world:

> The Indians keep burning an eternal fire, the sacred fire of the old dark religion. To the vast white America, either in our generation or in time of our children or grandchildren, will come some fearful convulsion . . . When the pueblos are gone. But oh, let us have the grace and dignity to shelter these ancient centres of life, so that, if die they must, they die a natural death. And at the same time let us try to adjust ourselves again to the Indian outlook, to take up an old dark thread from their vision, and see again as they see, without forgetting we are ourselves.
>
> For it is a new era we have now got to cross into. And our electric light won't show us over the gulf. We have to feel our way by the dark thread of the old vision. Before it lapses, let us take it up.[8]

From September 1922 to September 1925, Lawrence stayed in Taos, New Mexico, broken by a return of about a year to Europe and several journeys to Old Mexico. It is Mexico, old and new, that dominates his imagination for the whole three years. During this period, Lawrence produces *The Plumed Serpent, St. Mawr, The Princess* and *The Woman Who Rode Away*, besides, a travel book *Mornings in Mexico* and a few similar essays. In an essay "American Look to Your Own", he regards the primitive religions, mainly of the Indians, the Aztecs, the Mayas and the Incas, as very important spiritual resources to which Americans should be able to return. "It means a departure from the old European morality, ethic. It means even a departure from the old range of emotions and sensibilities . . . We must start from Montezuma, not from St Francis or St Bernard".[9] According to Hough's analysis, the modern white inhabitant of the United States, in terms of his conscious life, is farther away from his primeval roots than his European counterpart. He suggests the modern white man can still see in the Indian life of his own South-West a faint survival of the primitive spark.[10] Lilly in *Aaron's Rod* recognizes this primitive spark in the life of the Aztecs and the Red Indians:

> I would have loved the Aztecs and the Red Indians,
> I know they had the element of life that I am looking for.
> They had living pride . . . The American races—and the
> South Sea Islanders—the Marquesans, the Maori blood.
> That was the true blood. It wasn't frightened.[11]

Lawrence's own experience of living with Indians in New Mexico supplied him with substantial religious sources, and liberated him from the shackle of the modern civilization. He writes in "New Mexico":

> I think New Mexico was the greatest experience from
> the outside world that I have ever had. It certainly changed
> me for ever. Curious as it may sound, it was New Mexico
> that liberated me from the present era of civilization, the
> great era of material and mechanical development.[12]

He feels liberated because he has gained a "permanent feeling of religion" from the Red Indians:

> I had no permanent feeling of religion till I came to New Mexico and penetrated into the old human race-experience there. It is curious that it should be in America, of all places, that a European should really experience religion, after touching the old Mediterranean and the East. It is curious that one should get a sense of living religion from the Red Indians, having failed to get it from Hindus or Sicilian Catholics or Cingalese.[13]

In the Red Indians' "living religion", he is particularly touched by their reverence for the dark relationship between humanity and the living universe. During his first contact with "Red Men", listening to an old Indian ceremonial preaching, he felt "an acute sadness, and a nostalgia, unbearably yearning for something, and a sickness of the soul came over me".[14] He realized immediately the great distance between white civilization and the primeval religions. "The voice out of the far-off time was not for my ears", he writes in his essay "Indians and an Englishman", it is "issuing plangent from the bristling darkness of the far past", which makes his soul yearn for "the lost past": "The soul is as old as the oldest day, and has its own hushed echoes, its own far-off tribal understandings sunk and incorporated". At that moment Lawrence realizes that he and the old Indians must have had the same "dark faced" father.[15]

Most white Americans in their white consciousness would not acknowledge or be ready to accept what the Indians worship: the many nature-spirits of animism and the nature-inhabiting gods of polytheism. Nevertheless, they have to admit the fact that, in psychic terms, the aboriginal spirit of the Indians is actually indestructible as a part of the universal human heritage. Lawrence is finally aware of this common heritage after his real-life contact with the aboriginal religions and cultures. "I am no ethnologist", he writes in "Indians and an Englishman",

> The point is, what is the feeling that passes from an Indian to me, when we meet? We are both men, but how do we feel together? I shall never forget that first evening when I first came into contact with Red Men, away in the Apache country. It was not what I had thought it would be. It was something of a shock. Again something in my

soul broke down, letting in a bitterer dark, a pungent awakening to the lost past, old darkness, new terror, new root-griefs, old root-richnesses.[16]

It is the same blood or the same primeval root that generates both primitive and modern man. In one's deep layers of unconsciousness, there is the divine "primitive spark" which is waiting for modern man to pick up. Once having picked this up, modern Americans will discard their white consciousness, and then achieve a lively connection with all the presences of the universe, with the sun and the earth.

Lawrence perceives, even in the wild land of New Mexico, the rampancy of white consciousness, which he says is willful, negative, obstinate and resistant. "Everything in America goes by *will*", he writes, "A great negative *will* seems to be turned against all spontaneous life—there seems to be no *feeling* at all—no genuine bowels of compassion and sympathy".[17] While the Indians, though hostile, are different from bullying whites, their consciousness is particularly in opposition to that of the white egoistic consciousness. "The Woman Who Rode Away" is a story illustrating Lawrence's religious experiment of how a white woman abandons her white consciousness and submits her whole being to the Indian's primitive culture. While being kept in a high valley among the Chilchuis ("the descendants of Montezuma and of the old Aztec or Totonac kings", "the sacred tribe of all the Indians", who are said to keep up the ancient religion of the Aztecs, including human sacrifice),[18] she has gone through the rituals of the tribe. "The sweetened herb drink" has easily numbed her mind, and changed her state of consciousness:

> This exquisite sense of bleeding out into the higher beauty and harmony of things. Then she could actually hear the great stars in heaven, which she saw through her door, speaking from their motion and brightness, saying things perfectly to the cosmos, as they trod in perfect ripples, like bells on the floor of heaven, passing one another and grouping in the timeless dance, with the spaces of dark between.[19]

The power of the Indian consciousness triumphs over her white consciousness. The woman is to the Indian neither a friend nor an enemy, yet she receives from them at once a "curious impersonal solicitude" and "a strange, profound, impersonal hate".[20] The Indians' impersonal attitude towards the white woman is in opposition to the white consciousness of intense personality and individuality. When she watches the Indians dancing,

> Her kind of womanhood, intensely personal and individual, was to be obliterated again, and the great primeval symbols were to tower once more over the fallen individual independence of woman. The sharpness and the quivering nervous consciousness of the highly-bred white woman was to be destroyed again, womanhood was to be cast once more into the great stream of impersonal sex and impersonal passion.[21]

Living in a vital relationship with the cosmos, the Indians are able to view things in a particular way of impersonality and sexlessness. This story suggests that the Indians have never acquired the personal, egoistic consciousness that divides sun and moon, male and female. The young Indian remarks with contempt that white people "know nothing. They are like children, always with toys. We know the sun, and we know the moon". Now since the divisive egoism of white consciousness has triumphed, the boy says, we "have lost our power over the sun, and we are trying to get it back". So, according to their religious belief, it is of great significance and necessity to have a white female sacrificed to the sun and the moon, in order to unite the two, restore life to the Indians and "make the world again". When the white woman comes to "that other state of passional cosmic consciousness", she sees, in the eyes of the oldest man, "power, power intensely abstract and remote, but deep, deep to the heart of the earth, and the heart of the sun".[22] This power springs from the primeval source of the universe. However, the power the white woman's blood will win from the sun is only for the savage races, not for the white. Keith Sagar points out, though the woman did find the right trail leading to the oldest Indian consciousness and to their gods, there seems to be no hope for her to be reborn after "yielding her entire being to the Indian vision".[23] But for Lawrence, the purpose of this myth is not to prove that the woman can be finally liberated from her white consciousness with the help of the Indians; the myth has simply dramatized Lawrence's vision that the Indian's religious consciousness has finally triumphed over the white man's consciousness. In the case of the white woman's sacrifice, as I mentioned in the previous chapter, we come to understand that,

> More and more her ordinary personal consciousness had left her, she had gone into that other state of passional cosmic consciousness, like one who is drugged. The Indians, with their heavy religious natures, had made her succumb to their vision.[24]

Similarly, in *The Plumed Serpent,* Kate realizes that the aboriginal life in America was that of humanity "before the mental spiritual world came into being". The aboriginal consciousness is "the old mode of consciousness, the old, dark will, the unconcern for death, the subtle, dark consciousness, non-cerebral, but vertebrate". When the white men came to this country, their "mental-spiritual life . . . suddenly flourishes like a great weed let loose in virgin soil. Probably it will as quickly wither". Kate sees the need and possibility of a new type of human life "that will arise from the fusion of the old blood-and-vertebrate consciousness with the white man's present mental-spiritual consciousness. The sinking of both beings, into a new being".[25]

Living in Mexico and immersed in the Indians' primitive cultures, Lawrence is particularly aware of their cosmic consciousness. The essay "The Dance of the Sprouting Corn" vividly records Lawrence's observation of the Indian's ritual ceremony, which expresses the Indians' gratitude to the sky and the earth for the basic food they have received. In the "pale, dry, baked earth" of the Pueblo's desert,[26] the costumed Indians dance and chant under a white-hot sky. Their life is closely linked to "the wide universe":

> The sky has its fire, its waters, its stars, its wandering electricity, its winds, its fingers of cold. The earth has its reddened body, its invisible hot heart, its inner waters and many juices and unaccountable stuffs. Between them all,

the little seed: and also man, like a seed that is busy and
aware.[27]

With this knowledge, the Indians, through their chants and
"rhythmic energy of dance", bring down the influences from the
heights and bring up the influences from the depth. "And when
he eats his bread at last", Lawrence imagines, he partakes "of the
energies he called to the corn, from out of the wide universe".[28] In
The Plumed Serpent, Ramon, leader in reviving the primitive god
Quetzalcoatl, preaches about man's dependence upon the universe.
Before the rain, for example, he convinces his followers that the
"Bird" will "shake(s) water out of his wings", and goes on: "The
earth is alive, and the sky is alive . . . and between them, we live.
Earth has kissed my knees, and put strength in my belly. Sky has
perched on my wrist, and sent power into my breast".[29] When
Kate arrives at Sayula, Mexico, she is stirred by something in the
air. "The Other Breath in the air, and the bluish dark power in the
earth had become almost suddenly, more real to her than so-called
reality". The cosmic breath melts her consciousness of reality:

> Concrete, jarring, exasperating, reality had melted
> away, and a soft world of potency stood in its place, the
> velvety dark flux from the earth, the delicate yet supreme
> life-breath in the inner-air. Behind the fierce sun the dark
> eyes of a deeper sun were watching, and between the
> bluish ribs of the mountains a powerful heart was secretly
> beating, the heart of the earth.[30]

The cosmic consciousness for the Indians is their way of keeping
the individual's organic wholeness, and is for Lawrence the key to
the survival of modern man's civilization. The white man must get
ready to annihilate his own consciousness in order to comprehend
primitive thought and culture, so that he can rediscover the power
of the dynamic life of the cosmos.

The American Indians' religious insight into the spirit of place
enhances Lawrence's strong sense of man's intrinsic relationship
with land. The modern white men, he believes, have cut themselves
off from the land, so they are deteriorating mentally and physically,
whereas the ancient thought, or more precisely the Indians'
primitive consciousness, has its essential vitality in their worship

of the mother earth, and in their cosmic perception of everything sentient and insentient on the earth. Indians' relation to the land has its special significance as is suggested by Lawrence in "Dance of the Sprouting Corn": "the earth's red center" is "where these men belong, as is signified by the red earth with which they are smeared".[31] The primitive consciousness of the value of native land is the most ready material borrowed by Lawrence who conceives that the rich spirit of the place would effectively cure the diseased white consciousness among Western communities. Nearly all the primitive tribes have their religious rituals worshipping the vitality of the awesome earth. Gary Snyder, the most ecologically self-conscious of twentieth-century poets, writes on the value of the earth:

> As a poet I hold the most archaic values on earth. They go back to the late Paleolithic: the fertility of the soil, the magic of animals, the power-vision in solitude . . . the love and ecstasy of the dance, the common work of the tribe. I try to hold both history and wildness in mind, then my poems may approach the true measure of all things and stand against the unbalance and ignorance of our times.[32]

Lawrence shows similar understanding of the archaic values of earth through his presentation of countryside life, such as in *The Rainbow* and *Lady Chatterley's Lover*; and of the exotic religious rituals as in *The Plumed Serpent* and particularly in the New Mexico stories.

The religious ceremony of the snake dance manifests furthermore the aborigine's intuitive knowledge of the land. It also stirs in Lawrence's imagination the creative mystery and destructive cruelty of the earth. Lawrence writes of the significance of the snake dance in "The Hopi Snake Dance": According to the Indians' belief, there lies in unconscious nature a dangerous spirit, and there is "the dark sun" at the centre of the earth, which is "the terrific, terrible, crude Source" of all things in the world.[33] The dark sun issues energies to create the cosmos, but it is at once creative and destructive, so the Hopi has to sooth the rattlesnake before letting it go back into the earth. Man must expose himself to direct contact with nature's dangerous elements, and have the courage and strength to bring them to the service of his own life:

Man, little man, with his consciousness and his will, must both submit to the great origin-powers of life, and conquer them. Conquered by man who has overcome his fears, the snakes must go back into the earth with his messages of tenderness, of request, and of power. They go back . . . into the resistant, malevolent heart of the earth's oldest, stubborn core. In the core of the first of suns, whence man draws his vitality, lies poison as bitter as the rattlesnake's. This poison man must overcome, he must be master of its issue.[34]

The snake dance of Indian religion is meaningful to Lawrence for the duality of the land, which is vividly depicted elsewhere in his essay "New Mexico", in *St. Mawr* and particularly in *The Plumed Serpent*. Indian beliefs echo Lawrence's own insight that at the centre of this universe there is not a rainbow, but "poison as bitter as the rattlesnake's". Man's task is to "submit to" it in order to draw vitality from the core of the sun. In the essay "Indians and Entertainment", apart from the characteristic impersonality, Lawrence finds in the Indians a submissive attitude towards the mystery. He comments on the significance suggested by the dance movements:

The mind is there merely as a servant, to keep a man pure and true to the mystery, which is always present. The mind bows down before the creative mystery, even of the atrocious Apache warrior. It judges, not the good and the bad, but the lie and the true.[35]

Lawrence sees their dance as a return to the source, "the dark blood into the downward rhythm, the rhythm of pure forgetting and renewal",[36] or as an expression of their pride in the glory and power of life. He writes:

It is the dance of the naked blood-being, defending his own isolation in the rhythm of the universe . . . The creature of the isolated, circulating blood-stream dancing in the peril of his own isolation, in the overweening of his own singleness. The glory in power of the man of single existence. The peril of man whose heart is suspended like a single red star, in a great and complex universe, following its own lone course round the invisible sun of our own being, amid the strange wandering array of other hearts.[37]

Lawrence's essay "The Spring Corn Dance" also registers the Indians' submission to the "invisible influences" of the land and the universe.

Apart from its "terrible proudness and mercilessness", the land in New Mexico is so brilliant with sun that one could not help feeling the vital energies rushing through all things:

> In the oldest religion, everything was alive, not supernaturally but naturally alive. There were only deeper and deeper streams of life, vibrations of life more and more vast . . . To come into immediate *felt* contact, and so derive energy, power, and a dark sort of joy. This effort into sheer naked contact, without an intermediary or mediator, is the root meaning of religion.[38]

The Indians have a strong religious belief that the whole living universe is animistic. "This animistic religion", Lawrence writes to J. M. Murry, "is the only live one, ours is a corpse of a religion".[39] According to Lawrence's religious perception, there should be no distinction between self and the external world; man's life is not separate from the lives of other creatures and things. Instead, human beings should draw energies or qualities from all other forms of life on earth, such as the pride of the lion, the meekness of the lamb, and the power of the snake. He says in "Pan in America":

> Man, defenceless, rapacious man, has needed qualities of every living thing, at one time or another. The hard silent abidingness of rock, the surging resistance of a tree, the still evasion of a puma . . . man can be master and complete in himself, only by assuming the living powers of each of them, as the occasion requires.[40]

Lawrence regrets the loss of "the savage mind", hoping man can return to the status of Pan: "In the days before man got too much separated off from the universe, he was Pan, along with all the rest". A tree, he says, is still a Pan, "a strong-willed, powerful thing-in-itself, reaching up and reaching down . . . down between the earth and rocks, to the earth's middle".[41] The Indian, not cutting off from the Pan powers, assimilates the powers by entering into a relationship of reverence for the cosmos. Lou of *St. Mawr* feels a mysterious Pan power like "the eternal fire" hidden in the holy universe:

> Because, after all, it seemed to her that the hidden fire was alive and burning in this sky, over the desert, in the mountains. She felt a certain latent holiness in the very atmosphere, a young, spring-fire of latent holiness, such as she had never felt in Europe or in the East.[42]

Lou finally resolves to serve these "other, unseen presences". She comes to realize that this is the right way to "get our lives straight from the source, as the animals do, and still be ourselves". This is certainly a way of renewal for the Indians, and Lawrence seems to have experienced it too: "Somehow my life draws strength from the depths of the universe, from the depths among the stars, from the great 'world'. Out of the great world comes my strength and my reassurance".[43] In the same year (1924) when he writes *St Mawr*, Lawrence also revises Mollie Skinner's novel of the Australian frontier, which becomes *The Boy in the Bush*. The hero Jack Grant is learning to live spontaneously and directly from the source, in order to fulfil his deep desires towards his rival and his two women. With his cosmic consciousness, he visualizes "the Great God in the roaring of the yellow sun, and the frightening vast smile in the gleaming full-moon".[44] Jack, a representative of primitive cultures, thinks in blood and acts directly from the wild spirit within himself. He is, like the red Indians, living spontaneously in harmony with the great cosmic realities of the sun and the moon.

The Plumed Serpent, conceived and written between 1923 and 1925, is a serious effort in the restoration of ancient god in the Mexican tribe, which Lawrence regarded as his most important work. Lawrence's imagination was kindled chiefly by Leo Frobenius' account of the restoration of the ancient god in *The Voice of Africa*. Reading Frobenius, Lawrence realizes that a native population, debased and demoralized by European influences, needs to develop a vital culture and religion of its own.

The Mexicans' primitive culture, in *The Plumed Serpent*, has been destroyed by Christianity. The ambition of the heroes Don Ramon and Don Cipriano is to resurrect what Lawrence calls the pre-Aztec god Quetzalcoatl, so that the native Mexicans would revive their old religion, living in their blood consciousness un-subjected to the idealism and materialism of Western civilization. The way of revival, as Tindall concludes, is through those religious rituals: "by the aid of drum, dance, sermon, symbol, and the destruction of socialists, papists, and engineers".[45] The serpent in the novel again signifies a dual power, something malevolent, brutal, yet powerful and vibrant. It at once represents the powers of volcano and earthquake and the power to generate the plants and man's life. If Quetzalcoatl is resurrected as a young and shining god, the dragon—the horror of Mexico—will raise himself and assume his good aspect. The men of Quetzalcoatl name themselves Lords of the two ways, of heaven and earth, fire and water, day and night. Quetzalcoatl is also Lord of the Morning Star, as he stands between the day and the night, in the creative twilight or the time of rebirth. Don Ramon preaches with Aztec consciousness,

> Quetzalcoatl is to me only the symbol of the best a man may be, in the next days. The universe is a nest of dragons, with a perfectly unfathom- able life-mystery at the centre of it . . . And man is a creature who wins his own creation inch by inch from the nest of the cosmic dragons.[46]

The heroine Kate hates the horrors and the darkness of Mexico, but also hates what she calls the mechanical people of the civilized Western world. "Give me the mystery and let the world live again for me! Kate cried to her own soul. And deliver me from man's automatism".[47] Through her own experiences of questing for a source of renewal, Kate finally comes to a conclusion, justifying the two white men's devoted cause:

> No! It's not a helpless, panic reversal. It is conscious, carefully chosen. We must go back to pick up old threads. We must take up the old, broken impulse that will connect us with the mystery of the cosmos again, now we are at the end of our own tether.[48]

She finally surrenders herself to the two men by consenting to be their goddess.

Whether Ramon's transformation can save the country or not is questionable, but Lawrence is using the myths of the Aztecs to convey the message that the way to save ourselves is through the revival of mysteries of the primitive consciousness. His primitivism, in a sense, echoes our modern concept of "deep ecology". Patrick Marsolek argues in his website article "Deep Ecology and Man—A sacred Kinship" that "these early civilizations possessed highly developed mathematical, agricultural and medical capabilities in addition to their engineering skills", which might be "only the surviving colonies of a far-older culture, akin to Plato's Atlantis, whose records are lost to us". He then further clarifies:

> Many of these great civilizations and cultures also believed in the sacredness of the planet, naming their gods after the sun, earth, moon and stars; the air, earth, water and fire. We think of these mythical beliefs as primitive knowledge obtained before scientific under-standing. Yet, it is not without significance that almost every ancient culture, civilized or not, possessed myth and legends of great cycles of rising and falling and births and deaths of civilizations on a grand scale, e.g.—the Hopi Indians, the Maya . . .and so on. Did these myths arise from the experiences of cultures that lost their connection with the planet?[49]

He suggests a link between the rise and fall of all civilizations and physical changes of the earth. "Nature seems to experience periodic incarnation, death and resurrection, mirroring the rise and fall of humankind". If man fails to "affirm the importance of the lost vital connection with the sacred nature of the world", he is doomed to be destroyed, which is warned of in Hopi prophecy and ancient writings.[50] Lawrence, with the same deep reverence for the lost civilizations, sees the danger of modern man's turning away from his ancient roots and warns us of our destructions: "unless we proceed to connect ourselves up with our own primeval sources, we shall degenerate".[51] In a letter, he reaffirms his view: "I know there has to be a return to the old vision of life . . . It needs some welling up of religious sources that have been shut down in us: a great *yielding* . . . to the darker, older unknown, and a reconciliation". [52]

It is clear that Lawrence does not want to live among the savages, he is fully aware of the fact that the white man today will not be happy living in the past. "I am so tired of being told that I want mankind to go back to the condition of savages", he complains.[53] He writes in "Pan in America": "It is useless to glorify the savage. For he will kill Pan with his hands, for the sake of a motor-car . . . And we cannot return to the primitive life, to live in tepees and hunt with bows and arrows".[54] In "Indians and Englishman", he describes his feeling that he has no desire to be living with those 'dark-faced' men: "But I don't want to go back to them, ah, never . . . I don't want to live again the tribal mysteries my blood has lived long scene".[55] However, he argues, "To be civilized, we have to sow wild seed again. We have to cultivate our feelings", and so let us "Get back to the roots again for a new start".[56] Lawrence's seemingly contradictory remarks are justified by his viewpoint that in reviving the present civilization, "Every profound new movement makes a great swing also backwards to some older, half-forgotten way of consciousness".[57] This insight accounts for his yearning for the lost past: "Our darkest tissues are twisted in this old tribal experience, our warmest blood came out of the old tribal fire. And they vibrate still in answer our blood, our tissue. But me, the conscious me, I have gone a long road since then". Therefore, being with the Indians, he feels, "every thread in my body quivers to the frenzy of the old mystery".[58] He hopes that modern man, with the same roots, will learn from the savages to "un-tame" himself and to plough his soul in order to cultivate an organic relationship with the living universe.

* *

From 1913 to the time of his death, the revival of primitivism became an important issue in most of Lawrence's works. William Y. Tindall, in *Susan His Cow* and in the essay "D. H. Lawrence and the Primitive", has examined the legacy of Lawrence's primitivism. As well as his experiences on different continents, Lawrence has been influenced by the books of anthropologists, archaeologists, psychoanalysts and historians. Among those he owed considerable debt to, to list a few, are Frazer's *Golden Bough*, Jane Harrison's *Ancient Art and Ritual*, Tylor's *Primitive Culture*, Leo Frobenius' *The Voice of Africa*, and of course C. G. Jung's *Psychology of the Unconscious*. The comment he made in one of his letters in 1916 reveals his excitement in the knowledge:

> I read the *History of the East* . . . something in me
> lights up and understands these old, dead peoples, and
> I love it: Babylon, Nineveh, Ashurbanipal, how one
> somehow understands it. And I cannot tell you the joy
> of ranging far back there seeing the hordes surge out of
> Arabia, or over the edge of the Iranian plateau.[59]

In his essays and novels, we find a significant legacy of his knowledge of primitivism in the books he read. "The Crown" contains references to Dionysus, Moloch, and Egyptian animal worship; *Movements in European History* contains long passages about the Great Mother, the gods of fertility, and the worship of trees and the golden bough, which are obviously based on Frazer. Birkin of *Women in Love* loves African sculpture for its "mystically sensual" character, and is fond of ancient Egyptians, "whom he makes his models in mindless, vitalism, and polarity".[60] Count Dionys of "The Ladybird" is very much a primitive man whose symbolic ladybird is an Egyptian scarab, a pre-Roman equipment, and claims to be a devotee of the sun. Lawrence's *Apocalypse* is "plainly a study of the primitive baggage in man's unconscious, of the dragon now deep in our minds".[61] Tindall finds dozens of quotations and paraphrases taken by Lawrence from John Burnet's *Early Greek Philosophy*. Lilly of *Aaron's Rod* reads Frobenius to the music of Debussy: "His soul had the faculty of divesting itself of the moment, and seeking further, deeper interests. These old Africans! And Atlantis! Strange, strange wisdom of the Kabyles! Old, old dark Africa, and the world before the flood!"[62] The "strange wisdom" that Lilly yearns to recover is that of the great African civilization that the German ethnographer identifies as the legendary Atlantis. The themes of Frobenius' *The Voice of Africa* interested Lawrence deeply in the last decade of his life: the health and vigor of the ancient religion; the debasement and decadence caused by Europeanization of the black tribes; and the need to revive the "strange wisdom" of the past. Frobenius undoubtedly supplies clues invaluable to Lawrence in the latter's effort to recreate the ancient cultures and religions.

Living a simple life in the countryside is an effective way to gain one's primitive consciousness and to establish a closer connection with nature. In this sense, Lawrence depicts a world of woods and wildlife in *Lady Chatterley's Lover*, in which Mellors and Connie are able to live a life intuitively closer to the vitality of nature. Disappointed at the staleness of superficial modern industrial society, they enjoy a primitive mode of life in which man's sensual potential is reawakened, and they "lived breast to breast, as it were, with the cosmos, in naked contact with the cosmos, the whole cosmos was alive and in contact with the flesh of man . . ."[63] Mellors tells Connie that he wishes the people of England would drop "the whole industrial life" and live for immediate experience rather than for money:

> They ought to learn to be naked and handsome, and to sing in a mass and dance the old group dances, and carve the stools they sit on, and embroider their own emblems. Then they wouldn't need money. And that's the only way to solve the industrial problem: train the people to be able to live, and live in handsomeness, without needing to spend.[64]

This primitive Utopian society, Mellors believes, might help us to reawaken human beings' old values. As a representative of natural man, his immediate experience—a revival of meaningful "daily ritual"—radically excludes those concepts such as societal work and moneymaking, which he vainly hopes we could live without. In 1928, a year after *Lady Chatterley's Lover* was finished, Lawrence writes:

> We want a revolution not in the name of money or work or any of that, but of life,—and let money and work be as casual in human life as they are in a bird's life . . . you've got to smash money and this beastly possessive spirit. I get more revolutionary every minute, but for *life's* sake. The dead materialism of Marx socialism and soviets seems to me no better than what we've got.[65]

Unrealistic as it is in modern times, it might serve as a complement to our mechanical life, because in Lawrence's philosophy it is not the machine but "naked forces" that nurture our lives. It is the natural elements of the surrounding world that we should "struggle with", instead of modern mechanization which can only pull us away from the miracle of life:

> The more we intervene machinery between us and the naked forces the more we numb and atrophy our own senses. Every time we turn on a tap to have water, every time we turn a handle to have fire or light, we deny ourselves and annul our being. The great elements, the earth, air, fire, water are there like some great mistress whom we woo and struggle with, whom we heave and wrestle with. And all our appliances do but deny us these fine embraces, take the miracle of life away from us ... When we balance the sticks and kindle a fire, we partake of the mysteries. But when we turn on an electric tap, there is as it were a wad between us and the dynamic universe.[66]

In 1929, the year before his death, he writes in A Propos of Lady Chatterley's Lover that in one way or another there must be a renewal of the ancient rhythm and cosmic life: "The greatest need of man is the renewal forever of the complete rhythm of life and death, the rhythm of the sun's year, the body's year of a lifetime, and the greater year of the stars, the soul's year of immortality".[67] He then stresses again that modern man "must get back into relation, vivid and nourishing relation to the cosmos and the universe. The way is through daily ritual, and the reawakening".[68]

Lawrence's utopian vision of "primitive" life is at variance with the ethos of the modern industrial world, which undoubtedly meets with suspicion and rejection. According to his utopian vision, modern people living in an industrial civilization should not rely heavily on technology, neither should they be preoccupied with the accumulation of material wealth; instead, they should establish an immediate contact with "the dynamic universe". He writes to Trigant Burrow in 1927 that man has unfortunately cut himself from the "principle in the universe, towards which man turns religiously—a life of the universe itself". He then says the "cut-offness" is the result of the individualist illusion affected by a capitalist society that emphasizes possessions, egoistical exclusiveness, and the primacy of the individual.[69] The concluding message of his last non-fiction book *Apocalypse* sums up his concerns over our modern life: "What we want is to destroy our false, inorganic connections, especially those related to money, and re-establish the living organic connections, with the cosmos, the sun and earth, with mankind and nation and family".[70] Primitive people do not have that many inorganic connections, as their life is not directed by money or any material competitions. When he was in Taos, Lawrence noticed with admiration that the Indians seemed to care little about the moneymaking business, which he deems the main reason for their innocence and vitality. The white men on the contrary are living as if within "the golden wall of money", which is fatal because the money cuts them off from their connection with nature: "Our last wall is the golden wall of money. This is a fatal wall. It cuts us off from life, from vitality, from the alive sun and the alive earth, as *nothing* can . . . We are losing vitality, owing to money and money-standards".[71] Lawrence's seemingly absurd assertion is in its real sense a rebellious cry against man's money-oriented modern life. Similarly, Ben Wills in his *The Tao of Art* criticises modern man's ill-founded notion of treating the possession of money as a means of security: "Man had traded his peace of mind, creativity and inner freedom for the illusion of security", and as a result, he becomes "the pawn and slave of meaningless utilitarianism and dehumanised, pragmatic social formulas"[72], which is a tragedy of our civilization. The way to avoid this tragedy, he advocates, is return to one's primeval self, living according to one's inner desire and spontaneity instead of pining for the accumulation of money and property.

* * *

Lawrence has a religious passion not only for primitive cultures but also for the oriental and the occult. The increasingly developed materialist society brings him only intense discomfort and disappointment, which in a way accounts for his interest in the oriental philosophies: theosophy, yoga and astrology. His theosophy is actually part of his primitivism. Tindall devotes a whole chapter "Susan Unveiled" to the influences of different theosophists and Eastern philosophies on Lawrence. Lawrence, ever since his university days, was greatly influenced by Emerson and Thoreau, both of whom reject the rationalism of the eighteenth century, and found something useful in Hinduism, Buddhism, and other eastern systems. Emerson's theory of over soul, for example, comes from the *Vedas* and the *Upanishads*. Jessie Chambers writes in her memoir that Lawrence "read and liked Emerson's Essays and became wildly enthusiastic over Thoreau's *Walden*, especially the essay on The Ponds".[73] Thoreau called himself Yoga, and his hermit life style--built a hut in the woods and lived beside the pond--evoked Lawrence's nostalgic imaginations. Apart from Emerson and Thoreau's influences, Lawrence's understanding of Yoga was enlightened by *The Apocalypse Unsealed* written by James M. Pryse, also a theosophist. In the late nineteenth century, Mme Blavatsky[74] published two books, *Isis Unveiled*, 1877, and *The Secret Doctrine*, 1888, which offered spiritual release for those sensitive Americans and Englishmen by the occult powers and secret wisdom of the oriental philosophies.[75] Annie Besant was once a fervent atheist, a socialist and a thorough materialist, but her political career left her no spiritual satisfaction, and she finally found refugee in theosophy. Many of her works explaining Mme Blavatsky's secret doctrines inspired Lawrence deeply, and he alludes several times to her. Lawrence, coming upon the works of Mme Blavatsky, "found her congenial", for her response to civilization confirmed his existing doctrines in many aspects. Frieda told Tindall that Lawrence "read and delighted in all Mme Blavatsky's works and that, as he read, he used to smile at the 'mundane egg'".[76]

Lawrence was fascinated by the book of *Occultism*. It is "magic, astrology", he writes to Mark Gertler, "It is very interesting, and important—though anti-pathetic to me. Certainly magic is a reality. . . ."[77] The occult interpretation of the self and the enigma of nature apparently enrich his religious insight, and he later becomes an enthusiastic reader of *The Occult Review*. Tindall, when discussing Mme Blavatsky's theosophical ideas, points out:

> In the present cycle on this earth, primitive man was more spiritual than the modern scientist, who is at the lowest material point of development, limited to reason

and unable to know the truth by intuition and instinct. Without this useful capacity, which primitive man and Mme Blavatsky enjoyed, Huxley, for example, found it impossible to follow them in their contemplation of the various orders of spirits, such as fairies, salamanders, and vampires, of the meaning of sun, moon, cow, serpent, and lotus, of the mysteries of alchemy, astrology, yoga, and numerology, and of the beauty of Isis. . . .[78]

Unlike Huxley, Lawrence is familiar with theosophical symbols and ancient occult stories. He is proud of his knowledge, telling his Buddhist friend Brewster that "The Indian, the Aztec, old Mexico—all that fascinates me and has fascinated me for years. There is glamour and magic for me".[79] He is also fascinated by the different divinities worshiped in the east and the west. In *The Plumed Serpent*, Ramon lists those ancient gods, hoping they will someday come back. For example, he wishes "Thor and Wotan, and the tree Igdrasil" would come back to the Teutonic world; Tuatha De Danaan to the Druidic world; Hermes to the Mediterranean, Ashtaroth to Tunis; Mithras to Persia; Brahma to India, and the oldest dragon to China.[80] Many allusions throughout his later writings suggest his fascination at and long acquaintance with theosophy. The title of his essay "Him with His Tail in His Mouth" indicates the symbol of the tail-biting serpent by which theosophists suggest eternity, metempsychosis, and other matters. Quetzalcoatl's favourite symbol is a serpent with his tail in his mouth. Many symbols Lawrence used are reflections of those described in Mme Blavatsky's books. The lonely, self-begetting Phoenix is, according to Mme Blavatsky's *The Secret Doctrine*, an esoteric symbol of initiation and rebirth. The references to the "Third Eye" in St. Mawr, the thrice-greatest Hermes Trismegistus known to the hero of *Kangaroo*, the "mystic Om", and the Quetzalcoatl or Pryse's Kundalini in *The Plumed Serpent* are all theosophical. Besides, Mme Blavatsky's theosophical vision of a secret sun behind the apparent sun and her understanding of "the Great Breath" are also reflected in *The Plumed Serpent*. Isis, the ancient Egyptian goddess, is a much-admired symbol. "It is Isis the mystery/Must be in love with me", he writes in the poem "Don Juan".[81] The story of Count Psanek of "The Ladybird" also reveals much of Lawrence's knowledge and an interest in theosophy.

This mindless Czechoslovakian is "an initiate" in an old esoteric society, who knows "awful secret knowledge" about the sun, about the affinity between moon and water, about Egypt and Isis, and about hermetic gold. His symbolic scarab is decorated with seven spots; and on the base of his symbolic thimble is coiled a snake surrounded by seven spots. The cover of *The Secrete Doctrines* is also decorated with an annular serpent.[82] The mystic power of the snake is a repeated theme in Lawrence's work, which evidently shows Lawrence's fascination with theosophy.

To Lawrence, and also to Mme Blavatsky, the symbols of the Aztec are identical with those of the Egyptian, but more revealing is that the symbols such as the cross, the circle, the tree, the lotus, the sun, the wheel, the snake, the dragon and the bull reveal the same religious past. He says in *Apocalypse* that these symbols may go back "for four thousand years and even beyond that. The power of suggestion is most mysterious". And the profound truths embedded in the symbolism of old religious documents "may carry the unconscious mind back in great cyclic swoops through eras of time".[83] There are many remarks in *Apocalypse* on the symbolic clues to the past. The foreword to *Fantasia of the Unconscious* heavily carries Lawrence's theosophical view: "In the great world previous to ours a great science and cosmology were taught esoterically in all countries of the globe, Asia, Polynesia, America, Atlantis and Europe". Then after they are flooded:

> The refugees from the drowned continents fled to the high places of America, Europe, Asia, and the Pacific Isles. And some degenerated naturally into cave men, Neolithic and Palaeolithic creatures, and some retained their marvellous innate beauty and life-perfection, as the South Sea Islanders, and some wandered savage in Africa, and some . . . refused to forget, but taught the old wisdom, only in its half-forgotten, symbolic forms. More or less forgotten, as knowledge: remembered as ritual, gesture, and myth-story.
>
> And so, the intense potency of symbols is part at least memory. And so it is that all the great symbols and myths which dominate the world when our history first begins, are very much the same in every country and every people, the great myths all relate to one another.

And so it is that these myths now begin to hypnotize us again, our own impulse towards our own scientific way of understanding being almost spent. And so, besides myths, we find the same mathematic figures, cosmic graphs which remain among the aboriginal peoples in all continents, mystic figures and signs whose true cosmic or scientific significance is lost, yet which continue in use for purposes of conjuring or divining.[84]

This text reflects simple theosophy, but is important for our understanding of Lawrence's later work. The theme of *The Plumed Serpent* is "the recovery of lost Atlantis by means of myths and symbols",[85] which is similar to the theme of Mme Blavatsky's *Secret Doctrine*. Lawrence realizes that "all prophets such as Buddha, Mohammed, Christ, and Quetzalcoatl pointed consciously or unconsciously to the primitive wisdom",[86] and that they themselves serve as the symbols of primitive truth. Kate of *The Plumed Serpent* feels akin to the man of "that old pre-flood world" before the melting of the glaciers:

> When great plains stretched away to the oceans, like Atlantis and the lost continents of Polynesia . . . and the soft, dark-eyed people of that world could walk around the globe. Then there was a mysterious, hot-blooded, soft-footed humanity with a strange civilization of its own.[87]

Through *The Plumed Serpent,* Lawrence expresses his theosophical utopia, which is the fusion of the scientific European mind and the aboriginal life before the flood. His way to Atlantis is to revive the myth and symbols of Quetzalcoatl. Tindall argues that Don Ramon's plan generally follows Mme Blavatsky's: erecting a past Utopian world in the present, but with modern improvements. Among many theosophical elements in *The Plumed Serpent* are the references to "dragons in the cosmos", "the Morning star", and the earth-bound spirits (salamanders, for example) and water spirits in Ramon's fourth hymn. Ramon is even excited at the names of Mexican gods, exclaiming that the gods' names "are like seeds, so full of magic, of the unexplored magic . . . How wonderful! And Tlaloc! Ah! I love them! I say them over and over, like they say *Mani Padma Om*! In Thibet".[88] He believes that the chanting of the magic names of their old gods will gradually enable the Mexicans to return to their lost past. Lawrence seems to acknowledge himself as a theosophist, and his theosophical mind "cries" in his writings:

> You may be a theosophist, and then you will cry: *Avaunt! Thou dark-red aura! Away!!!—Oh come! Thou pale-blue or thou primrose aura, come!*
> This you cry if you are a theosophist. And if you put a theosophist in a novel, he or she may cry *avaunt!* To the heart's content.
> But a theosophist cannot be a novelist, as a trumpet cannot be a regimental band. A theosophist, or a Christian, or a Holy Roller, may be *contained* in a novelist.[89]

It is right to say that the theosophist who wrote *The Plumed Serpent* is contained in Lawrence as a novelist. Being a theosophist, Lawrence sees great significance in reviving local cults and divinities, no matter whether their origins are in the East or West.

Lawrence's interest in theosophical occult again seems foolish or sounds ridiculous, but those familiar with the origin and development of his beliefs would not think of him in that way. Tindall in *D. H. Lawrence & Susan his Cow* analyses the reason why Lawrence and the other artists take interest in theosophy and the occult. Artists and sentimental intellectuals in history and especially in modern times feel discomfort in adjusting themselves to the changing and disordered world. Science, industry, and sceptical reason have driven them either to religion or to spiritual consolations in nature, in the exotic, the ancient and the mysterious. Primitivism and theosophy become a substitute for an unbearable reality. Lawrence is no exception in his response to the changing world. Unwilling to adjust his emotions to industrialised civilization, he takes refuge in all that seems opposite, in strange cults and mysteries, in philosophies of nature's vitalism, in primitivism and theosophy. Feeling disappointed in Christian doctrines, he has established his own private religion—his worship for the natural world, in which the flower, the bird and the sun have their own religious meanings and sacred values. Lawrence's philosophy and insight in a way help us to understand the behaviour and emotions of many other artists who are his contemporaries and predecessors. To Lawrence, ancient philosophies not only provide a refuge for his unconventional thought and emotion, but also become an indispensable part of his art. For us, the study of Lawrence's primitivism and theosophy may lead us to "a better understanding of some of the problems of our literature, society, judgement, and taste".[90]

[1] *The Letters of D. H. Lawrence*, James T. Boulton, ed., vol. III, p. 689.

[2] *The Collected Letters of D. H. Lawrence*, Harry T. Moore, ed., Vol. I, p. 380.

[3] Ibid., p. 390.

[4] Ibid., pp. 375-6.

[5] Raymond Williams, *Culture and Society 1780-1950*, p. 202.

[6] William Y. Tindall, *D. H. Lawrence & Susan His Cow*, p. 86.

[7] *The Collected Letters of D. H. Lawrence*, Harry T. Moore, ed., Vol. II, p. 759.

[8] D. H. Lawrence, "Certain Americans and an Englishman", *New York Times Magazine*, December 24, 1922, p. 9.

[9] D. H. Lawrence, "America, Listen to Your Own", *Phoenix*, p. 90.

[10] Ibid., p. 119.

[11] D. H. Lawrence, *Aaron's Rod*, Ch. 9, p. 119.

[12] D. H. Lawrence, "New Mexico", *Phoenix*, p. 142.

[13] Ibid., p. 142.

[14] D. H. Lawrence, "Indians and an Englishman", *Phoenix*, p. 95.

[15] Ibid., p. 99.

[16] Ibid., p. 95.

[17] *The Collected Letters of D. H. Lawrence*, Harry T. Moore, ed., Vol. II, p 721.

[18] D. H. Lawrence, "The Woman Who Rode Away", in *The Woman Who Rode Away and Other Stories*, p. 49.

[19] Ibid., p. 73.

[20] Ibid., p. 77.

[21] Ibid., pp. 70-1.

[22] Ibid., pp. 72, 74, 83.

[23] Keith Sagar, *The Art of D. H. Lawrence*, p. 149.

[24] D. H. Lawrence, "The Woman Who Rode Away", in *The Woman Who Rode Away and Other Stories*, p. 76.

[25] D. H. Lawrence, *The Plumed Serpent*, p. 431.

[26] D. H. Lawrence, "Dance of the Sprouting Corn", in *Mornings in Mexico and Etruscan Places*, p. 64.

[27] Ibid., p. 70.

[28] Ibid., pp. 70-1.

[29] D. H. Lawrence, *The Plumed Serpent*, p. 211.

[30] Ibid., p. 118.

[31] D. H. Lawrence, "Dance of the Sprouting Corn", in *Mornings in Mexico and Etruscan Places*, p. 67.

[32] *The Poetry of Gary Snyder*, quoted in Dolores LaChapelle, *D. H. Lawrence, Future Primitive*, p. 103.

[33] D. H. Lawrence, "The Hopi Snake Dance", in *Mornings in Mexico and Etruscan Places*, p. 76.

[34] Ibid., p. 87.

[35] D. H. Lawrence, "Indians and Entertainment", in *Mornings in Mexico and Etruscan Places*, p. 63.

[36] Ibid., p. 58

[37] Ibid., p. 59.

[38] Ibid., pp. 146-7.

[39] *The Letters of D. H. Lawrence,* Aldous Huxley, ed., p. 610.

[40] D. H. Lawrence, "Pan in America", *Phoenix*, p. 29.

[41] Ibid., p. 24.

[42] D. H. Lawrence, *St. Maw*, in *St. Mawr and Other Stories*, p. 178.

[43] D. H. Lawrence, "The Real Thing", in *D. H. Lawrence, A Selection from Phoenix*, p. 379.

[44] D. H. Lawrence, *The Boy in the Bush*, p. 185.

[45] William Y. Tindall, *D. H. Lawrence & Susan His Cow*, p. 113.

[46] D. H. Lawrence, *The Plumed Serpent*, p. 285.

[47] Ibid., p. 114.

[48] Ibid., p. 147.

[49] http://www.irfs.com/ DeepEco.html, 20 June 2005.

[50] Ibid., website.

[51] D. H. Lawrence, "The Novel and the Feelings", *Phoenix*, p. 758.

[52] *The Letters of D. H. Lawrence*, Aldous Huxley, ed., p. 605.

[53] D. H. Lawrence, "We Need One Another", *Phoenix*, p. 194.

[54] D. H. Lawrence, "Pan in America", *Phoenix*, p. 31.

[55] D. H. Lawrence, "Indians and an Englishman", *Phoenix*, p. 99.

[56] D. H. Lawrence, "The Novel and the Feelings", *Phoenix*, pp. 758-9.

[57] D. H. Lawrence, *Apocalypse*, p. 50.

[58] D. H. Lawrence, "Indians and an Englishman", *Phoenix*, p. 99.

[59] *The Letters of D. H. Lawrence*, Aldous Huxley, ed., p. 318.

[60] William Y. Tindall, *D. H. Lawrence & Susan His Cow*, p. 102.

[61] Ibid., p. 121.

[62] D. H. Lawrence, *Aaron's Rod*, pp. 128-9.

[63] D. H. Lawrence, *Apocalypse*, p. 159.

[64] D. H. Lawrence, *Lady Chatterley's Lover*, p. 312.

[65] *The Collected Letters of D. H. Lawrence*, Harry T. Moore, ed., Vol. II, p. 1110.

[66] D. H. Lawrence, "Dana's Two Years Before the Mast", in *Studies in Classic American Literature*, p. 134.

[67] D. H. Lawrence, *A Propos of Lady Chatterley's Lover*, in *D. H. Lawrence, A Selection from Phoenix*, p. 354.

[68] Ibid. p. 355.

[69] *The Letters of D. H. Lawrence*, Aldous Huxley, ed., p. 688.

[70] D. H. Lawrence, *Apocalypse*, p. 200.

[71] D. H. Lawrence, "Reflections on the Death of a Porcupine", in *D. H. Lawrence, A Selection from Phoenix*, p. 459.

[72] Ben Wills, *The Tao of Art*, p. 136.

[73] Jessie Chambers, *D. H. Lawrence: A Personal Record*, p. 101.

[74] Mme Blavatsky founded a Theosophy Society in New York (1875) and came to England in 1887.

[75] According to Mme Blavatsky, the central element of theosophy is metempsychosis, the evolution of individuals under the law of Karma from spirit to matter and back again seven times in seven planes around a chain of seven planets, of which this earth in this plane alone is visible. Reference in William Y. Tindall, *D. H. Lawrence & Susan His Cow*, p. 127.

[76] Ibid., p. 133.

[77] *The Letters of D. H. Lawrence*, Aldous Huxley, ed., p. 440.

[78] William Y. Tindall, *D. H. Lawrence & Susan His Cow*, pp. 127-8.

[79] Earl Brewster, *D. H. Lawrence: Reminiscences and Correspondence*, p. 38.

[80] D. H. Lawrence, *The Plumed Serpent*, Ch. 17, p. 261.

[81] *The Complete Poems of D. H. Lawrence*, Vivian de Sola Pinto, ed., p. 196.

[82] William Y. Tindall, *D. H. Lawrence & Susan His Cow*, p. 135.

[83] D. H. Lawrence, *Apocalypse*, p. 126.

[84] D. H. Lawrence, "Foreword" to *Fantasia of the Unconscious and Psychoanalysis and the Unconscious*, p. 8.

[85] William Y. Tindall, *D. H. Lawrence & Susan His Cow*, p. 144.

[86] Ibid., p. 145.

[87] D. H. Lawrence, *The Plumed Serpent*, p. 431.

[88] Ibid., p. 68.

[89] D. H. Lawrence, quoted in William Y. Tindall, *D. H. Lawrence & Susan His Cow*, p. 148.

[90] William Y. Tindall, *D. H. Lawrence & Susan His Cow*, p. viii.Conclusion

Conclusion

Lawrence and Ecological Consciousness

Having examined Lawrence's transcendental attitude towards nature, including his preference for primitivism, intuition, spontaneity, blood consciousness, togetherness, and man's lifetime effort to establish an organic relationship with the whole universe, we are in a position to assert that Lawrence's work is an outstanding example of twentieth-century Romanticism. Furthermore, in Lawrence and in his work, we see a prominent figure in the development of a new environmental consciousness in literature.

William Y. Tindall in his *D. H. Lawrence & Susan His Cow* defines Romanticism thus: "Romanticism has been described as the return to nature and as nostalgia for the remote in time or place; it has been said to involve wonder, strangeness, imagination, mysticism, unreason, or even sickness and perversity".[1] Lawrence's work displays all these characteristics of Romanticism. Untouched nature is for Lawrence, as for other Romantic writers, both a heaven away from the unbearable distastefulness of industrial civilization and a medium for the pursuit of spiritual truth. He enjoys a simple life in a secluded country and yearns to build a Utopian society with his friends. With a strong desire to reform the then decadent Western culture, he travels all over the world, not just for the purpose of escape but with an expectation to find practical and effective remedies. His way of saving mankind and the world from falling apart is, through his writing, by urging people to gain a living wholeness, a fulfillment of man's primal relationship with the universe. Tindall says that Lawrence's hope for the regeneration of the wasteland of western civilization centres in his essentially Romantic view of man, nature and the cosmos. Study of his view of nature reveals abundant elements of contemporary Romanticism in his life and work. Tindall concludes: "In his transcendental attitude toward nature, savages, the past, intuition, and the relations between men and women and in his devotion to Susan, the central religious tendency of recent romanticism is plain".[2] Roger Ebbatson expounded in his *Lawrence and the Nature Tradition* that Lawrence's views of nature are deeply rooted in the Romantic traditions and in writers of the eighteenth and nineteenth centuries. He points out:

> The Nature tradition in the novel took the form of synthesis of Romantic visions of Nature as revelation and deliverance and Darwinian pictures of man's ordeal in the natural world. It is a tradition of great variety and complexity, and it culminates in the work of D. H. Lawrence.[3]

Thus, Horace Gregory calls him "an heir of the Romantic tradition in English literature".[4]

In accordance with his life and his Romantic view of nature, Lawrence is fairly labelled, apart from Romantic, by other names such as monist, pantheist, vitalist, transcendentalist and a worshipper of primitivism. Through these names we come to have an overall insight into an organic characteristic of Lawrence, which reflects his intense consciousness of nature in all its aspects. Some ecologists call this consciousness "Future Primitive", which suggests an environmental consciousness rooted in a sense of primitive ecology.

Lawrence, during his last visit to his home town Eastwood, is sadly aware of the fact that industrial materialism has changed his living environment in a rather ugly way, and that is to him "the real tragedy of England". He says, "The country is so lovely: the man-made England is so vile". He sees life in his boyhood surroundings as "a curious cross between industrialism and the old agricultural England of Shakespeare and Milton and Fielding and George Eliot".[5] This situation of "curious cross" has been a crucial concern of his environmental consciousness and has always remained in the background of his thoughts and major works.

Through his essays and novels, particularly *The Rainbow, Lady Chatterley's Lover* and *The Plumed Serpent*, Lawrence elaborates on possible ways to regain man's living wholeness with the earth and the natural environment. For him, this living wholeness, being unfortunately destroyed by modern industrialization, can only be revived through the practice of the old mode of life.

The internationally renowned ecologist and biographer Raymond Dasmann[6] writes in his essay "Future Primitive": "I cannot see much hope for the future of either parks or people, unless some of the old sense of belonging to the natural world, of being a part of nature, and not hostile to it is restored". He then mentions that Jerry Gorsline and Linn House have used the term of "Future Primitive", and quotes from their essay: "We have been awakened to the richness and complexity of the primitive mind . . . where culture is integrated and employs for its cognition a body of metaphor drawn from and structured in relation to that ecosystem". This is exactly the voice behind Lawrence's proposal of the adjustment of modern life to the ecosystem. Dasmann finally concludes: "I would propose that the answer for nature conservation in the South Pacific as elsewhere, will be found to lie in the direction of 'Future Primitive'".[7] Primitivism does not mean barbarism or savageness with backward cultures and superstitious beliefs. Dasmann, after explaining the etymology of the original meaning of the word primitivism, points out that primitivism "refers to widely distributed, well-organized institutions that had already existed just prior to the rise of ancient civilizations, it does not imply historically an inchoate time of cultural origins".[8]

Modern civilizations are not necessarily superior to primitive ones. Our industrial development and scientific advances do not inevitably bring us the good life, or any particular peace in our mind or society. The modern way of life, or the human ego, has destroyed the equanimity and balance of nature. The ever-growing degenerating environment is due to modern society's incessant economic development in line with man's insatiate desire for material possessions, or for greater sensuous enjoyment out of the reformation of the natural environment. Recently while developed Western countries have begun to reflect on the damage modern civilizations have caused to nature, and are embarking on environmental protection, many developing countries are struggling to catch up with Western standards of economy and life-style through intensified economic competition and the exploitation of natural resources. As a result, many nations eat the fruits of natural disasters caused by men's intention to improve their lives. The ecology scholar Stephanie Kaza points out an alternative solution to the environmental crisis: "It is clear to many leading environmental thinkers that science, technology, and economics alone will not solve the environmental crisis. Instead they call for cultural transformation based on religious, moral, or spiritual values of deep care of and concern for the earth."[9]

Future primitive could help to solve the environmental crisis through cultural transformation, transforming one's sentiments, attitudes and outlook in accordance with the great reality of nature. *The Plumed Serpent* is Lawrence's experiment in cultural transformation; the revival of the Aztec god Quetzalcoatl is aimed at rescuing the lost primitive consciousness. The prehistoric culture of "Plato's Atlantis" and other legends and ancient cultures he describes in *The Plumed Serpent* and *Fantasia of the Unconscious* are good supplementary materials in drawing our attention to the urgency of the re-establishment of a vital relationship between the individual and his land and the whole living environment. The pursuance of this vital relationship is an ultimate element in the practice of future primitive, which means the pursuance of the "old ways" of harmonious and balanced living on the earth. The primitive approach of life is for Lawrence and for many other ecologists as well, a model indicating the direction for a cultural transformation of our civilization. It is of vital significance in sustaining a healthy environment for generations to come.

Patrick Marsolek points out:

> The periodic destruction of whole species and genera of flora and fauna, followed by 'large gaps' in the record, after which whole new species appear seems to answer certain important questions about the causal relationship between deep ecology, man and Gaea.[10]

The extinction of primitive cultures suggests a close link between man's destination and nature's behaviour. Earthquake, tsunami, global warming, air pollution and the large scale of destruction of rainforests—a mixture of natural and man-made disasters—are the main causes for the crisis in our ecosystem, which might bring forth in the near future the end of our civilization. The greatest danger is however from human beings, as man's exploration of nature is causing damage to our earth and environment every day. Lawrence sees the earth as a victim of man's destructive attitude: "But if we persist in our attitude of parasites on the body of earth and sun, the earth and the sun will be mere victims on which we feed our louse-like complacency for a long time yet". [11]

Nature is indifferent, but also "vengeful" once it is harmed. Considering the fact, as ancient Buddhism teaches us, that the world is an endless net of causality where every event sends ripples throughout the whole fabric of the universe, there is reason for us humans to be more aware and more fearful of the consequences of what we do to nature. Any anthropocentric belief that man can conquer the world or reform it or heal it is naive and arrogant. Lawrence asserts that we make a choice between living to conquer the universe and living in a real relationship with it. He proclaims: "a conquered world is no good to man . . . We need the universe to live again, so that we can live with it . . . a conquered universe, a dead Pan, leaves us nothing to live with. You have to abandon the conquest, before Pan will live again". [12]

Nature is forever unknowable and incomprehensible, and whatever human beings do to it, as man's power and knowledge are limited, they face unexpected consequences, regardless of their good or bad intentions. Lawrence is fully aware of the fact that the mystery of nature is beyond human comprehension, "it is a non-human mystery, it has its own great ends, man is not the criterion", he writes in *Women in Love*. Exploiting the environment is in violation of the natural laws of the universe; even protection movements aiming to improve nature do not always produce positive outcomes. Therefore, prudent behaviour and action known as Wu Wei, the great virtue in Taoism, could be a wise solution (Wu Wei not only means taking no action against nature, but also suggests an effective way of solving problems). Lawrence shows his own Wu Wei attitude in his objection to industrialism and materialism, and in his assertion of rejecting money- making business as a sole means of life. Through Mellors' final letter to Connie in *Lady Chatterley's Lover*, Lawrence urges people to drop "the whole industrial life" and live for immediate experience rather than for money.[13] "Owing to money and money-standards", Lawrence says, we are cut off "from life, from vitality, from the alive sun and the alive earth . . ."[14]

Lawrence's writing, by eulogizing the intrinsic value of the natural world, has applied ecological principles to literary texts. In view of modern ecology, his work has presented a new world with a perspective of "future primitive". Del Ivan Janik summarizes Lawrence's living wholeness and his advanced ecological consciousness at the end of his essay "D. H. Lawrence and Environmental Consciousness":

> Lawrence was a revolutionary writer . . . He had a profound respect for the land, the plants, and the animals which Western man had come to view as mere instruments of progress toward human ends. He saw the short-sightedness of modern man's ever-increasing reliance on technology and his substitution and creative community. In his later works he offered hints toward a restructuring of human society based on a recognition that man is not, after all, the measure of the universe. That his name has been invoked and his ideas have been echoed so often by writers who came to share his post-humanistic philosophy, from William Carlos Williams and Aldous Huxley to Kenneth Rexroth and Gary Snyder, is evidence that Lawrence stood at the beginning of the development of a new environmental consciousness in literature.[15]

The study of Lawrence's philosophy of nature, I hope, will enable us to have a better understanding and appreciation of Lawrence's insight into man's life and its symbiotic relationship with nature, and further, to value the natural environment in both metaphysical and ontological senses.

1 William Y. Tindall, *D. H. Lawrence & Susan His Cow*, p. 193.

2 Ibid., p. 199.

3 Roger Ebbatson, *Lawrence and the Nature Tradition*, p. 26.

4 Horace Gregory, *D. H. Lawrence: Pilgrim of the Apocalypse: A Critical Study*, p. xvi., quoted in James C. Cowan, *D. H. Lawrence's American Journey*, p. 24.

5 D. H. Lawrence, "Nottingham and Mining Countryside", *Phoenix*, p. 137.

6 Raymond Dasmann, Senior ecologist at the International Union for the Conservation of Nature at Morges, Switzerland.

7 Raymond Dasmann, quoted in Dolores LaChapelle, *D. H. Lawrence, Future Primitive*, pp. ix-x.

8 Ibid., p. 181.

9 Stephanie Kaza, "American Buddhist Response to the Land: Ecological Practice at Two West Coast Retreat Centers", quoted in Mary E. Tucker, *Buddhism and Ecology*, p. 187.

10 Ibid. p. 4.

11 D. H. Lawrence, "The Crown", in *Reflections on the Death of a Porcupineand Other Essays*, p. 306.

12 D. H. Lawrence, "Pan in America", *Phoenix*, p. 29.

13 D. H. Lawrence, *Lady Chatterley's Lover*, p. 312.

14 D. H. Lawrence, "Reflections on the Death of a Porcupine", in *D. H. Lawrence, A Selection from Phoenix*, p. 459.

15 Del Ivan Janik, "D. H. Lawrence and Environmental Consciousness", in *Environmental Review*, p. 371.

Bibliography

Primary Sources:

Lawrence, David Herbert.
Aaron's Rod. Harmondsworth, England: Penguin Books Ltd. (first published 1922), 1968.
Apocalypse. With an introduction by Richard Aldington. New York: The Viking Press (first published 1931), 1967.
Apocalypse and the Writings on Revelation. Edited by Mark Kalnins. Cambridge: Cambridge University Press, 1980.
The Boy in the Bush. Harmondsworth, England: Penguin Books Ltd. (first published 1924), 1983.
"Certain Americans and an Englishman". *New York Times Magazine*, December 24, 1922.
The Collected Letters of D. H. Lawrence. Edited with an introduction by Harry T. Moore, 2 Vols. London: William Heinemmann Ltd. (first published 1962), 1970.
The Collected Short Stories of D. H. Lawrence. Bungay, Suffolk: Richard Clay (The Chaucer Press), Ltd., 1975.
The Complete Poems of D. H. Lawrence. Collected and edited with an introduction and notes by Vivian de Sola Pinto and Warren Roberts. Harmondsworth, England: Penguin Books Ltd. (first published 1964), 1984.
The Complete Short Stories of D. H. Lawrence. Phoenix edition, 3 Vols. London: William Heinemmann Ltd. (first published 1955), 1965.

D. H. Lawrence, A Composite Biography. Edited by Edward Nehls, 3 Vols. Madison: The University of Wisconsin Press, 1957-1959.

D. H. Lawrence, A Selection from Phoenix. Edited by A. A. H. Inglis. Harmondsworth, England: Penguin Books Ltd., 1971.

England, My England and Other Stories. Cambridge: Cambridge University Press (first published 1922), 2001.

Fantasia of the Unconscious and Psychoanalysis and the Unconscious. The Phoenix Edition. London: William Heinemann Ltd. (first published 1923), 1971.

The First Lady Chatterley. London: Penguin Books Ltd. (first published 1944), 1973.

Kangaroo. Harmondsworth, England: Penguin Books Ltd. (first published 1923), 1972.

Lady Chatterley's Lover. Harmondsworth, England: Penguin Books Ltd. (first published 1928), 1993.

Lawrence on Hardy and Painting. Edited with an introduction by J. V. Davies. London: Heinemann Educational Books Ltd. (first published 1936), 1973.

The Letters of D. H. Lawrence. Edited with an introduction by Aldous Huxley. London: William Heinemann Ltd., 1932.

The Letters of D. H. Lawrence. Edited with an introduction by James T. Boulton and Andrew Robertson, 3 Vols. Cambridge: Cambridge University Press, 1979, 1981, 1984.

The Lost Girl. Harmondsworth, England: Penguin Books Ltd. (first published 1920), 1976.

Love Among the Haystacks and Other Stories. Harmondsworth, England: Penguin Books Ltd. (first published 1930), 1970.

Love Poems. London: Duckworth & Co., 1913.

Mornings in Mexico and Etruscan Places. England: C. Nicholls & Company Ltd (first published *Mornings in Mexico* 1927 , *Etruscan Places* 1932), 1960.

Movements in European History. Oxford: Oxford University Press, (first published 1921), 1981.

Mr Noon. Edited by Lindeth Vasey. Cambridge: Cambridge University Press, 1984.

Phoenix: The Posthumous Papers of D. H. Lawrence. Edited with an introduction by Edward D. MacDonald. London: Heinemann (first published 1936), 1970.

Phoenix II. New York: The Viking Press, 1968.

The Plays of D. H. Lawrence. London: Martin Secker, 1933.

The Plumed Serpent. Harmondsworth, England: Penguin Books Ltd. (first published 1926), 1966.

The Prussian Officer. Harmondsworth, England: Penguin Books Ltd. (first published 1914), 1981.

The Rainbow. Cambridge: Cambridge University Press (first published 1915), 1989.

Reflections on the Death of a Porcupine and Other Essays. Edited by Michael Herbert. Cambridge: Cambridge University Press, 1988.

Sea and Sardinia. Edited by Mara Kalnins. Cambridge: Cambridge University Press (first published 1923), 2001.

Selected Essays. Harmondsworth, England: Penguin Books Ltd., (first published 1950), 1969.

Selected Literary Criticism. London: Heinemann Educational Books Ltd., 1969.

Sons and Lovers. Harmondsworth, England: Penguin Books Ltd. (first published, 1913), 1966.

St. Mawr and Other stories. The Cambridge Edition. Edited by Brian Finney. Introduction by Melvyn Bragg. London: Granada Publishing Ltd. (first published 1925), 1984.

Studies in Classic American Literature. London: Penguin Books Ltd. (first published 1923), 1977.

Study on Thomas Hardy and other Essays. Edited by Bruce Steele. Cambridge: Cambridge University Press (first published 1923), 1985.

The Tales of D. H. Lawrence. London: Martin Secker, 1934.

The Trespasser. Cambridge: Cambridge University Press (first published 1912), 1982.

Twilight in Italy. Harmondsworth, England: Penguin Books Ltd. (first published 1916), 1981.

The Virgin and the Gipsy. Harmondsworth, England: Penguin Books Ltd. (first published 1930), 1973.

The White Peacock. Harmondsworth, England: Penguin Books Ltd. (first published 1911), 1966.

The Woman Who Rode Away and Other Stories. Harmondsworth, England: Penguin Books Ltd. (first published 1928), 1960.

Women in Love. Cambridge: Cambridge University Press (first published 1921), 1987.

Secondary Sources:

Aldington, Richard. *Portrait of a Genius, But . . . .* London: William Heinemann Ltd., 1950.

Allen, Walter. *The English Novel: A Short Critical History.* London: Phoenix House, 1963.

Alldritt, Keith. *The Visual Imagination of D. H. Lawrence.* London: Edward Arnold Ltd., 1971.

Andrews, W. T. (editor). *Critics on D. H. Lawrence.* London: George Allen and Unwin Ltd, 1971.

Asquith, Cynthia. *Remember and Be Glad.* London: James Barrie, 1952.

Asquith, Herbert. *Moments of Memory: Recollections and Impressions.* New York: Scribner, 1938.

Balbert, Peter and Phillip L. Marcus. *D. H. Lawrence: A Centenary Consideration.* Ithaca and London: Cornell University Press, 1985.

Barbour, Ian. G. (editor). *Earth Might Be Fair: Reflections on Ethics, Religion, and Ecology.* Englewood Cliffs, New Jersey: Prentice-Hall, Inc., 1972.

Bate, Jonathan.
—*The Song of the Earth.* Cambridge, Massachusetts: Harvard University Press, 2000.
—*Romantic Ecology, Wordsworth and the Environmental Tradition.* London: Routledge, 1991.

Bateson, Gregory. *Mind and Nature: A Necessary Unity.* New York: E. P. Dutton, 1979.

Beal, Anthony. *D. H. Lawrence.* Edinburgh and London: Oliver & Boyd Ltd., 1966.

Bergson, Henri. *Creative Evolution.* Mineola, New York: Dover, 1998.

Blyth, R. H. *Zen in English Literature and Oriental Classics.* Tokyo: Hokuseido Press, 1948.

Brewster, Earl and Achsah Brewster.

—D. H. Lawrence: Reminiscences and Correspondence. London: Martin Secker, 1934.

—D. H. Lawrence and the Body Mystical. London, Archer, 1932.

Brown, Keith (editor). *Rethinking Lawrence.* Milton Keynes: Open University Press, 1990.

Burgess, Anthony. *Flame Into Being: The Life and Works of D. H. Lawrence.* New York: Arbor House, 1985.

Burns, Aidan. *Nature and Culture in D. H. Lawrence.* London: The Macmillian Press Ltd., 1980.

Callicott, J. Baird and Roger T. Ames (editors). *Nature in Asian Traditions of Thought: Essays in Environmental Philosophy.* Albany: State University of New York Press, 1989.

Carswell, Catherine. *Savage Pilgrimage: A Narrative of D. H. Lawrence.* London: Secker and Warburg, 1951.

Carter, Frederick. *D. H. Lawrence and the Body Mystical.* New York: Haskell House Publishers Ltd., 1972.

Cavitch, David. *D. H. Lawrence and The New World.* New York and London: Oxford University Press, 1969.

Chambers, Jessie (E. T.). *D. H. Lawrence: A Personal Record.* Edited by J. D. Chambers. London: Frank Cass & Co. Ltd., 1965.

Clark, Colin. *River of Dissolution: D. H. Lawrence and English Romanticism.* London: Routledge and Kegan Paul, 1969.

Clark, L. D. *Dark Night of the Body: D. H. Lawrence's Plumed Serpent.* Austin: University of Texas Press, 1964.

Clayre, Alasdair (editor). *Nature and Industrialization.* Oxford: Oxford University Press, 1977.

Cobb, Edith.

—"The Ecology of Imagination in Childhood", *Daedalus,* 88 (Summer,1959) pp. 537-48.

—The Ecology of Imagination in Childhood. Dallas: Spring Publications, 1993.

Cowan, James C. *D. H. Lawrence's American Journey: A Study in Literature and Myth.* Cleveland, Ohio: The Press of Case Western Reserve University, 1970.

Delavenay, Emile. *D. H. Lawrence and Edward Carpenter: A Study in Edwardian Transition.* London: Heinemann, 1971.

Dohetty, Gerald. *Theorizing Lawrence: Nine Meditations on Topological Themes.* New York: Peter Lang Publishing Incorporated, 1999.

Ebbatson, Roger. *Lawrence and the Nature Tradition: A Theme in English Fiction 1859-1914.* Atlantic Highlands, New Jersey: Humanities Press Inc., 1980.

Eiseley, Loren. *The Unexpected Universe.* London: Victor Gollancz Ltd, 1970.

Eliot, T. S. *After Strange Gods: A Primer in Modern Heresy.* New York: Harcourt, Brace and Co., 1934.

Erikson, E. H. *Childhood and Society.* New York: W. W. Norton Inc., 1950.

Fernihough, Anne.
—*D. H. Lawrence: Aesthetics and Ideology.* Oxford: Clarendon Press, 1993.
—(Editor). *The Cambridge Companion to D. H. Lawrence.* Cambridge: Cambridge University Press, 2001.

Fingarette, Herbert. *Confucius: The Secular as Sacred.* Illinois: Waveland Press, Inc. 1998.

Ford, Ford Madox, *Portraits From Life.* Boston: Houghton Mifflin Co., 1937.

Foster, E. M. *Nation and Athenaeum.* 1930.

Frank, E. T. *D. H. Lawrence, A Personal Record.* London: Cass and Co. Ltd., 1965.

Frazer, Sir James. *The Golden Bough: A Study in Magic and Religion.* New York: Macmillan Co., 1943.

Freeman, Mary. *D. H. Lawrence, A Basic Study of his Ideas.* Gainesville: University of Florida Press, 1955.

Fung, Yu-lan. *The Spirit of Chinese Philosophy.* London: Routledge and Kegan Paul Ltd., 1962.

Gerhardi, William. "Literary Vignettes II", in *The Saturday Review*, London, June 20, 1931.

Gilbert, Sandra M. "D. H. Lawrence's Uncommon Prayers" in *D. H. Lawrence: The Man Who Lived.* Carbondale: Southern Illinois University Press (April, 1979), pp. 73-93.

Goodheart, Eugene. *The Utopian Vision of D. H. Lawrence.* Chicago: Chicago University Press, 1963.

Gregory, Horace, *D. H. Lawrence: Pilgrim of the Apocalypse, A Critical Study.* New York: Grove Press, Inc. Evergreen Books Edition, 1957.

Grigg, Ray. *The Tao of Being.* England: Wildwood House Limited, 1990.

Herzinger, Kim A. *D. H. Lawrence in His Time: 1908-1915.* London and Toronto: Associated University Press Ltd., 1982.

Heywood, Christopher (editor). *D. H. Lawrence: New Studies.* Houndmills: Macmillan Press, 1987.

His, Chu. *The Philosophy of Human Nature.* Translated by J. Percy Bruce. London: Probsthain and Co., 1932.

Hochman, Baruch. *Another Ego, The Changing View of Self and Society in the Work of D. H. Lawrence.* Columbia: University of South Carolina Press, 1970.

Holderness, Graham. *D. H. Lawrence: History, Ideology and Fiction.* Dublin: Gill & Macmillan, 1982.

Hough, Graham. *The Dark Sun: A Study of D. H. Lawrence.* London: Gerald Duckworth and Co. Ltd., 1970.

Janik, Del Ivan. "D. H. Lawrence and Environmental Consciousness" in *Environmental Review* (Winter 1983), pp. 359-71.

Jastrab, Joseph and Ron Schaumburg. *Sacred Manhood, Sacred Earth.* New York: Harper Collins Publishers, 1994.

Jefferies, Richard. *The Story of My Heart.* London: Constable and Company Ltd., 1947.

Jung, C. G. *Modern Man in Search of a Soul.* London: Routledge & Kegan Paul Ltd., 1962.

La Chapelle, Dolores.
—*D. H. Lawrence, Future Primitive.* Texas: University of North Texas Press, 1996.
—*Earth Wisdom.* Los Angeles: Guild of Tutors Press, 1978.
—"System Thinking and Deep Ecology: A Historical Overview" in *Earthday X Colloquium: On the Humanities and Ecological Consciousness.* Denver, Colorado: University of Denver (April, 1980), pp. 21-4.

Lao Tzu. *Tao The King.* Translated as *Nature and Intelligence,* by Archie J. Bahm. New York: The Continuum Publishing Company, 1988 (English version).

Lao Tzu. *Tao Te Ching*. Betty Radice (advisory editor). Translated with an introduction by D. C. Lau. London: Penguin Books Ltd., 1963 (English version).

Laozi. *Dao De Jing*. Shuhai Publish House, 1996 (Chinese version).

Lawrence, Ada and G. S. Gelder. *Young Lorenzo: Early Life of D. H. Lawrence*. New York: Russell & Russell, 1966.

Lawrence, Frieda. *Not I, But the Wind . . ..* New York: The Viking Press, 1972.

Leavis, F. R.
—*Thought, Words and Creativity: Art and Thought in Lawrence*. London: Chatto & Windus, 1976.
—*D. H. Lawrence: Novelist*. New York: Alfred A. Knopf, 1956.

Liu, Xiaogan. "Non Action (WU WEI) and the Environment Today: Conceptual and Applied Study". Cambridge, Massachusetts: Harvard University Press, 2001.

Luhan, Mabel Dodge. *Lorenzo in Taos*. New York: Alfred Knopf, 1932.

Maddox, Brenda. *D. H. Lawrence: The Study of a Marriage*. New York: Simon and Schuster, 1994.

Malpas, Jeff and Robert C. Solomon. *Death and Philosophy*. London: Routledge, 1998.

Marshall, Tom. *The Psychic Mariner: A Reading of the Poems of D. H. Lawrence*. London: Heinemann, 1970.

Marsolek, Patrick. *Deep Ecology and Man—A Sacred Kinship*. http:// www.irfs. com/DeepEco.html. 20 June 2005.

McLean, George F. (editor). *Man and Nature: 2nd International Conference of the International Society for Metaphysics*. Oxford: Oxford University Press, 1978.

Merrild, Knud. *With D. H. Lawrence in New Mexico, A Memoir of D. H. Lawrence*. London: Routledge & Kegan Paul Ltd., 1964.

Meyers, Jeffrey.
—*D. H. Lawrence: A Biography*. London: Macmillan, 1993.
—*D. H. Lawrence and Tradition*. Amherst, Massachusetts: University of Massachusetts Press, 1985.

Miller, Henry. *The World of Lawrence: A Passionate Approach*. Edited with an introduction and notes by Evelyn J. Hinz and

John J. Teunissen. Santa Barbara, California: Capra Press, 1980.

Moore, Harry T. *The Life and Works of D. H. Lawrence*. London: George Allen and Unwin Ltd., 1951.

Murry, J. M. *D. H. Lawrence: Son of Woman*. London: Jonathan Cape, 1954.

Nahal, Chaman. *D. H. Lawrence: An Eastern View*. New York: A. S. Barnes & Co. 1971.

Nixon, Cornelia. *Lawrence's Leadership, Politics and the Turn against Women*. London: University of California Press, Ltd., 1986.

Niven, Alastair. *D. H. Lawrence, The Novels*. Cambridge: Cambridge University Press, 1978.

Panichas, George A. *Adventure in Consciousness: The Meaning of D. H. Lawrence's Religious Quest*. The Hague: Mouton, 1964.

Partlow, Robert B. Jr. and Harry T. Moore (editors). *D. H. Lawrence: The Man Who Lived*. Carbondale: Southern Illinois University Press, 1979.

Pearce, Joseph Chilton. *Magic Child*. New York: E. P. Dutton, 1977.

Poplawski, Paul. *Promptings of Desire: Creativity and Religious Impulse in the Works of D. H. Lawrence*. London: Greenwood Press, 1993.

Preston, Peter. *D. H. Lawrence in the Modern World*. London: Macmillan, 1989.

Prichard, R. E. *D. H. Lawrence: Body of Darkness*. London: Hutchinson University Library, 1971.

Sagar, Keith.
—*The Art of D. H. Lawrence*. Cambridge: Cambridge University Press, 1966.
—*D. H. Lawrence and New Mexico*. Salt Lake City, Utah: Gibbs M. Smith, Inc., 1982.
—*D. H. Lawrence: Life into Art*. Penguin and Viking, 1985.

Salgado, Gamini and GK Das (editors). *The Spirit of D. H. Lawrence: Centenary Studies*. Basingstoke: Macmillan, 1988.

Sanders, Scott. *D. H. Lawrence: The World of the Major Novels*. New York: Viking Press, 1973.

Scheckner, Peter. *Class, Politics, and the Individual, A Study of the Major Works of D. H. Lawrence*. London: Associated University Presses, 1985.

Schneider, Daniel J.

—*The Consciousness of D. H. Lawrence: An Intellectual Biography*. Lawrence, Kansas: University Press of Kansas, 1986.

—*D. H. Lawrence: The Artist as Psychologist*. Lawrence, Kansas: University Press of Kansas, 1984.

—"'Strange Wisdom': Leo Frobenius and D. H. Lawrence" in *D. H. Lawrence Review* 16, No. 2 (Summer 1983), pp. 183-93.

—"The Symbolism of the Soul: D. H. Lawrence and Some Others" in *D. H. Lawrence Review* 7, No. 2 (Summer 1974), pp. 107-26.

Shepard, Paul. *Man in the Landscape, A Historic View of the Aesthetics of Nature*. New York: Alfred. A. Knopf, 1967.

Sklar, Sylvia. *The Plays of D. H. Lawrence: A Biographical and Critical Study*. London: Vision Press Limited, 1975.

Spilka, Mark. "Lawrence's Quarrel with Tenderness" in *Critical Quarterly* 9, No. 4 (Winter 1967), pp. 363-77.

Stewart, Jack F. *The Vital Art of D. H. Lawrence: Vision and Expression*. Cambridge: Cambridge University Press, 1999.

Tindall, William York.

—*D. H. Lawrence & Susan His Cow*. New York: Cooper Square Publishers, Inc., 1972.

—"Introduction" to *The Later D. H. Lawrence*. New York: Alfred A. Knopf, 1952.

—"D. H. Lawrence and The Primitive" in *Sewanee Review* (April-June, 1937), pp. 198-211.

Toropov, Brandon and Chad Hansen. *The Complete Idiot's Guide to Taoism*. Indiana: Pearson Education Company, 2002.

Tucker, Mary Evelyn and Duncan Ryuken Williams (editors). *Buddhism and Ecology: The Interconnection of Dharma and Deeds*. Cambridge, Massachusetts: Harvard University Press, 1997.

Vivas, Eliseo. *D. H. Lawrence, the Failure and the Triumph of Art*, London: George Allen and Unwin Ltd., 1961.

Watts, Alan W.
   —*Nature, Man and Woman*. London: Wildwood House, 1973.
   —*The Way of Zen*. London: Thames and Hudson, 1957.
Wheeler, Reuben. *Man, Nature & Art*. London: Pergamon Press Ltd., 1968.
Whelan, P. T. *D. H. Lawrence: Myth and Metaphysics in 'The Rainbow' and 'Women in Love'*. Cambridge: Cambridge University Press, 2000.
Williams, Raymond. *Culture and Society 1780-1950*. New York: Columbia University Press, 1958.
Willis, Ben. *The Tao of Art*. London: Century Hutchinson Ltd., 1987.
Worthen, John.
   —*D. H. Lawrence, The Early Years 1885-1912*. Cambridge: Cambridge University Press, 1991.
   —*D. H. Lawrence and the Idea of the Novel*. London: Macmillan, 1979.
Wright, Terry R. *D. H. Lawrence and the Bible*. Cambridge: Cambridge University Press, 2000.
Zhuangzi. *Zhuangzi*. Edited by Zhong Kanglei. China: Shuhai Publishing House, 1996 (Chinese version).